To Sandy + Jim
With warm good wishes!
M. Nora McClanahan
7-23-78

Give Me A Mountain Meadow

D1616423

Charles Fayette McGlashan

Give Me A Mountain Meadow

The Life of Charles Fayette McGlashan (1847–1931)
Imaginative Lawyer-Editor of the High Sierra,
Who Saved the Donner Story from Oblivion
and Launched Winter Sports in the West

M. Nona McGlashan

Fresno  1977

Copyright © 1977
by
Valley Publishers

Library of Congress 77-79315
ISBN 0-913548-41-3
Paper Edition ISBN 0-913548-42-1

Manufactured in the United States of America

Introduction

During the stupendous and satisfying task of building and maturing a nation based on the revolutionary principles of the Founding Fathers, nineteenth century Americans developed a plethora of heroes toward whom they could look for example. Some, such as Mike Fink the keelboatman or Jim Bridger the mountain man, stimulated the spark of adventure that eventually made America's destiny manifest, while others, a Ralph Waldo Emerson or a Mark Twain, satisfied the urge for intellectual achievement so sought after by a frontier society. Still others, an Eli Whitney or Elias Howe, for example, invented the tools of the expanding industrial revolution, then in the process of working dramatic changes into the life of the nation, while Andrew Carnegie or John D. Rockfeller provided a picture of what could be accomplished in the way of personal wealth through the use of those tools. Yet of all the American heroes of that century, the man, and, on very rare occasions, the woman, who was most revered was that "universal genius," the individual recognized as outstanding in a variety of pursuits, particularly those of a cultural or scientific nature, at the same time supporting himself or herself in good style with a useful economic endeavor. Thus, Samuel F. B. Morse, remembered now chiefly for the telegraph code to which his name is attached, became a highly respected American hero, renowned as a painter, sculptor, and founder of the National Academy of Design, as well as inventor.

Although he was a member of that select group of nineteenth century universalists, and even carried over into the twentieth century, Charles F. McGlashan is known only to a few students of California and the American West, and to them merely as the author of *The History of the Donner Party*, the first, and in many ways still the best of the multitude of books on the subject. Now, through the adoring, but not uncritical eyes, and very considerable writing talents of his granddaughter, M. Nona McGlashan, historians, students, and the general public alike can come to know this truly remarkable man.

Faithful to the nineteenth century ideal, Charles McGlashan came up the hard way. Better educated than many boys of his time, he nevertheless had to struggle to establish himself financially, and, due largely to his omniverous and ever-changing interests combined with his innate generosity, McGlashan had to work hard throughout his life to make ends meet. In that sense he failed to achieve the American Dream, and that may account for his relative obscurity. He started out in rags, but never quite made it to riches, at least the monetary kind. Along the way, however, there were compensations. McGlashan met enough challenges, accomplished enough tasks, and had enough fun to satisfy several lifetimes.

Whatever struck his fancy he tried, whatever would benefit his town or region he promoted. Schoolteacher, scientist, sports promoter, lawyer, administrator—he tried them all, not infrequently at the same time. McGlashan not only owned and operated his own newspaper more than once, but earned a well deserved reputation as one of America's first investigative reporters. Basing his story on site visits and personal interviews with those involved, he was the first to bring to the world the factual story of the so-called Mountain Meadows Massacre, while the tale of his tribulations in tracking down the Donner survivors and obtaining their statements reads like a detective novel. His efforts to commemorate the Donner experience led to the establishment of the Donner Monument. Butterflies were another obsession and led to a collection of over 20,000 specimens which he displayed in airtight glass cases of his own invention. When it became time for McGlashan to design and build his own unique house, his keen observations of the winds and weather of the Sierras enabled him to so slant and face the roof that the heavy snows of winter could not stick. He invented a train telegraph device which prevented many a wreck and saved countless lives.

Add to this litany a fascinating personal life, one which did not exactly conform to the accepted Victorian standard, and you have all the ingredients for an engrossing biography. In the following pages you will necessarily become an admirer of this man who has so much to tell us about his times and region, and, upon reflection, about ourselves. I commend you to the care of Nona McGlashan, and through her, to Charles McGlashan. You will not only enjoy the experience, but be better for it.

Richard E. Oglesby, *University of California, Santa Barbara*

Acknowledgements

My heartfelt thanks to the cousins, my peers among the grand-children, who gave me unflagging moral support over the ten years of this writing. Special thanks are due Naida Palmer (nee Gilmore) for her unstinting generosity with family photos and memorabilia, and Alicia (Dukie) Kelley, widow of Dr. Douglas M. Kelley, for hours of discussion, as well as for invaluable notes dictated by June Kelley, law partner (and daughter) of C. F. McGlashan. I thank my aunt Ximena Howard for the "butterfly princess" story and for her account of the mineral springs enterprise.

I thank Ruth Mason (Mrs. E. M.) Calderwood, now deceased, for help with the story of her grandmother, Ella Keiser Webber, and for other insights into the Keiser narrative.

I am deeply indebted to librarians for countless favors, partic-ularly those of the California State Library, and Bancroft, at Berkeley. The interest and efficiency of librarians in my local libraries at Oxnard and Ojai also smoothed my path unnumbered times. I particularly thank Fern Middough, librarian at Ojai Valley School.

I thank Mr. C. F. Katzenmeyer of the Beaver Dam Chamber of Commerce for delving into cemetery records in search of Elizabeth McGlashan's grave. This revealed that a number of McGlashan families settled the Beaver Dam area.

For the Healdsburg years I am indebted to Mr. Edwin Lang-hart, City Clerk, for maps that led me to the site of the Cloverdale cabin built by Peter McGlashan, and to the location of his house in Healdsburg. Mr. Langhart also furnished the photo of Sotoyome Institute. His research into old newspapers supplemented Fay-ette's journal and correspondence to give a strong picture of those youthful years.

I am very grateful to Mr. Arthur L. Hepworth, former dean of

Williston Academy; to Mr. and Mrs. Guy R. Carpenter for research that illuminated the Williston experience with unexpected depth; and to Mr. Joseph Lucier, Alumni Secretary, and Mr. Donald Lightfoot, Director of Development, for their assistance with photographs of Williston.

For much of the Donner chapters I thank Vera (Mrs. Ralph D.) Cornell, who obtained for me a typescript of the McGlashan-Eliza Donner Houghton correspondence from the Huntington Library in Pasadena. This gave me my grandfather's personal account of his adventure in writing the Donner history.

For the restoration of the ice palace and other old photos, I thank Paul Waring of Ventura, California. To him I also owe gratitude for the sharp reproduction of the carnival medallion. I thank his wife, Gayle Waring, for the drawing of the map. To Jeanine Oppewall, special thanks for the butterfly photos, the star map photo, and that of the bottled Murphy cabin splinters.

I thank all Truckee people who helped me with memories of the "old days." Foremost among these are Minnie (Mrs. Peter) Martini and her daughter Gladys (Mrs. A. R.) Matcham; Stella (Mrs. Wm. E.) Englehart; and Mr. and Mrs. Todd McGinnis, now of Oroville, California. I thank, too, my uncle, Dr. George F. Kelley, now deceased.

My indebtedness is great to Mr. Roy Baker, President of the Truckee-Donner Historical Society, for his belief in the manuscript and his active, helpful interest in its progress. I thank him and all members of the Historical Society for their encouragement.

I thank Bert Troelsen, former superintendent of Donner Memorial State Park, for extensive help at the initial stages of research. And I salute, too, Mr. Thomas J. Lee, Headmaster of Ojai Valley School, for granting me a sabbatical summer in which to complete the final draft.

Finally, but not least, I wish to express my appreciation to my publisher, Mr. Charles W. Clough, of Valley Publishers, and his staff, for their lively and helpful interest in my book.

March 30, 1977   M. Nona McGlashan
Ojai, California

Chapter One

On any day of the new moon, my grandfather recruited my keen young eyes to scan the skies over Truckee. This was a year-round ritual, but we enjoyed it most on summer evenings when the ground was dry and the mild air warm. Then, immediately after supper when the sun had barely slipped behind Donner Summit, he sent me scampering outside to find the whispery crescent in a blue still charged with daylight.

"Nevertheless, Maqueda..." He called me by my mother's name, for only my grandmother was Nona to him. "Nevertheless, it's the best time to look for it—while it's still above trees and telegraph poles."

This was important, I knew, for we played a game that was more than a game to both of us. If he saw the new moon (how I saw it didn't count) clean and clear of cloud, branch, or any other obstacle, the month ahead augured well. If, on the other hand...

But it was my job to see to it there was no other hand. On this depended my reward exceeding great—invariably, a silver dollar. That the employment of a scout was cheating fate, we both would have denied—I hotly, he with his cropped white head thrown back in a shout of laughter.

After all, hadn't he done the same for his own father? He had told me about it gravely in one of our bedtime story sessions.

"When my sisters and I crossed the plains in an ox wagon, our father's sight began to fail. The hot glare of the sun on desert sands tortured his eyes and inflamed them. He asked us children to find him the new moons then and ever after. We all liked to believe our mother sent him a message from heaven by the clear little moon, you know."

1

Charles Fayette McGlashan in 1912.

"What if the moon was in clouds, Papa?" My grandparents had adopted me after my mother's death and I called them Papa and Mama.

"Oh, that was a warning. Not of bad trouble necessarily. Delays, perhaps. A broken axle..."

I knew nothing was wrong with Papa's sparkling brown eyes, for he never wore glasses, not even for reading. No, where our moon omen was concerned, understandably he was not taking chances. And I, I was only the honest agent of whomsoever on the other side managed the lunar signals for him.

"I see it!"

My triumphant squeal brought them both from the dinner table, for Mama went along with the game, gently smiling. Papa gallantly draped her cream-white shawl about her cushiony straight-backed little figure while I hopped up and down in glee.

2

Our floppy-eared water spaniel, Brownie, joined sound and hubbub to the procession we made past the big black kitchen range and out along the plank runway that bridged our house to the uneven turf of our backyard. For we lived on a hill where all around us the ground dipped and rose like sea waves frozen in a photograph.

For dramatic suspense, Papa always delayed conceding he saw my moon. But at last he slid a hand into the pants pocket of his brown suit and produced the dollar. Then, if the air was pleasantly cool, he offered Mama his arm and we took a walk along the dirt road that climbed our hill from the town below. This road traveled past our house and on to the crest of the hill where the high school stood. There it sloped down to McIver's dairy and joined the highway to Donner Lake. Brownie and I cavorted ahead, followed by the aging couple's firm, even steps, paced to Mama's best speed.

Neighbors hailed us, smiling and waving from high porches where they sat out the evenings to watch the trains below disgorge passengers and take on freight in the unending drama of the Southern Pacific depot.

Beyond the tracks the narrow Truckee River plunged eastward. Across its turbulent stream the forest, darkly green, mounted the southern ridge. For we lived on the north rim of a saucer, sharing an unbroken panorama that stretched from Mt. Rose in the east near Reno to the towering cliffs of the western summit, rising two thousand feet above Donner.

The string of homes ended at the high school's granite wall. There the road became a rutted path that trickled down to the highway among warm milky smells and occasional mooings from the McIver barns. We could either follow it and turn back at the barns, or circle homeward behind the school by way of Mother Rock.

"Which way, my love?"

"Oh, I think, Mac, I'd like to rest a minute on Mother Rock...if you'd like, too."

And seated on the smooth wide lap of the enormous beige-gray boulder, my grandparents often fell silent. Even I, who was perpetually rock-hopping and climbing, quieted too, guessing at

Leonora (Nona) G. McGlashan in 1908.

their mood. For I was the last child in their child-happy lives. My mother had scrambled over this rock with her six sisters and brother, Earl, as well as a foster sister named Lizzie May. In fact, all my huge granite friends—Blunderbore, the Three Giants, Aladdin's Cave, and this fat-thighed rock with the hollow like a giant thumbprint—these were my inheritance from Nonette, June, Elizabeth, Lotus, Earl, Ximena, Bliss. They were gone on to grown-up lives and had children of their own—except for my mother Maqueda, the daughter who died when I was born.

"This child keeps us young," Papa always said when someone suggested that in taking me on the McGlashans had bitten off an unlikely chunk for people in their sixties.

"And from loneliness," Mama might have added. For I often saw her gray eyes spill tears when we were alone together. I'd reach my short arms about her aproned waist to give comfort while her strong kind hand pressed my cheek into her stomach's rounded softness. Her touch was always carefully gentle. She never forgot her scratchy fingertips, calloused by years of plucking the strings of her cherished Martin guitar.

At these moments I would believe the silence of our big high-ceilinged rooms oppressed her, or that she listened to remembered shouts and laughter. When I was only four or five, sudden gusts of grief for my mother would storm through her short compact frame.

"Queedie, oh Queedie!" She gasped the pet name over and over. As suddenly as it overtook her, she controlled the storm, wiping her softly wrinkled wet cheeks with the edge of her apron. "She would have loved you, dear."

In summer her joy returned, for as soon as schools let out in June, her children came home. Their father had purchased a tract of eighty wooded acres near the head of Donner Lake and wisely deeded each one a chosen lot. Thus his clan-loving Scottish heart assured annual family reunions as long as he and their mother lived. And long beyond that, it was his hope.

For a week or two in June we welcomed new arrivals almost daily in cars stuffed with camping gear and topped with boy and girl cousins, already barefoot and itching to hike and swim. All our spacious rooms rang with life for the few days they spent with us. The dining room table, a gift from Sam Davis, Governor of Nevada, stretched to the length of all its leaves to seat a daily fifteen to twenty.

While the adults finished their meals at leisure, my cousins and I were excused to play outside around the house and grounds.

Now this was no ordinary house.

For thirty-four years, until it burned in 1935, the McGlashan home commanded the hill beside the rocking stone in Truckee—a soaring castle in effect, with flashing windows flanked by smooth white columns. A high-swung wooden footbridge joined it to a matching tower set atop the great rock.

An unabashed departure from anything else in the small mountain town or, for that matter, in the entire Sierra Nevada,

our house sang out from the hill, conspicuous as a wedding cake, lyrical, imaginative, large-souled and free. It was an architectural portrait, in short, of the man who built it—Charles Fayette McGlashan, my grandfather—designed largely by my grandmother, his wife Nona, born Leonora Gertrude Keiser.

A high circular wall of rough-hewn granite blocks grew from a lower point down the hill to the level of our stone basement. This wall was no barricade. It simply shored up the hillside, embracing a large front yard casually sown by bird and breeze with orange poppies and blue bachelor buttons. The only imported plant was the matilija poppy whose white crepe-paper petals blew open each July—a memento of three years spent long ago in Santa Barbara, California and of a baby daughter buried there. A tree of lavender lilacs, as well as a wildly scented hedge of yellow roses along the northern curve of the wall, were planted but indigenous.

It was the round tower, of course, perched on top of the adjoining great rock, that most suggested a castle. The illusion was strengthened by a two-story rotunda that fluted out from the southeast corner of the residence, repeating the turret-like lines. The Rocking Stone Tower, as we called it, housed my

Panoramic view of Truckee, taken after 1900. At far left is Meadow Lake High School. At left center is the McGlashan home, "conspicuous as a wedding cake" among the utilitarian designs common around the turn of the century.

grandfather's museum—his renowned butterfly collection, all relics of the Donner party tragedy not returned to survivors (some were not returnable), numerous Indian baskets and other artifacts of the Washoe tribe, and myriad curios from all parts of the world.

In point of time, the museum preceded the house by seven years. Papa had purchased the phenomenal balanced stone and its hill above town as early as 1891. With it had come a nagging anxiety. Children had played at the base of the parent rock since earliest settlers came. But hoodlums had begun scaling the giant, thirty feet high, to test their muscles on the rocking stone, a sixteen-ton boulder centered and balanced on its flat top. A baby's hand could set this stone quivering; a gentle push made it rock slightly back and forth; but so fine was the balance, only a strong man with tools, it was believed, could unseat it. However, if this rock should ever roll with children below it . . . My grandfather wondered if he shouldn't destroy it himself. Mean-

7

while, he fenced it around with a picket fence.

And then he thought of the museum.

"Do you think it would work?" he asked Mama. She did, and they sat down together to plan it—a thing of beauty, princely yet practical, and filled with light. She sketched as they talked and when he recalled white columns he had fancied in New England, she drew them in. The final design showed a two-story circular wall of fourteen panels, all window glass but for the back, which would be needed for tier upon tier of shelves. Slender columns, joined by Roman arches, separated the tall panes. The pillars seemed to support a slightly overhanging flat roof on which, lest it look too stark, she etched a crown of iron filigreed railing, then fashionable. That nothing whatsoever might be lacking, they added a flagpole in the center.

By 1893 it was done. To the flagpole Papa attached a large arc light that lit up the hill at night, bathing in ghostly glow the white sculpture of the little Rocking Stone Tower. During the day, visitors climbed a ladder to the entrance, a door at the rear that left the encircling glass panes uninterrupted almost all the way around the circumference.

The children were taught to guide tourists through, as I did in my later time. I remember the narrow staircase that wound upward past a shark's toothy skull, a red-and-blue beaded tomahawk fastened to the wall with several Indian baskets, and my great-grandfather John Keiser's Civil War uniform (blue). The stair led to a circular balcony from which we stared down at the top of the rocking stone. Here we unfolded standing hinged cases filled with Papa's moths and butterflies—20,000 brilliant-winged jewels, arranged by my grandmother in the colorful geometry of a kaleidoscope. (Most of the collection remains intact in the airtight glass cases patented by C. F. McGlashan in 1886. It is displayed at the County Court House in Nevada City, California.)

On the first floor the relics of the Donner tragedy were of major interest. I recall vividly one only labeled: Woman's Little Toe Bone, Found On Hearth.

But the pivotal attraction was always the rocking stone itself. According to the legend of the Washoes, they could thank the wind god for the rocking stone. Around its base, high above thieving animals, they were able to dry and store their venison. Most wonderfully, even their grain was safe there, for birds looked askance at the rocking stone, which any obliging breeze pushed into motion.

John Muir examined the phenomenon with my grandfather and called it a glacial wonder. The ancient ice had left many such "ducks on rocks" in the high Sierra.

But Papa was not satisfied.

"Look at this floor. Show me another rock on a floor sheared off like this one."

True, today as then, it looks like an apple with the top sliced off. The surface seems tool-cut in its glazed crystalline flatness. There does exist another theory: A race of giants...?

And it was this floor (top of the parent rock) thirty-three feet in circumference, not the rocking boulder, that captivated my grandfather's attention. For one thing, it shed all snow in winter, a virtue fully appreciated by the Indians. With his friend, Charles Burckhalter, he had long ago measured the almost imperceptible slant of the floor and found a gradient of one-half inch to the foot, sloping in a northeasterly direction.

"I'm going to experiment, Nona," he said. "I've got something here."

"What are you going to do, my dear?"

"You watch and you'll see. But I'll tell you one thing that's sure. I'm *not* going to shovel snow off of any house I build."

At this time he owned the town's water works and, kissing his twinkling wife goodbye, he went out to order construction of a huge water tank. Its roof sloped one-half inch to the foot, northeasterly—as did the roof of the Rocking Stone Tower.

Throughout the winter both the tank and the tower sloughed off their weight of snow, to his immense satisfaction.

For seven years the flat-roofed tower and tank, watched cynically by unbelieving townsmen, took care of their own snow. And when he built the large meadow of his residence roof, fellow Truckeeites assured him he was out of his mind.

"I'll give you a hand with the shovel, Mac, anytime."

"I won't need it. Thanks anyway."

And using the slope of the rocking stone's floor, he never did.

When at last his home rose complete, united in design and by a bridge with the little tower, he still had a landscaping problem to solve.

A plenitude of bulky boulders made a warty patch all the way to our door. These must either be hauled away or pulverized; and yet they served the purpose of holding up the hill. To substitute for this function, he decided to create an expanse of filled-in ground, shored up by a granite wall. The boulders he took out didn't yield enough stone for this wall and he cast about for more rocks of good size, near enough to haul.

This began to worry two of his younger daughters. They knew that Blunderbore and the Three Giants had every qualification for walldom. Lotus, eleven, and Ximena, nine, abandoned all discretion one day and voiced their fears at the lunch table.

"You won't blow up Blunderbore, pa, will you?"

"Please don't, papa. Or the Three Giants either."

"Of course he won't, sillies!" hissed one or both of the teen-agers, Earl and Elizabeth, impaling the worry-warts with black looks. Maqueda, barely through the teen portal, still identified with the younger faction. It was her special gift of wisdom to keep her mouth shut in crises. So now she only gave the anxious seven-year-old, Bliss, a reassuring kick under the table.

Whether or not this was to be a "situation" depended, of course, on Papa. He had ordained from the start of their earthly journey that meals were sacrosanct to intelligent and, if possible, entertaining conversation that was, above all, peaceable. He was never to be heckled, whined at, or forced to referee while he ate. And if permissions were demanded at this sacred time, the answer was *ipso facto* "No."

But he was not now about to make an issue of the little girls' choice of table talk. He was no niggler. And the rock problem engrossed him enough to gather his family into his mental orbit. Therefore, he pushed back his chair, crossed his legs, and otherwise signalled his wish to talk.

"I'll need a mammoth boulder. More than one, of course. This wall will take a couple of hundred blocks, as I see it. As you all know, we used up the best rocks on the hill for the basement."

The basement, a half-story high, allowed extensive storage for the winter woodpile, a room for Mama's preserves, and a windowed studio for Nonette, the oldest and a sculptress. Moreover, a quantity of rock had gone into three flights of stone steps to two entrances—one on the front or east side and a longer stair on the south side.

"Pa, I have a thought."

Eyes turned to June, second oldest, home with her new degree from Hastings Law School to begin partnership with her father in the firm of *McGlashan and McGlashan*.

"Good. No, wait. Let's retire to the rotunda."

That got everybody on their feet while Papa gallantly saw to it that Mama led the way.

The rotunda, ringed with windows, became henceforth the family's favorite gathering place. Here, Papa gave himself up to the fat arms of his black padded leather chair that faced Donner Peak in the west. Wreathed in smoke from his Brown Owl cigar, he beamed satisfaction with chair, family, and that house so open to the world. At his left, Mama's highbacked upholstered rocker symbolically faced her own realm of tranquil influence— the entire "inscape" of the house. Her immediate vision, however, took in only the big living room—the kettle-shaped stove that devoured railroad ties in winter; the worn couch; the wall telephone; the lamps and tables embossed with the priceless patina of her children's usage.

"Now, June, let's hear your idea," Papa said when the family was seated, the younger children on the floor.

All eyes turned to the tall slim girl, admiration shining frankly or shyly, according to temperament, from each child's face. June looked her "Portia" role. Even as she sat she held herself erect and controlled. Standing, she had the presence and carriage to project dignity and forceful purpose in a courtroom even though she still tied her dark curls with a ribbon at the nape of her neck and looked more eighteen than twenty-one. In the family group she spoke with authority, for she and Nonette were second in command to their mother.

"I was thinking of the Hooligan Rock, pa."

He paused with his cigar halfway to his lips. "The Hooligan

Rock! Why, of course! It's perfect."

"And it's not too far."

"True. Only a mile or so on the road to the lake, and near the road, to boot."

Mama's face tried to harden over a frowning thought. "I think that rock *ought* to be dynamited. It's a blot on Truckee's name and always has been."

"You're right, love. What a thought! To break up the Hooligan Rock and turn it to a good cause!"

Midway between Truckee and the eastern edge of Donner Lake, the great granite rock towered in a clearing just off the road—an Olympian of the forest. But during Truckee's early days, the monarch had been forced to an ignoble posture. Men had made it the backdrop of ugly secret scenes—floggings in the night, scalding tar and a smother of feathers, curses and screams for mercy. The perpetrators were sometimes citizens pushed too far too long by thieves, arsonists and crooked gamblers. But the aura of evil came from a different group—haters and bigots, whose victims were usually Chinese.

"I'll look into that this very afternoon," Papa promised.

And thus it came to pass that the Hooligan Rock atoned. It became our patient, supportive wall. Today it still stands although the house is gone. Seventy-five years old and buckling, it will give its stalwart best to the end. Two large remnants of the original rock may be seen at the historic spot of its days of infamy, owned by Richard Joseph and his sister, who have fashioned their garden around its granite flanks.

12

Chapter Two

My grandfather was keenly aware of my solitary state of only child in the household, for his own experience of family life had been entirely large-scale. He therefore gave me his own companionship when he could, and valiantly tried to share with me his joy in botany, entomology, and all the marvels of natural science.

Here communication between us floundered. I had been born devoid of scientific curiosity. Give me the proper classification of flower, bird or star and you blighted all my pleasure in it. I know I must have disappointed him. However, he had learned long ago the futility of answering questions that were not asked and, instead, told me that which I liked best to hear—stories of his boyhood in the distant past.

For these stories, usually told at bedtime, we sat in the living room near the wide white doors opening on the library-music room we called "the parlor". Here, beside a three-legged floor lamp, we faced the silver-gray iron stove and a stack of pine railroad ties, sawed-off for winter fire.

This was a meditative spot in summer with the gathering shadows of dusk around us, and in winter, as well, when we sat in the magic circle of the lamp's peach glow. I would climb on Papa's knees in my nightgown—an athlete on the mark, set for the mental gymnastics that earned me my story.

"Now, Maqueda, let's hear you name the books of the Old Testament."

"Forward or backward?"

"Why, forward first, of course. Genesis..."

"Genesis, Exodus, Leviticus, Numbers, Deuteronomy..." on I marched through the thirty-nine books of the King James edition, to the smashing finish—"Zechariah, Malachi." It was an eye-popping performance for any random guest.

"All right. Now can you give me the books of the New Testament?" He knew I could. He hadn't programmed me overnight. Then, having delivered those twenty-seven titles, I heard the expected, "Now, backward."

"All of them?"

"Well, maybe just the Old Testament tonight..."

Done at last, we said the Lord's Prayer together, ending with my solo affirmation, never omitted, "I am God's child, no harm can come to me." This came out in a rush too triumphant for reverence, marking as it did the end of my performance and the beginning of his.

We didn't attend a church in my time, although both my grandparents were deeply religious. Years before, the family would walk down the hill to the steepled Methodist-Episcopal on Church Street. But this custom had abruptly come to an end one Sunday when, after the fuss and furor of getting eight children dressed and polished, they arrived at the moment the minister began to speak. Grimly, he halted while the McGlashans filed in—the children in steps by size, followed by Mama in her best hat, and Papa carrying the baby.

Inevitably, the only empty pews were at the front. These the family filled while the waiting pastor compressed his lips in a silence ominous as the roll of drums. When at last he spoke, he flung tact to the winds.

"Now the McGlashan tribe is settled, we shall proceed."

At which Papa whispered a command along the line and the family rose, about-faced, and proceeded back out the door, never to return for services again.

However, Sabbath observance was by no means abandoned in our home. Papa had taught Sunday School for years in his youth and had even believed, for a time, that he had "the call" himself. Now, with charts and colorful Bible pictures and texts in bold print, later used for my own instruction, he set up Sunday School in our dining room.

"Now, what story do you want tonight?"

They were all re-runs that I demanded again and again. I was enthralled by the poverty of his childhood and loved to hear about heartrending Christmas mornings when the boy Fayette (he was called by his middle name) and his sisters found nothing, nothing at all, in their stockings.

"But why? Why didn't Ann or your other big sisters make you toys out of sticks or anything? Just *anything* for a present?"

"We were so poor that our father didn't want us to expect things. I suppose he thought that would only make for worse disappointments."

This I could not accept. Either I must dislike my great-grandfather Peter for a dour Scot, or come up with another answer. And who is to say my romanticizing mind did not approach the truth? From all the stories told me and my own long thoughts on my pillow, the following picture of Papa's father, mother and early life formed as vividly in my mind as if I had lived it personally.

Peter McGlashan, not yet twenty, left the highlands near Pitlochry and sailed to America during the hard times of the late 1820s. He came with several families of clan McGlashan, a sept of the Stewarts of Atholl.

Energetic Scots with shrewd restless minds, the McGlashans brought varied skills and interests to their new homeland. Peter himself taught music. The violin was his love, but he taught voice and pianoforte as well, and he sang in a tender lyric tenor.

Arrived in New York, he soon parted with kin who wanted to farm, as well as those who hankered after urban enterprise. Alone, he set out on foot to find pupils in the scattered settlements. In short, Peter was a pioneer only by necessity. Instinctively, he took up the life he would have followed anyway if he'd never left Scotland.

One golden autumn day, tramping along a winding road toward the village beyond, he spotted a trail that angled off into the woods. On the chance it might be a shortcut, he took it—and was immediately glad he did. High noon had touched off a wild conflagration of crimson and gold in a maple grove. Above his head, sunbeams slanted in luminous benedictions through a ceiling of tangled branches.

He walked a few paces reverently, hushed with delight, on a carpet of leaves like fallen stars. Then, as soon as he made sure the path meandered in the right direction, he quickened his step, abandoned himself to its lead, and opened his mouth to sing.

No sound left his throat.

Before him rose a rustic house in a natural clearing ringed with white birch. And *he* was standing in its unfenced backyard. Not alone.

A dark-haired girl faced him squarely from behind a huge round tub brimming with sudsy garments. Her long rich hair shone in the sunlight and tumbled loosely over her breast and shoulders. She stood as if frozen with elbows akimbo, her bare arms immobile in the soapy water.

Blue eyes riveted on brown in a shared paralysis of mind and muscle. Not only her arms were bare, he saw. Her shoulders gleamed equally naked. Appallingly, unmistakably, her clothes were in the tub. All of them.

"And that's how I met your mother," Peter grinned, telling their daughters in years to come.

"Mother! How awful!" Adelia, or Ann or Lib responded on cue. "Tell us again what you did."

Elizabeth, smiling, went on mending or cooking while she answered.

"I was in a predicament, all right. There stood this young man, embarrassed witless, with his mouth open, and his eyes— well, I thought he was going to cry."

"The truth, love, the truth! My eyes were popping with the vision of Aphrodite riding the foam."

"Fiddlesticks! Your pa, girls, didn't know whether to drop through the ground or turn tail and run. I felt so sorry for the poor boy I forgot to be embarrassed myself."

"Cool as a cucumber, the brazen hussy."

"I said, 'Turn around, if you please, and keep your eyes tight shut, sir.' Which he did. His neck was 'like the red, red rose'."

Sometimes Peter sobered down at this point and leaned toward his wife as if only the two were in the room.

"And there she stands, when I can look, in a green dress dripping bubbles. Shy? Not a bit of it. Like the queen of England herself she bids me come in for a cup of fresh milk."

"And you said yes, pa."

16

"I always say 'aye' to a mermaid. I've been saying it ever since, if you've noticed."

He would reach out a hand and pat her wrist or knee, or rub a knuckle down her cheek. Theirs was a demonstrative love. The children were used to Peter's romantic lapses, with the consequent transfiguration of their mother's face.

Elizabeth Waterhouse McGlashan, French Canadian by birth, was not as pretty as she seemed to be. Each feature had its imperfection—nose too long, mouth too strong, chin slightly left of center. But the glowing softness of her large dark eyes and the swift animation of her smile unified her features with attractive charm.

A schoolteacher when Peter met her, Elizabeth gave up teaching when they married. As long as his pupils supported them, they stayed in a quiet village of western New York. However, music lessons were a luxury in the farming community and pupils dropped off with every disappointing crop. They began to feel anxious when Adelia was born and Elizabeth soon conceived again.

"Come to us, Peter," wrote cousin John McGlashan from a new settlement in Wisconsin Territory called Beaver Dam, located in Black Hawk country, north of Janesville. "There's something here for everybody, even for music masters."

Why not? As babies came along, the alternative would be the city, which they both rejected. They wanted a life that was simple, noncompetitive, far from industry's smoke and din.

There is reason to believe an infant son was born and died about this time. Elizabeth would bear, in all, seven living children, spaced with predictable regularity—except for a four-year gap between Adelia and Ann.

That the baby was a boy may be surmised from the fact that the sixth child, the only living male we are sure of, was called Charles Fayette.

"It's a name handed down in my family, love," Peter said, "but there's a curse on it. If the first-born male is christened Charles Fayette, he dies. In infancy or early childhood."

"Superstition!" Elizabeth scoffed affectionately.

Nevertheless, would Peter have taken the risk of naming a

first-born son so recklessly? Or would Elizabeth have shadowed his joy in a son by insisting on a name he feared? She loved her husband's fey side. Every new moon she played his game of spotting the faint curved sliver while it rode clean and clear, uncrossed by a portent of trouble. It is more believable that my grandfather, Charles Fayette, was simply not their first male child.

At Beaver Dam Peter built a log house among others like it. Genial neighbors helped him plant crops, acquire chickens, hogs, a cow.

Tranquil days flowed into months and years. Peter wasn't enslaved by his farm. He had time for music, books, good friends, wife, and daughter after daughter.

Ann was born on a crisp September tenth in 1837. Every two years thereafter, Elizabeth brought forth another girl until, in addition to Adelia and Ann, they had Elizabeth (Lib), Isabel and Martinette (Nette).

Like all women of pioneer communities, Elizabeth was on call for any illness, confinement, or emergency. At home, she taught her girls early to bake bread, patch a torn dress, darn socks, cut a pattern. More than that, she sat them down daily to reading, writing, spelling and ciphering.

It was her passionate goal to see her daughters educated. Peter admired her determination and fostered it with family reading every night after supper. In addition to his violin and a melodeon, he had brought from New York every book they had acquired, including volumes of Sir Walter Scott, Shakespeare, classic myths, *Pilgrim's Progress, Scottish Chiefs,* and the English poets.

By Christmas of 1846, Nette, who had been born on Valentine's Day of that year, toddled in her mother's wake like a small tug-boat. Elizabeth now knew a summer baby was started and the girls began their favorite game of wagering on a brother.

This time, at last, they were to win.

During the months that this baby grew in his mother's womb, a tragedy was being enacted far out west in the Sierra Nevada. From November to March of 1846–47, the men, women and children of the Donner party floundered in a white deathtrap of wild blizzards, savage snowstorms, and sub-zero cold.

18

Scarcely four months after rescuers brought the last survivors down the mountain, Charles Fayette McGlashan was born at Beaver Dam, on a sweltering August 12, 1847.

Thirty years later, he and the survivors of the Donner Party would meet. The meeting would alter his life, and theirs as well.

—•—

When Fayette was two, the McGlashans celebrated a new milestone in their marriage. In November, 1849 Adelia married a prospering young rancher named George W. Balis, from western New York. Since Elizabeth was pregnant again and due at Christmas, Adelia would have postponed the wedding, but Elizabeth would not hear of it.

Immediately after the wedding, Christmas preparations began in full force. Elizabeth had always made Christmas memorable from start to finish.

"And it starts a month ahead," Peter groaned. For weeks he could expect to blunder into secret workshops and hideaways, suffering outraged glares from his daughters. At the same time, he confessed, odors of cinnamon and clove soaked the rafters, quince and cranberry jellies bubbled on the stove, and the house was a heaven of delicious fragrances.

This 1849 Christmas must be no different, Elizabeth said. In case the baby came on the Eve or on the very day, they must prepare well ahead.

But for this Christmas, they could not prepare.

Elizabeth's time came and it was a bad time.

Neighbors spread the word. From far reaches of the settlement women came to help. Peter was banished to wherever he chose to pace alone and pray to God for her. Kinsmen gathered the children in. Adelia came home to stay by her mother's bedside.

At last, for an hour or so, tensions eased. A baby girl was born and breathed and cried. But Elizabeth...

When it was over, they tried to comfort him.

"She was a good wife and mother."

"God rest her soul."

"She lived thirty-eight years? For a woman, these days... out here... that's good."

"Don't worry about the children, Peter. Leave them with us until . . . And we'll find a wet-nurse for the wee one. Laurie? Laura. A bonny name."

He stared at them, dry-eyed with shock and disbelief, nodding his head in mute thanks.

—•—

For awhile, George Balis brought Adelia to the house once a week to help twelve-year-old Ann and check on them all, but Adelia was pregnant in early spring, and her visits tapered off.

This suited Ann. She had taken hold with shrewd practicality and the methods of a marine sergeant. Farm and house chores hummed smartly under her command. In frigid January pre-dawns, she smacked a laggard's bottom while she stripped the bedding off her juniors at four o'clock sharp.

Her father was her main worry. From a fun-loving, affectionate, singing man he had become an absent man—dull-eyed, humorless, moody.

They were all sorrowing, comforting each other, rocking the small ones when they cried. Only Peter they could not comfort.

"We must just be good and do our chores," Ann said.

Christmastime came again. Peter made it an anniversary of mourning and forbade every sign of celebration, other than church-going. Thus it would be for years to come.

But in 1851, when the baby was two and Fayette three and a half, he told them astounding news.

"George and Adelia are going to California. We shall go, too."

A silent moment paid tribute to the enormity of this announcement.

"*We* are going?"

"We are going. I have thought on it, and we are going."

"When, Pa?"

"We must begin now, straight off, to make our plans. We need to buy oxen and a wagon."

Ann saw his eyes flicker with tiny resurrections of light and life. He told what they must do (get rid of much); what adventures might befall (Indians); and what hardships they must endure boldly (short rations).

20

"Where will our home be, Pa, when we get there?" Lib asked.

A bewildered look of loss and loneliness twisted across his face. He shook his head roughly, like a horse persecuted by the same old fly.

Lib had spoiled the rare, close-gathered warmth of the moment and Ann swiftly rallied them all: "Come on, everybody. Time to feed the hogs. We'll be back, Pa."

Outside, she slid an arm around her sister's plump shoulders.

"Don't ask where we'll live, Lib. What does it matter? 'Delia and George are going. Maybe lots of people we know."

"But why, Ann? Why leave here? This is home!" Tears tracked the girl's flushed cheeks.

"Because it's away, that's why," Ann answered sharply. "Don't you understand anything? Pa has to go away, that's all."

Thus began in spring, 1851 a flight so dogged by bad luck it seemed likely never to get off the ground.

In Missouri, sickness struck the children down, including Adelia's child, Marella. At the camp near St. Joseph, cousin John's wife helped Ann and Adelia nurse them. Then their company's turn came to cross the river.

"Go on ahead, George," Peter said. "Take Adelia and the baby, if she can travel. I'll wait it out."

If a train didn't move by mid-May, it must sit out the seasons until another spring. They camped among a multitude of tented wagons, shivering through winter blasts, sweating under summer sun. The year took its toll of equipment and clothing. Hunger moved into their lives like an uncongenial boarder, but not yet the enemy it would become.

At last they moved with a train to Salt Lake. Again they camped. Another year passed.

Meanwhile, the children grew in stature, age, and toughness. By the time the pasture greened again in 1854, heat, cold and short rations had made four-year-old Laurie and Fayette, six, as durable as young Sioux.

In May they began the long final journey, and just to be moving refreshed Peter's parched spirit. Excruciating facial pains had felled him during the long encampments. Perhaps he could fend them off in action.

Indians they met were friendly. Peter gave out yardage of calico, brought along for appeasement. Ann and Lib beguiled one party with hot biscuits while Bell produced tunes on the little melodeon they were never to jettison.

Once there might have been trouble. The McGlashan wagon dropped behind one afternoon, while Peter repaired an axle. Suddenly, a group of painted braves materialized from a clump of boulders.

"How!" Peter said, raising his palm in greeting.

The Indians frowned in silence. Peter knew he must quickly demonstrate that they beheld a peaceful man, alone with a wagonload of harmless children. He was glad Ann and Lib were inside the wagon tent. In their teens, both of them, they could be considered squaw material. He called out without turning his head.

"Annie, dig out two bolts of calico, and both of you stay out of sight. Fayette! Laurie! Do what I tell ye, hear?"

These two had been staring, enthralled by paint and feathers.

"Go to the wagon and fetch the cloth. Quickly! Ye'll give it to the gentleman in front there, d'ye hear?"

The red man watched stolidly while the boy with sunburnt hair and the small doe-eyed girl entered the wagon's flapdoor. When they came out, they lugged between them two planks of red and blue cloth. Beaming with curiosity and friendship, they walked to the leader and placed their burden at his feet.

He made no move. An awkward moment wavered, out of focus on the afternoon. Suddenly inspired to good manners, Fayette slapped a hand on his stomach and bowed. Then he grabbed Laura's hand, about-faced and walked her to their father.

When he turned, the Indians and the cloth were gone.

—•—

When the worn but jubilant caravan trundled down the Carson Road into Hangtown, officially named Placerville the previous June, George and Adelia were cheering with the throng that turned out to welcome them. Chubby-legged Marella rode on her father's shoulders. Adelia carried a year-old child in her arms. George had struck gold and invested in a boarding house for steady income, and it was there the Balises took Peter and the children.

For the time being, Peter must rest and recover. The pains in his face had returned cruelly during the trek across glaring sands.

By the following spring, he was ready to try a small farm near Cook's Bar in Sacramento County, but the oppressive summer heat convinced him he should move north.

He heard of vast ranches, former Mexican holdings in Sonoma County, up the Russian River—acres now open to squatters. This proved to be only rumor. Actually, the Sotoyome ranch, owned by Captain Henry D. Fitch's widow, was being parceled and sold at public auction.

Peter had arrived too late. The prices of leftover lots had risen beyond his means. People who knew the region tried to help. Three squatter families, they said, had taken land west of a turn-off ten miles north along the wagon road. One man drew a map. With all of their possessions in a wagon, the family set out to follow it.

Peter had bought a horse and mare and he let them take their time. It was fall and the ripe wheat fields stretched to the base of the rounded hills of the Coast Range. Trees lined the road for several miles, then gave way to meadows of waist-deep clover. Before they reached the turn-off shown on the map, the predicted ten miles had become fifteen.

At the turn-off they followed wagon tracks directly seaward—and came face to face with craggy brush-bound hills. Soon they were toiling up a rutted tortuous trail that climbed only to plunge as steeply down.

Silence had long since settled on them. They were all thinking the same thing—this couldn't be right. The map was misleading. Then the sound of rushing waters reached them from beyond another hill. The map said Beatty's Creek was near the squatter land. Hopeful, they pushed on.

When they descended the last hill to the banks of a wide tumultuous creek, the trail leveled off and their spirits revived. Another mile and they saw a cabin through the high brush. The map had not failed them.

—•—

"Man, turn back," squatters Taylor and Wilkinson both advised. "Nothing grows here. Nothing! The hills are too steep for cows or sheep, even if there was any pasture, which there ain't. We boil a stubby oat for mush, ourselves. Game there is, and fish. Not much of anything in winter, though. Take your young 'uns and go back. Children need fruit and greens."

However, before they could decide to leave, a storm trapped them. Driving rains obliterated the wagon tracks and turned the hills into cascading rivulets of mud. The sympathetic families took them in, dividing the children among them.

When the rains stopped, Peter built a shelter. Now they must wait for the earth to dry out.

But it stormed again. Peter built more securely. He took Fayette into the wilderness to shoot rabbit and quail. With the father's eyesight worsening, the boy, now nine, must provide them with game. Taylor went with them to help them find the stream's best fishing.

From the kindly Taylor, Bennett, and Wilkinson women, Ann and her sisters learned what could be made of the strange oat and wheat grasses.

Chapter Three

One day in the spring of 1860, a stranger walked up the green banks of the creekbed to their cabin door, and offered two dollars in gold dust for rattlesnake rattles.

Fayette didn't have to risk his father's wrath. He could have kept his mouth shut. But gold dust! It had been nearly four years since the family had had anything but hens' eggs to barter with.

He heard his father saying, "I'm afraid we dinna have ... "

"Pa, I've got some."

Peter wheeled on him, scowling, "Some what?"

"Rattles. I've got a whole box full."

Too elated to see the storm signals clouding his father's brow, he scurried into the house and came back with a hand-made box crammed with dry feather-light husks.

The gold-dust man whistled between sparse teeth and reached for the box with both hands. Dumping the rattles on the earth, he counted them, one by one. Then he untied the pouch secured to his sweaty belt and prepared to measure out his payment by pinchfuls into a crumpled square of soiled cloth.

While the children watched the tiny mound grow, Peter was concerned with moral issues. True, he had taught the boy to secure a snake's head with a forked stick, but he hadn't meant it for a game. The fact he'd kept the rattles hidden proved that Fayette knew the foolhardy business would be forbidden. He had been deliberately deceitful. Peter toyed with the notion of refusing the payment, to prove that good does not come of evil, but the rapt young faces told him the lesson would be lost.

He therefore gravely concluded the transaction and pointed the stranger's way upstream. Then he took his son behind the house.

In the morning, the boy's empty bed, neatly made, stated he'd gone respectfully, but he had gone.

Peter forbade any search. "The boy should come back on his own," he said.

Smoldering gloom, compounded of shock and anxiety, settled on the household.

Five days and four April-cold nights passed; then Ann could wait no longer. Her narrow face thundery with decision, she went to her gaunt, graying father in the chicken yard where he was mending the melodeon's cracked boards.

"Ye'll let us go look for the boy now, Pa."

Her words came bluntly, with no saving grace of an upcurved tone implying doubt or question. She was glad her sisters couldn't hear, for this was mutiny. She braced herself as for a blow, although Peter never struck the girls—only the boy. And him for the last time, she thought, even if he does come home.

Even in profile she could follow her father's thoughts. What else had she done since she was Fayette's age? She was twenty-one now and until this minute she had upheld Peter's word as law. If he should turn on her with a roar, she could scream back, "I've earned the right, Pa. I've earned the right to speak my mind."

But no roar came. Clearly as if he spoke aloud, the message reached her:

"That ye have, lass, that ye have."

A slowly climbing flush softened her plain face. Deep within, she felt a trickle of joy, as if she had received an award, or a diploma.

"Look, Pa, he'd have gone to the settlement. You know he would. And Bell and I can be there tomorrow if we take the wagon."

She mended her tone so he could straighten now and face his daughter fully, shading his eyes with a lean forearm.

"Ye know my stand on it, Annie. The boy went off on his own. On his own he should come back."

"But Pa..."

"I wash my hands of it. You're a woman now, do what ye will. I say no more." He turned away and bent over his work.

The words saved his pride, she knew, and the burr growled

26

gently on his tongue. In pity, she yearned to put her arms around the stooped shoulders, to let him know she understood he suffered her anxiety, too. But his manner repelled any overtures.

He has to go on blaming the boy, she told herself, or admit he was unjust. Too often, of late years, he'd lashed out at his son in sarcasm or with blow.

"It's the headaches, dear." she had told Fayette.

There was more to it, she knew. Fear of blindness, as much as unrelieved and nauseating pain, had paralyzed Peter's will, trapping them all here on the barren side of the Coast Range. She suspected he told himself every day, "Tomorrow we'll get out of this wasteland." The tomorrows were already a river four years long.

While Laurie helped Ann and Lib hitch the mare to the wagon, Peter worked on, ignoring the commotion.

Lib, second in command, had grown into the Brunhilde of the family. She was tall, blonde, full-bosomed. Nettie, fourteen and skinny, might grow as tall. Isabel had the flower-pretty face and sweet temper, they all agreed. Dark-eyed Laurie would be tiny like Ann.

When all was done, Isabel and Ann came to kiss their father goodbye. He swiped his mouth with the back of his hand and kissed them, but gave no parting word of blessing.

"We're riding with them to the hill," Lib shouted.

He waved consent and bent lower over the melodeon until the creaking wagon scraped off and the garrulous stream drowned the girls' treble chatter.

Alone, with no posture of righteousness to maintain, he let his thoughts run free. After a moment, he dropped his knife and strode into the spice-blown thicket, taking a trail the boy followed when he played alone. His booted toes stubbed against rocks and knotty roots as he stumbled along the path, blindly shoving branches from his face with bare forearms.

Soon, as he knew it would, a natural amphitheatre opened before him, made of encircling boulders, oaks, and spring-green plumed bushes. Here was Fayette's playground.

Seated on a humped blue stone, he opened his spirit to the influences around him. Everywhere the image of his son burned

Map of Sonoma County, circa 1867, showing location of Peter McGlashan's cabin in the Cloverdale wilderness. Note that his last name was misspelled.

through—the unruly orange-brown hair; the vibrant face, lightly freckled like a firm-cheeked apricot; the fleet-footed carriage, erect as an Indian. He saw him in the spiny, wet-green oak leaves, in the puckering elfin apples of satin-barked manzanita, in the smile of pale sky, glimpsed through long strong branches. And in the sandy dust he saw the scuff and scrape of his footprint.

Peter moaned, covering his face with long, flat-tipped sensitive fingers, and listened with closed eyes. Latent in the air were the sounds of his son, for here he let out the yells that were in him. Here he whooped, hollered, whistled, and mimicked the hooting, screeching wildlife whose habitat they shared.

Suddenly, surrendering to the turbulence of remorse and love, Peter did something the man Elizabeth had known might have done. He knelt on the earth and kissed the boy's footprint.

Laurie's bare feet had brought her silently along the same trail.

She would have called out to her father if, at that moment, he had not done what he had done.

With consummate good sense in one so small, she never let him know that she saw. She only stole back to the house and, at bedtime, whispered it to Lib.

—•—

Ann's hunch was correct. Fayette had headed for Healdsburg.

Once out of the wilderness and into the fields of clover, he carefully avoided the cluster of houses near the general store. On the level wagon road, with his nose pointed straight toward the town at last, he made good time. But as the sun climbed the sky, hunger plagued his stomach, and he wished he had made some provision for it. Thirst was hardest to ignore, and he could have whooped with joy when he spotted a frame house not many yards to the right.

A woman was crouching over a berry patch near one side of the house and he approached her with his best manners showing. Wishing her a good day, he was about to ask for a cup of water from the well when, instead, he heard himself say, "Do you need a berry picker, ma'am?"

Her sun-dried face peered up at him from a deep bonnet. He knew she was judging his thievery-potential, so he beamed a politician's open smile at her until slowly she unbent and stood up. With a large-knuckled hand she offered him a nest of juice-stained boxes.

"All right. Take these boxes and fill 'em up. Mind you don't bruise them berries."

She stalked into the house, leaving him parched with thirst and his stomach hunger-knotted, to pick the ripest, juiciest, sweetest-smelling strawberries of his life.

But he tasted not one.

This wasn't lost on the woman, who peeked from behind flimsy curtains. When he brought in his finished work at last, she was benignly ready with his reward and, that hour, he relished two things new to his experience. One was berries with sugar and cream. The other was independence. His stomach, he saw, could be as full as hands, feet and back were willing.

—•—

Charles Fayette McGlashan at age 12, when the family moved to Healdsburg, California.

He found Healdsburg greatly expanded. It now had two sections, served by merchants, saloons, stables, and a butcher shop. Here, he found the aproned owner sweeping up the soiled sawdust.

"Can I do that for you, sir?" He gave the deferential little bow instinctive to him, which so astonished the butcher he handed over the broom without a thought. Only after a customer had come and gone did he ask the boy his name.

"Grant. Grant Gray."

This was the only thing he'd planned ahead. Grant—like granite, flinty and hard—a man's name. As for Gray, this was a non-lie really, he told himself. Hadn't his father said McGlashan meant gray-green in Gaelic? In England, McGlashans even changed the name to Gray or Greene.

He then volunteered an autobiography, supplying himself with a home two miles north. He would gladly come every day, he said, to sweep or run errands in return for a piece of sausage.

The butcher liked him, didn't entirely believe him, and shook hands to seal the bargain.

The next day, he swept the butcher shop and had time to hire out his usefulness to Dutcher's General Store as well. By midweek, he was not only enjoying two fair meals a day through his own diligence, but had prospects of supplying other needs, such as soap, a comb, and, not impossibly, a pair of store pants from Dutcher's.

At night he slept under the oaks and slender madrones on the riverbank. The way to this chosen campsite led him past the impressive new two-story schoolhouse, where he stood awhile on the edge of the playground, staring up at the belltower and trying to picture the classrooms. From snatches of talk, he had learned that a hundred and fifty pupils were already enrolled. It was called Russian River Institute now, but would be changed soon to Sotoyome.

Hot yearning flooded him. He had to go to that school—or some school. And oh, he would, he would. Ann always said, "Your life is what you make it, little brother." Well, he would make it take the shape he wanted, but he had to begin with school.

On the fifth morning of his new life he woke up with fiery knives lacerating his throat at every swallow. He went to work at the butcher shop, but before noon his employer noticed the feverish brilliance of his eyes and laid a meaty-wet hand on his hot forehead.

"Lie down in the back room, son. I'll take you home later in the wagon. And I'll tell your mother she should keep you home a day or two."

Too sick to answer, too sick to care that the jig was up and his lie would now be revealed, he did as he was told.

—•—

There had been a long darkness. He didn't open his eyes although he saw the play of light on his eyelids. An ocean of softness, demanding identification, bore him up. He fanned an exploratory leg from side to side. A bed. He lay on a billowy wide bed.

"Grant? Do you hear me, Grant?"

He turned his head toward the muted voice, a woman's.

"You're going to get well fast now, dear."

Warm gray eyes smiled down at him when he looked. The plump, motherly face of Mrs. Dutcher hovered over him.

"You've been a sick boy, but you'll be fine now we can fatten you up."

She pummeled the goose-feather pillow under his head. When he tried weakly to lift himself on an elbow, she gently pushed him back and tucked the blankets under his chin.

"I'm going to bring you a hot bowl of cereal. And after that.." She tweaked the hump his foot made under the covers. "After that, you have a big surprise coming." With a wink, she backed out of the room and softly closed the door.

Left to himself, Fayette's eyes roved the high-ceilinged room. He had experienced a real home before, during the few weeks in George and Adelia's boarding house. He wanted to live in a decent house with real chairs, not boxes, to sit on. His sisters, too, should have skirted dressing tables and long mirrors like the ones in this room.

Later, while he downed oatmeal and warm milk, he shrank from questions Mrs. Dutcher was sure to ask. He was beginning to wonder why she didn't ask them when he heard the clop-clop of horses' hooves come to a halt below his window.

"There! I told you I'd have a surprise." Mrs. Dutcher glanced out the window, then rapidly smoothed his blankets and whisked away the tray with its emptied bowl. After another wink, she bustled through the door and clumped down the stairs.

Almost immediately, women's voices and footsteps ascended to his room and the door was flung wide.

"Fay!"

"Darling boy!"

Ann, with Isabel behind her, crossed the room in two strides and pressed his head to her hard, narrow shoulder. Over and over she kissed his hair, eyes, cheeks. Tears trickled from her face and over his nose, and this made them laugh...

The strawberry woman had given the first clue, Ann said. Once in Healdsburg, they had gone straight to Dutcher's store, sure he'd be errand-boy there or elsewhere.

"You see, I know you!"

Fayette laughed and listened, enjoying his sisters' voices and faces, aware how much he'd missed them. But his guard was up. The moment must come when Ann would talk of taking him home.

It came. "Mrs. Dutcher thinks you can travel in a day or two. Will you go back with us, Fayette?"

His jaw dropped in surprise. She had made it a question, as if he had a choice. He couldn't believe it. Pulling the covers up to his ears, he squinched down in the bed.

"I'm not going back. I won't go back."

Bell, who had been strolling around the room fingering the unfamiliar fabrics of curtain and chair, stared at him.

"What do you mean? Of course you're going back."

"Bell, please," Ann interposed. "Let me." She patted the covers, tautly gripped around the boy's tense form. But Isabel, usually so placid, insisted hotly.

"Annie, no! I'll talk. It's Pa I'm thinking of. Fay, what are you doing to Pa?"

She had dug into the sore spot. He burrowed his face deeper into the pillow. Relentless, Bell stamped around the bed to glare down at her brother's head. Knuckles on her slim hips, she prodded with her voice.

"Think how you've hurt him, Fay."

"Pa hates me. He don't want me back." The words erupted in muffled explosions.

"Don't want you back! What's got into you? Don't want you back!"

Ann repressed a comical urge to say "*doesn't*" to both of them. "Hear me, both of you," she ordered. "This is no time for decisions. We'll come back later on. Fay will rest now, and we can enjoy looking around the town, since we've found him at last."

She walked to the door, commanding Bell with a look to follow suit. Fayette, sullen and mistrustful, slowly turned his head to watch them go. Ann added a final word.

"We're going to visit that new school. I've a Scotch hunch you young ones will go there soon."

Two faces stared at her in mute amazement. She walked back to the bedside. "It's true, dear. We're moving to Healdsburg. As fast as we can get out of that hole back there."

"But Pa...?"

"He will agree. If a twelve-year-old boy can earn his way, what can't the lot of us do!"

Fayette struggled to sit up. "You promise?"

Ann sat on his bed, pushing him gently back against the pillow. "I promise." She hesitated, about to say more, but her eyes filled with tears and she only kissed the boy's cheek, then joined Bell at the door.

"Sweet dreams, little brother."

—•—

For the next two days, sunbursts of euphoria dazzled all three. Fayette ate ravenously and gained strength from hour to hour. Ann directed her energies to learning answers her father was certain to demand of her. And Bell, charged with the list of staples and dry goods, schemed on paper how best to spend the pouch of gold dust provided by Fay's rattlers.

Ann's first business was a talk with the school's principal. He assured her Fayette could sweep halls and do yard work for tuition. She didn't beg for Nette and Laurie. Somehow she would raise those costs herself.

She almost danced away from the interview. "Fulfillment," sang her thought, "for the boy, and for us all!" For herself, what did she ask of life except to put her brother on the road to—what? Greatness? Yes. She'd see him "a statesman in the land"—a statesman in the land! Why not? With education, who could stop him? Not Pa, not anyone...no one but the boy, himself. With strong guidance from herself now, while he was young, he would follow through, most likely. But that would be up to him.

From the school she drove to Dutcher's store where Bell was making their purchases. No sooner had she hitched the mare to

34

Sotoyome Institute. C. F. McGlashan graduated from this school, and taught there at age 17, in 1864–65.

the porch railing than her sister called out so musical a greeting that Ann's breath caught on an instant of question.

Inside, young Lyman Dutcher leaned across a counter heaped with bright bolts of calico, cotton, silk and wool. Beneath his dazed and glowing eyes, a pink flush heightened the tan of his honest face. Ann saw she'd guessed the truth—her pretty sister and Mrs. Dutcher's boy smiled from some capsuled realm apart.

At the Dutcher's table that night, Ann related her experiences of the day and the family promised to give every help in their power when the McGlashans moved to town.

With Lyman a willing escort, the girls explored the settlement next day and found an old but suitable house. Ann paid a month's rent to hold it.

On the following day, in the morning's first light, Mrs. Dutcher fed them all a hearty sausage and pancake breakfast, after which Lyman and his father loaded the wagon with their purchases.

"Come back to us now."

"We will, we will!"

"Tell your pa we'll help him all we can."

"Thank you for everything!"

They set out for the Cloverdale turn-off that would point them to the final lap of the journey back. They didn't talk much after the first few miles. Each of the three had private thoughts to mull before they reached the house they no longer called home.

Chapter Four

Of the Healdsburg years, I gathered bits of scene and color that, in mature years, my mind saw whole like a Seurat landscape, whose tiny dots of paint are blended by the eye.

If the McGlashans lived frugally in their house on Tucker Street, nevertheless they had been transplanted to rich soil spiritually. It was a time of excitement and delight, with all of them pulling together to support the home and keep the three youngest in school. They were fully alive now, growing in every way among new-found friends and neighbors. Even Peter, now completely blind, taught the melodeon with Martinette's help. Ann taught common school. Isabel, engaged to Lyman, took care of the meals and housekeeping while Lib hired out as a seamstress. Fayette swept halls after school for tuition at Sotoyome Institute. Laura's after-school time was given to helping Isabel.

"We were able to go to church again when we moved to Healdsburg," Papa told me once. "I owned only one pair of shoes, of course, and didn't want to wear them out. So I always carried them to the church door, put them on for services, then carried them home again."

For a couple of years all their new moons sailed high above the tangled branches. A major joy and celebration spiced their lives when Lib married a rancher named Henry Briggs. Isabel's wedding would be next, they said. But everyone knew she was putting it off because she was so needed in the home. This worried Ann, who wondered if she oughtn't to quit teaching and take over the household from Bell. "But the money!" she would think. "We have to have the money I earn."

Then suddenly, one day, Ann came home from school, shaking with chills, burning with fever. The doctor diagnosed "consumption." She must get away to a drier climate. She went to Adelia's home in Placerville, for the foothill town seemed a sensible choice, both for climate and proximity to her sister's care. But once the acuteness of her fever abated, she found idleness unendurable. When she learned of a teacher's class in the Spencerian method of penmanship, she enrolled.

"I'm sure that teaching penmanship will be less arduous than common school," she wrote Fayette, "and it pays well. Anyway, I'm going to try it."

Meanwhile, sorrows began for the family. A scourge of fever nearly took Fayette's life, and did take his sister Isabel's. Bell's death was a heart-breaking loss to Fayette and his two sisters in school, for the sweet-tempered young woman, barely twenty-one, had replaced Ann as "mother" in the home. Fayette would long feel her gentle, protective influence.

Numerous deaths saddened the river settlement during that dark January of 1864 and neighbor joined neighbor in mourning. News of Bell's death reached Ann late, for she had moved to the little village on the road to Coloma where the penmanship course was offered. Heavy storms held up the Wells Fargo mailcoach, and apparently Adelia and George, still living in Placerville only eight or ten washed-out miles away, assumed she had word, or were unable to send a messenger through the storm. When she finally learned the tragic news, her impulse to hurry to Peter's side was blocked by the common-sense injunction from Lib, who quoted the doctor, to stay where she was. She mustn't throw her own life needlessly to the pestilence. Her only comfort lay in long letters to Fayette, now sixteen, and to Lib, who assured her that their father and the household were under her own watchful eye.

Very soon after Bell's death, Adelia's two smallest children, one an infant, died.

"Adelia is an old woman in all but years," Ann wrote.

The Balis family decided then to move to Red Bluff, in northern Tehama County, where George wanted to invest in a sheep ranch. Ann was alone indeed. Soon, however, she was able to arrange for young Laura to enroll in St. Catherine's, a private school in Benicia, a town much nearer to Ann although scarcely to the edge of the foothills. Then, to their joy, Nette passed the teacher's examination and was herself assigned to a school at Benicia. They began to believe their luck had turned, but it had not. A short time later, Lib's husband, Henry Briggs, died, leaving her with a small son, James, and a barely successful sheep ranch.

Lib asked her father and Fay to come live with her, but Peter liked the house on Tucker Street. "Fayette and I will manage," he told her. He knew his way around the little house, for one thing, and things he used or needed were ready to his hand. He liked his routine, as well, with the boy reading to him after supper—which Lib might prepare and bring over, if she liked—so his answer was, "Thank ye, lass, but we'll manage."

According to Ann's letters, Lyman dropped by often and made sure Peter lacked nothing from the store. After Bell's death, Lyman continued close as a son and brother to the McGlashan family.

In 1864, Fayette graduated from Sotoyome and was asked to join the faculty. For one not quite seventeen, this was an honor, and he accepted proudly. But the following year, he was teaching near Ann in the Mother Lode, at a mining camp called Cold Spring.

All of Ann's dreams and efforts revolved about her brother's future. She had set her heart on a prep school for Yale or Harvard and had written to three or four in the east. It took months for her letters to go and the replies to come, by steamer and stagecoach. But the waiting was rewarded when replies came at last. Of them all, the letter from Marshall Henshaw, headmaster of Williston Seminary (now Academy) at Easthampton, Massachusetts pleased her most. She wrote again, explaining that her brother must work for tuition, board and room, if the school accepted him. Fayette enclosed his own letter, expressing his desire and giving his academic qualifications.

The second letter from Henshaw sent them into a delirium of shouting, laughing, tearful joy. All the dreams were to come true. He qualified, Henshaw said, and would be given every chance to earn his way.

Now he must save for a decent suit, steamer passage around the Horn, and money to meet the immediate needs of the first month or two in New England. They estimated this would take him a full year, since he gave a portion of his salary to Peter's support.

By June, 1868 he had the money to go. And that same month the happening he most feared befell. Ann had returned to Healdsburg the year before. She was forced to rest from even the tutorial work of penmanship classes. Chills and fever had wasted her slight frame. Every violent coughing spell seemed beyond her strength to survive.

One of her friends from the foothills teaching circuit lived in San Francisco and, early in the spring of 1868, urged her to visit and rest at the family home. They knew a doctor, she said, who might ease Ann's condition.

Ann decided to accept this invitation. Possibly she hoped that in spite of her terminal illness she might gain strength to be active once more before death took her. But in June, she died. She would have been thirty-one in September.

Fayette came to the funeral and saw the sister who had been his mother, confidante, and best friend buried in San Francisco's Lone Mountain Cemetery.

Adelia and George came down from Red Bluff, too late for the funeral but able to comfort Peter and make the sorrowful occasion a reunion of the entire family—the last they would share with their father, but they did not know it.

In July, Fayette sailed on *The Golden Gate*. During the sea journey he copied all of Ann's letters into his commonplace book, branding their counsels on his mind and heart. Grieving for Bell he had suffered acute shock and a sorrow that he could express in wracking sobs and tears. But in Ann's death he had lost so much he found himself dry-eyed, his grief locked in.

Strangely, the very enormity of his loss exalted him. He felt hurtled out of himself and above himself, cleansed of self-interest. He would do his level best always—for Ann. He would make her dreams for him come true, not for ambition's sake, but for her whose dreams they had been. He would make his life a tribute to her who had sacrificed so much for him and for them all.

Arrived in Massachusetts, he quickly learned he had chosen one of the most progressive intermediate schools in the land.

Williston Seminary in East Hampton, Massachusetts, circa 1855.

Williston Seminary offered not only the classical foundation required by all major professions of the day, but daringly led the field with the innovation of a science department.

This had been the dream of founder Samuel Williston, a successful button manufacturer. As early as 1841, he had reasoned that an economy based heavily on productivity was bound to open up new careers requiring a preparation in the sciences rather than in Latin and Greek.

Successive headmasters, all classicists, either ignored his wishes or openly opposed them. After all, they implied, let a businessman endow education, not meddle with it.

Then, in 1863, Marshall Henshaw came—a quiet, gray-haired unassuming man, whose mild exterior sheathed an iron will. His gray eyes, magnified behind steel-rimmed spectacles, had the suffused visionary look of genius. The aging Samuel Williston rejoiced at last in a kindred mind that caught fire from his own. By the time Fayette enrolled, Henshaw had almost implemented Samuel's plan exactly.

"Our science course is still entirely separate from the classical," he told Fayette, who sat facing him across the big oak desk in his office. "Someday we'll offer a course that combines the two."

Fayette read the question in the headmaster's kindly face and knew what his own face must plainly show. He longed for the sciences. He never looked at the stars or an unknown tree, or heard a strange bird-call without chafing at his ignorance. But what would science fit him for in life? At that moment and in that day, the vocational world admitted law, medicine, teaching. What else? Too, he must remember Ann's dreams for him.

"I'm thinking of law," he said.

"I see." The headmaster seemed to check himself from saying more. He shuffled through some papers and selected a form.

"Register for Classical, then, of course."

As word got about that they had a Californian in their midst, the boys crowded around him, curious and friendly. He observed that, at five-feet-ten, he stood as tall or taller than most, and that his classmates ranged in age from fifteen up. He was one of the oldest, but he would not be the only freshman over twenty.

42

They, in turn, were impressed by the westerner's confident grace and subtle dignity. Such was their notion of the far frontier they would have been less than surprised if he had stalked into the halls of Williston and started shooting from the hip. Instead, he gave them the dry handclasp and direct gaze of self-control and discipline, while his modesty in words and manner revealed a gentleman. They raised their brows at the countrified cut of his suit and grinned at his accent, but they liked him and accepted him.

Immediately and permanently, they called him Mac.

"Show us how you shoot, Mac."

"Oh, any number of you are probably better shots than I am. I've been teaching, you know, not doing whatever it is you think we do out there."

But he let himself be drawn good-naturedly to a spot under the gracious campus elms. Since he had packed his handgun and shoulder holster in his luggage, someone went off to find a pistol which was put into his hand.

"All right. What target?"

"That's up to you, Mac."

They stood within a few yards of the white picket fence and, having checked out the weapon, he walked to the fence and fixed a match upright in a threadlike crack at the top of one of the pickets. He than stepped off twenty paces and scraped a mark in the dust with the toe of his shoe.

"Will someone light that match for me?"

Someone did. With the first shot he quenched the flame. With the next, he disposed of the match.

"Lady Luck," he said, handing over the pistol to its owner. "Now can we choose our rooms?"

Escorting him like a hero, they trouped jubilantly to the newest dormitory. Here, he soon found, the lady of fortune had gone ahead to wait for him. Every room in the year-old building exhaled the smell of excellence and fresh paint, but the boys agreed on the superiority of a certain corner room on the second floor. For one thing, its windows framed two pleasant views and also allowed cross ventilation.

"Why don't we draw lots for it?"

"Who's got a toothpick?"

"Here. Break up these two."

Within minutes, Mac was reaching out his hand to choose his fraction of wood.

He won. But this time his luck was met with a dampered enthusiasm. After a long and almost silent moment, one good-looking young man about his own age spoke.

"Look. I'll give you fifty dollars for this room. What do you say to it?"

What did he say? He thought the fellow must be joking. Why, fifty dollars was more than a month's teaching salary back home.

"I mean it, Mac. I want the room. I can get the money for you right now if it's a deal."

"No, no. If it means all that to you . . . " About to say, "Take it," he suddenly checked himself, remembering something out of the past.

He had been fifteen when he played a certain chess game on the splintery wooden porch of Dutcher's store. A stranger in Healdsburg had been challenging—and beating—every man who would take him on at chess. Then someone pushed Fayette McGlashan forward, saying "Here's one you won't checkmate straight off."

The man looked him over, amused; then he held up a five-dollar gold piece.

"All right, sonny. Sit down. If you win, this is yours."

Fayette did win. With great good humor and a kind of surprised respect, his opponent took out the gold piece and handed it over.

But Fayette drew back. "No, no. I couldn't take that."

"Go on, boy, take it. You won it fair and square."

"Really, sir. It's enough for me, just to win."

After a thoughtful stare, the man spoke with finality in his tone. "All right. I've offered it and you've refused. Now here's what I'm going to do. I'm going to teach you a lesson I hope you won't forget. I'm taking this gold piece and putting it back in my pocket. And the next time an honest man offers you honest money, honestly won, you take it."

"Well, Mac?"

44

He brought himself back to the present.

"You've got a deal."

They shook hands and the other went off to get the money while Mac looked for another room.

No meals were served on campus that first night, and Mac went with his new friends to a neighborhood cafe. Most of the second-year students took their option to eat in the town—it was not a freshman's privilege—so a momentary hush fell on the room when a disdainful group, flaunting the traditional top hats and canes of seniors, walked in and commandeered a table. Tomorrow their tyranny over the freshmen would begin, but for tonight they must be content to awe the scum with the mere sight of their own exalted dignity.

It had come to the attention of this segment of the senior class that the western fellow was carrying fifty dollars in his pocket—money taken in a deal, therefore "easy come, easy go."

"It behooves us to make this Californian feel welcome," said one. His companions turned in chorus to scrutinize Mac's table with deadpan gravity.

"Right you are. He must be entertained."

"Introduced to local night spots, I'd say."

"Shown where to spend his money."

They drew out their little skit, milking it of witticisms which they, as cast and audience, appreciated richly. By the time they were ready to put their scheme into action, however, enemy spies had caught their drift and revealed it to Mac's table. He was therefore ready with a smooth inoffensive evasion when the Greeks finally came bearing gifts. The plotters withdrew, foiled and angered.

It was a clear victory for the freshmen and the disgruntled seniors made a haughty exit from the cafe amid a silence that immediately exploded into a back-slapping, table-pounding celebration far out of proportion to the event. But every boy in the room sensed that celebration was in order, for something invisible had happened. Thrillingly, the hot current of *esprit de corps* had fused them into the solidarity of one for all and all for one. Less than an hour before, they had gathered at the restaurant, a crowd of strangers. They walked out proudly, the Class of 1870.

None felt the joy of spontaneous unity more keenly than Mac. He had dreamed of brotherhood—unselfish, passionately idealistic brotherhood—as he had longed for the comrades he had never had. Every free hour after school he had worked while other boys were playing. Immediately after graduation, he had taught his peers in classrooms they had shared. From then on he was expected to give good example. And he had done so, while secretly he mourned his lost boyhood.

For the next two years, only the intensely involved life within the microcosm, the tiny kingdom of Willistonia, bore the force and immediacy of reality for him. He gloried in his studies, vying for top grades with John Eden and one or two others. But above everything, he exulted in the new friendships—John, Frank, Paul, Mendenhall, Dickinson, Brewer—the litany of names and nicknames would never fade from his friend-hungry heart.

His friendships were not confined to the campus, for he volunteered to teach Sunday School at Payson Congregational Church, named for Samuel Williston's father, the Reverend Payson Williston, pastor for forty-four years. This church functioned as Williston's great hall for graduations, concerts and other formal programs, and it was also the official spiritual home of the academy. Residents of the community at large came to its Sunday services. Thus the Sunday School class introduced Mac to neighborhood folk.

At Christmas, when the school was deserted and he alone could not go home for the holidays, this stood him in good stead. On that first Christmas, however, he was too new for his plight to be known, and he found himself wandering the snow-clogged streets, wistfully gazing at festive wreaths and decorations with an acutely homesick heart. Before one gate he paused. The early gloom gave him a sharp glimpse of a delightful scene inside the house. Candles flamed on a lavishly ornamented dinner table. A brilliant fire danced on the hearth. He recalled his childhood Christmases when he had stood in the snow, as now, peering through windows at the festive family joy of other homes. He would have liked even now to tiptoe closer and imagine he shared the warmth and conviviality inside.

Suddenly the door opened and a white-haired man waved a

46

beckoning arm. "Come in!" he shouted.

Horribly embarrassed, thinking the man must be angry, he hurried up the walk to apologize and explain.

"Oh, but we've been expecting you," the man said. "Please come in and join us at table."

Amazed, he found himself seated, an honored guest at the family table. And it was not the last time. He would often be their guest. He learned that every year they waited for an Unknown Guest to share their Christmas feast, a custom he vowed he too would adopt when he had a family of his own.

During the summer holidays of 1869 he found a job in Springfield, Massachusetts with the W. J. Holland Book Company. Door-to-door book selling was just taking hold, and he proved a successful salesman. He knew the value of listening. Let a man tell you his life story, he told himself, and he'll probably buy—out of gratitude, if not a sense of fair play.

Back at school for the fall term, he sported the top hat and cane of a senior and savored the ambrosia of popularity. He was elected student-body president, and president of the elite debating society of the Classical department, called Adelphi. This carried the prestige and exclusiveness of a college fraternity. His final year at Williston began building early to a huge success, academically and socially. In sports, he shone in calisthentics rather than games; and he found his extracurricular forte in oratorical contests and debates.

Along with friendly rivalry for academic honors, he and Eden shared credit for originating some of the wilder pranks the "Classicals" perpetrated on the "Scientifics" in the name of nonsense. In fact, Mac's reputation for imaginative plots got him the name of "an originator," a classification with ambivalent connotations. All his life he would be "an originator," and called so with the same curious question as to whether the term was praise or blame, used in spite or admiration.

Headmaster Henshaw accepted the fact that pranks were part of student tradition; nevertheless, the sigh he breathed over some of '70s escapades was not entirely resigned.

Josiah Clark, the second principal in Williston history, was often quoted for his words: "At Williston we do not try to turn boys into men, but conserve the boy in the man." Henshaw went along with the idea of not curbing the enthusiasm of youth. At the same time, his endurance was wearing thin. Proud as he was of his seniors, both Classical and Scientific, he feared their hell-raising antics were giving the upcoming class a fund of ideas for the next year. He wondered, too, what limits he should put on patience.

If the boys ever flaunted his absolute orders . . . ? But he trusted they wouldn't go that far.

And then, within weeks of graduation, three seniors were invited to a Sunday program at the Mt. Holyoke Seminary for young ladies.

"It's an afternoon exhibition of gymnastics," they told the headmaster. "We can be home by supper. May we go, sir?"

For a reason known only to himself, Henshaw shook his head. "I think not, this time. I'd prefer you didn't go."

The young men swallowed their surprise and made attempts to change his mind. But without offering a reason for it, he remained adamantly negative.

The request seemed so innocuous that even the uninvited seniors grumbled at the decision, which was spread about by the three involved. Unfortunately, two teachers sided with them in their discontent and went so far as to say they'd go along if the boys could leave and return surreptitiously.

They could, and did. Teachers and students arrived at Mt. Holyoke after enormous risk and ridiculous mishaps along the way, only to find the event had been postponed. Steathily they crept home to Williston.

Henshaw learned of it. The complicity of faculty rendered a cloudy affair pitch black. Henshaw had never had the full sympathy of his teachers in his efforts to implement a science department and he was therefore constrained, he felt, to defend his position strongly.

After considerable thought in the solitude of a wakeful night he decided to make an example of one student. It so happened that one of the culprits was universally popular, as well as class valedictorian. Henshaw chose this one to expel.

Shock and fury rocked the campus. Questioned by classmates, the other two revealed they had not even been asked to apologize for their misdemeanor. "Injustice!" The inflammatory word crackled and hissed like a lit fuse circulating around the campus. The town heard of the headmaster's edict, for the students paraded through the streets of Easthampton, denouncing it to the accompaniment of raucous noisemakers.

In assembly the next day, Henshaw let it be known that anyone who participated in another such parade would face expulsion; whereupon Mac and nine fellow Adelphians went to him in his office afterward and respectfully stated their grievance: Why had not the three been punished equally?

But Henshaw stared up into their faces, meeting the hostility of their eyes, and turned away. He went to the long window and stood with his back to them, his shoulders sagging in the familiar crumpled gray coat they knew so well. He said not a word. Perplexed, the students withdrew into the hall.

"If John goes, I for one go with him."

Who said it? No one would remember, for they had all known that one of them must say it sooner or later. It was the code of honor among youth for all time.

"If he goes, we all go."

The ten shook hands on it; then they went forth to tell the world. The microcosm, that is. And there they met acclaim. They were hailed as "The Sacred Ten," and while they wrote an ultimatum for Henshaw beginning "WHEREAS...", someone shouted that the entire student body should walk out with them.

This caught on like a flame in dry grass—and died as quickly. Two of the Sacred Ten dropped out, and then there were Eight.

That night the Sacred Eight were paraded through town, enthroned on a horse-drawn cart. Everyone cheered for Nobility, Loyalty, Courage... and forgot that this second raggle-tale, theatrical march had been strictly forbidden.

The next morning the Eight read their statement to Marshall Henshaw, who heard it without comment. They swore to leave if their classmate and brother Adelphian was expelled without at least a hearing. They left him to think it over, and this he did.

He marvelled how mad the school had gone over the whole affair. Not one remembered that he had forbidden last night's parade, threatening participants with dismissal. Even the best, the most retiring, the most conservative, had drowned their judgment in the whirlpool of "mobdom." The Eight were leaders of the senior class, scholastically and every way...and yet... although they hadn't instigated the parade, they had been its heroes, its inspiration.

On the following morning, he made known his decision to the assembled student body. The Eight, he said, had become "too Sacred for Williston." They were not to have the chance to walk out in protest. They were expelled.

"The entire Classical will leave with us," one of them later blustered, believing it true. It wasn't. The parades and shouting over, the heroes walked their noble path alone.

Bewildered, numbed by the blow, the Eight were unable to grasp how Henshaw, whose fatherly concern had embraced them all, could now turn from them coldly. Willistonia had been their environment on every level for a timeless period. They were not to step now through the golden door of graduation into the brilliantly illuminated Next Phase. Only darkness and the unknown waited. The Alma Mater had aborted them.

They began to pack.

That night Mac took out his commonplace book. Was there any word from Ann to comfort him? Somewhere she'd written: "There are three ways to get out of a scrape—keep out, back out, or fight out. The second is the hardest. Resort to the last only if you know you are right."

Fight out. He had done that and lost. Back out? Never. Anyway, it was too late now. Keep out. Should he have kept out? His friend, his brother, had been unjustly treated. Injustice made him sick. No, he'd had no choice but to do what he'd done. Ann would have understood that.

He didn't leave Easthampton at once. A classmate's family invited him to stay at their home until he decided what to do. He gratefully accepted, for he had other commitments, to his Sunday School class and to the two lodges he had joined, the Masons and the Good Templars. He saw no reason to leave summarily for he believed in the course he had followed and had done no wrong.

On February 7th he had received the Third Degree of Masonry in Ionic Lodge at Easthampton. This was important to him, and the support of brethren in town helped him through this dark time. These were men, not boys. After all, he was a man of twenty-three himself now, not a boy of eighteen. He learned that others of the Eight were pulling wires to go on to the university without Henshaw's backing. Should he try to do the same? No, he must get on with his life now, not prepare for it forever.

Churning with the events of the previous weeks, he soothed his feverish soul by writing, in collaboration with a Miss Kate Hickey, a tract they called "The Chronicles of the Great Rebellion." Written humorously but with sharp wit, the tract put before the world the story of the unjust (as he saw it) expulsion and the Sacred Eight's position on it. But it did more. The "Chronicles" actually related the entire story of his two years at Williston. In its pages he relived the intense *comedia* of the rivalry between the "Classicals" and the "Scientifics," and in so doing, he regained perspective on Willistonia.

He saw that he had been in Lilliput. He had thrown away his dream of Yale, posturing and blowing off in great style on the victimization (as he saw it) of a classmate—nay, a brother Adelphian.

Meanwhile, to his chagrin, rumors came that the same brother would soon be on his feet again. It so happened that his family had position and power to see that their son realized his goals in spite of everything.

What had he done, oh, what had he done to his own life?

He soon went to Springfield and got back his old job with Holland Books, and about this time, letters came from Laura and Nette. Peter had quietly died, with Lib and Lyman at his side.

"Tell Fayette always to be a gentleman"—this was his dying legacy to his son.

They buried him near Isabel in Dutcher's plot, a pine-shaded nook in the Healdsburg graveyard.

Nette had taken his change of plans with equanimity and sisterly concern for his future. At Christmas she wrote that Placerville High School was reopening and that she had spoken to influential friends who remembered him. She was sure he could have the principalship if he applied, but hurry!

He had thought he was done with teaching. However, this was

administrative work, as well, and it would take him home, thank God. He wired her to submit his application and qualifications.

By mid-January he had the reply: "Come at once."

He hadn't been waiting in anxious uncertainty. He was packed, his affairs wound up, his goodbyes said.

He had unexpectedly seen a bewitching new moon, sailing high above the Berkshires, and he'd known what the answer would be.

Chapter Five

I don't know when I first became aware that Papa had been married once before. But when his daughter Undine, born of that earlier union, came to visit us with her two children, I asked my grandmother about it.

"Well, you see, dear, your father was a . . . a divorced man when I married him. His first wife, Jennie, was the sister of my best friend, Lyda Munson. What happened was . . . well, it seems Jennie said she loved someone else."

This stunned my nine-year-old mind, blotting out further questions. From then on, I tuned in to any family talk that would light up for me that unimaginable patch of time when — O treason! — Papa loved a woman who was not Mama.

It wasn't from sparse crumbs dropped at table, nor even from innuendoes of tone and eyebrow that I deduced the rocky course of that first marriage. I simply guessed what had happened when, in my own mature years, I tallied up his activities over the five-year span. They told me this: Love, for my grandfather, apparently detonated the artillery of his manifold talents. Ardent romantic that he was, love seemed to liberate the entire range of his creativity. New ideas fountained up from his joy-filled heart in the fiery showers of a Fourth of July sparkler, sending him out to take on the world—while his beloved waited at home.

A rare woman might understand this, but only an extraordinary woman could put up with it for long. Jennie probably did not pretend to be either.

He was eighteen and teaching at Cold Spring when they met. Pretty, popular Jennie Munson scarcely noticed the boyish schoolmaster at the time. He was almost bone-thin and desperately trying to dignify the pleasant regularity of his features with a reddish-brown brush under his nose. This only added a certain fierceness to the brown blaze of his eyes—which probably served him just as well, since most of his male pupils matched him in size and brawn.

It is unlikely, too, that he noticed Jennie at this time, since his mind was wholly centered on saving money for the eastern prep school. Each month he put aside what he could for Williston, and finally sailed east around the Horn in the summer of 1868.

When he returned in the early spring of 1871 as principal of Placerville Academy, from Jennie's point of view, he came back "swept and garnished." He was twenty-three, his physique had filled out handsomely, the mustache was a trimmed and glistening sable and, icing to the cake, he comported himself with the easy aplomb of a man of the world. Moreover, he knew how to dress. Hers was not the only feminine heart to tremble.

As for himself, he was glad to be back in the ebullient young west. His New England experience quickly faded to a dream. He would always remember Easthampton's purposeful, moderated pace with respect and fondness, but he knew now he needed the west's ferment. Its restlessness was his own. They were young together, their future illimitable.

He was glad, too, to be near his sister Martinette, now a spinster of twenty-five, regally tall, with ice-blue eyes and a coronet braid of straw-blond hair. Her mind was curious and hungry like his own, and he enjoyed arguing with her just to sharpen his own quick wit.

He didn't take seriously the fact that her seniority made her feel protective of him. But she had not missed the female glances which swooned in her brother's direction and had secretly decided she must, for his own good, steer him toward matrimony. Her only question was, which girl?

This was soon answered by her closest friend, who happened to be Jennie Munson.

"Oh Nette, I'll just die if Fayette doesn't ask me to the Masonic picnic. Oh dear, I think I'm in love. Oh Nette, what shall I do?"

A few weeks later, when Jennie wept over his indifference, sobbing "I'll kill myself if he doesn't propose!" Nette decided to give her brother a nudge in the right direction.

"You know, Fay, ministers and principals are always married men. Have you thought of a wife?" Then she gave him Jennie's melodramatic quote.

If she expected him to snort with laughter, he did not. Instead, he took another look at Jennie, whom he had always thought attractive but light-headed. Now he wondered. Had he done her an injustice? She cared so much? To kill herself! Could she have undiscernible depths?

He was the son of his Victorian times. He believed in two kinds of women—the good and the bad. And the good, he would have sworn, were scarcely of this earth. He knew he had been spoiled in his friendships with women, for he had known not just the angelic but the elect, the kind a man could talk to about books, politics, ideas. But as far as he could determine, Jennie had the limited repartee of a flirt.

However, Nette was right. He ought to marry. He did want love, children, a home. He began to court Jennie and soon, without a struggle, fell in love. The wedding was set for the following Christmas.

With romance accelerating all his energies, it is not surprising that during this time he discovered his two lifelong studies—butterflies and stars, and his journalistic avocation as well. The first came about this way:

One day he took his science class on a four-mile walk to Negro Hill, a mining settlement named for a black minister who had been the first to build there. As prearranged, an amateur scientist, one Mr. Oldfield, welcomed them to his house and led them to the backyard to gaze through a five-inch telescope.

While the pupils took turns with the telescope, their teacher's interest was captivated by something else. Cloth-lined breeding cages for moths and butterflies stood near the back porch. Even as he peered inside, several moths emerged from cocoons which Oldfield had arranged in such a way that newborn insects could perch, wings downward, on the sides of the cage to dry.

The queer little creatures with their big heads and soft moist bodies hardly looked like moths. Delighted, he gathered the class around the rare sight. Before they left for the long walk home, he had jotted down the names of books on entomology and had made an appointment to return alone.

Through this solitary Canadian, called "Mr. Oldfield, the Englishman" by local people, my grandfather began his two absorbing hobbies. He had little desire for lone pursuits, but the stars he could and did share—not only in rooftop viewing and instruction, but later with pocket fold-out maps he patented, which showed the seasonal positions of the stars. Each packet contained the diagramed constellations of the season, together with a comprehensive picture of the heavens in the western hemisphere. Intensely practical, the little maps easily slipped into a shirt pocket and each fold-out sold for a nickel.

As for lepidoptera, he soon learned that specialists in the field were eager for specimens from the Far West. Moreover, through Oldfield, he began a long correspondence with the Reverend Charles J. S. Bethune, founder of the Entomological Society of Canada, and later president of the Entomological Society of America. Since nothing was written for the amateur, his correspondence with W. Henry Edwards, Albert Koeberle, J. J. Rivers and other entomologists supplemented the reading he did at their suggestion. In exchange for samples, Edwards classified all the specimens he sent. In time, Rivers would name one of Mac's two discoveries *Melitaea macglashanii*, a butterfly (now called *Euphydryas chalcedona macglashanii*, a subspecies), and Edwards named *Hepialus macglashanii*, a moth still recognized as a distinct species.

If he was disappointed that Jennie shuddered at "those bugs" when, excited and enthused, he tried to explain them to her, he was not dismayed for long. They would have a whole life to share. And there were thousands of other things they could talk about.

At this point he should have named one.

As the wedding date neared, his thoughts revolved about money. A teacher's pay, albeit a principal's, was not enough for the good life he wanted for the family of his dreams. He began to think of writing—short pieces for quick sale. At sixteen, he had thought of writing as a career. He had bought his commonplace book for that purpose, declaring on the virginal first page, "I intend to write herein at least something every day" for the improvement of literary skills. At Williston, too, he had sold a short story to a Springfield paper. His thoughts turned now to California's leading newspaper, the *Sacramento Record-Union.*

At the earliest opportunity he caught the stage to Sacramento with a story in his coat pocket. Arrived there, he went directly to the *Record-Union* building, where, after a cooling wait, he was led to the desk of editor W. H. Mills, who attacked the proffered story with a black grease-pencil and tossed it across the desk.

"You have a good eye. Maybe a nose. Tell me about yourself."

When he had heard enough, Mills reached for the ruined paper and looked down the length of the top page.

"All right. Here's what I want in a story. And I'll tell you too what I won't stand for."

That day began—and he knew it—not only his journalistic career, but the strong bond of discipleship between himself and the editor. Through Mills he would develop a vigorous, incisive style. And he would find him a concerned friend when he needed one most.

— • —

After the wedding and turn of the New Year 1872, Jennie's family moved up the mountain to Truckee, from which her younger sister Lyda wrote frequent ecstatic letters. To her joy, Nona Keiser lived there. They had been classmates at boarding school and now the two girls, both seventeen, were entering hand in hand, so to speak, the magic years when every young man might be the prince. Lyda's dreams played a romantic light over all she wrote, as if her pen moved to Strauss waltzes.

Her mother wrote to a different tune. She missed Jennie and wondered why the couple didn't think of moving to Truckee. She had heard of an opening in the schools there, by the way. Her son-in-law might want to look into it.

He did, and liked what he found—a superintendency as well as principalship. Both the larger scope and higher pay appealed to him greatly.

He applied and was accepted, to begin the new term near his twenty-fifth birthday on August twelfth.

"Boy, you're out of your mind to move to Truckee," one old

foothill billy hooted when the news was out. "Why, it's only got three seasons: July, August, and WINTER."

Perhaps so, he'd conceded. After all, the town was some 6,000 feet up. He knew the high Sierra, for he had come by stagecoach more than once, returning to the foothills shaken by the primitive grandeur of the mountain country. He had heard of hundreds of lakes like spilled jewels, hidden in the blue-green forests. Knee-deep in a gleam of golden wyethia, he gazed, bemused, at meadows of sunny buttercups mixed with the burnt-orange of tiger lily and red columbine.

"I'm coming back with my net for you," he promised the million dancing butterflies.

At night he marveled at the stars, so reachable in that rare atmosphere, and said, "I must bring my telescope."

On those days he felt that he walked in a living Biblical psalm. He understood those verses, rococo with joy and love, wherein "the mountains skip like rams and the hills like little lambs." He heard "the trees of the forest shout with joy" and the waters "clap their hands."

Although he had vision, he would never be content with insubstantial dreams. Even in the enthusiasm of his hobbies, practicality ruled him. Therefore, while the esthetic wonders of the high Sierra moved him, at the same time he informed himself fully on Truckee's prospects. All that he learned convinced him that a young man could do worse than gamble his future on the five-year-old town.

This was the railroad age and Truckee was a railroad town. It was still the Comstock's hour and Truckee fed timber to insatiable Washoe mines. Snows came early and stayed late, but from May until October the good sounds of industry rang on the alpine air. Mill whistles tooted, donkey engines chugged and whined, and the blunt staccato of steel on anvil danced over blacksmith shops from dawn to dusk. And the best sound of all, in whooped the trains on schedules east and west. Between Sacramento and Ogden, Utah what Central Pacific terminus matched Truckee for good hotels, good food and raw whiskey?

That wasn't all. In June, he knew, vast droves of sheep, nasally baaing, undulated over and down the stony summit slopes to

58

graze on the lush pasture of the Truckee Basin. And up from scorched valleys, butter men shipped their herds to feed in the cool meadows of the river and its tributary.

Overnight, it seemed to everyone he talked to, cattle ranches and dairies dotted the surrounding valleys of Martis Creek, Prosser Creek, and Sierra Valley. Dazed by its luck, Truckee found itself the hub and supplier of outlying wealthy settlements.

Meanwhile, the vigorous little bronco river galloped eastward from its source, the blue "mountain sea," Lake Tahoe. It bragged, he thought, of all it had done and would yet do for the basin. Lumber mills, dependent on its swift current, lined its southern edge, and spreading back from its northern banks was the town. Not only that—five miles east, in the Boca dam, it froze to solid blocks in winter for a burgeoning ice industry.

Straight through the town like twin backbones ran the river and the railroad track. By each, Truckee lived.

Parallel to the town ran the old emigrant road along which the merchants continued to build. (This is now Commerical Row.) Here stood the first beginnings—a feed and water stop called Coburn's Station until the C. P. knighted it with the status of a terminus, complete with roundhouse, and gave it the river's name. (The river was named for Captain Truckee, Fremont's Indian guide.)

Such was Truckee, California in 1872.

Such, that is, was the bright side of the coin. On the dark side were serious problems of which he was well aware, for who was not? Newspapers of rival towns down the mountain made jokes of its location on the shooting end of Nevada County's pistol-shaped outline. In violence it almost equalled notorious Bodie.

The fact was that two sub-populations threatened Truckee's foundations. The first was a nebulous, changing swarm of transients that continually drifted down like soot from defunct or dying mining camps. Vandals, hoodlums, gamblers and con men, as well as wanted criminals who looked for a haven in the border town—these had become a plague. Moreover, isolation rendered the mechanics of justice slow and bumbling. The nearest jail, at Nevada City, the county seat, was hours away by train. When constable Jake Teeter escorted a felon to jail anything could happen back home and generally did.

Murders were frequent, not only among the criminal element but among the Jibboom Street girls and their pimps.

Jibboom was the nickname for Back Street, an alley of frame shacks snuggled behind Front Street's saloons and poker parlors. Here a blatant night-blooming life, shrill, often violent, played strident accompaniment to the intense respectability of Truckee's reputable citizenry and literally under its Victorian nose. Housewives peeked down askance from windows on the hill above. Directly below, the rouged and glittering floozies operated a flamboyant red light district, notorious across the nation.

Just as disturbing to townsmen was the other sub-populace, the sprawling despised Chinese colony shantied along the river's edge, east of the bridge.

The coolies had been tolerated when the C. P. brought them from Canton to hew and chew the railroad's path through granite cliffs. That done, they should vanish, go home—just go. But they had returned to Truckee for the same reason white men did. They could earn a living there. They hired out in platoons for a pittance, and white loggers, idled thereby, hated them murderously.

Townspeople, for their part, shuddered at the ugly eyesore of the crowded, noisesome shacks, a constant fire threat. Moreover, the colony's morals affronted them. Opium dens were thriving in dark back rooms. Slave girls, routinely imported from China, were often forced into prostitution.

Every man had his tong to back him. No private squabble could be less than a full-scale riot. And when fights broke out, pandemonium rocked the mountain.

Chapter Six

In order to settle in before school opened, they made the move to Truckee a month early, arriving July 12th on the afternoon train. As the great wheels braked for the station stop, Mac stood in the crowded vestibule with Jennie, who was trimly gloved and hatted despite the dry heat. He slid a steadying arm around her small waist while the cars lurched to a gradual groaning halt.

Through a small rectangular window high in the closed exit door he glimpsed the string of stores, saloons, rooming houses and cafes that made up Front Street. Two staircases, he recalled, ran up from its plank sidewalk to a weathered porch that protected the street in winter while it served as an upper deck for residents who owned businesses below.

Behind Front Street he saw a backdrop of low hills, haphazardly sown with frame houses whose peaked roofs and high thin stovepipes told their own story of winter snows.

Could this be his destined port at last? A sudden sting of tears suffused his vision and, surprised at his own emotion, he blinked away the moisture as a porter clanged open the door.

"We may be home, my dear," he murmured into Jennie's beribboned hat while the smiling porter positioned the steps below them.

Whatever he was trying to say, she didn't hear. She was delightedly waving her tiny lace handkerchief to the searching upturned faces of her mother and sister among the crowd on the depot platform.

Surrounded and kissed, hugged and patted, she stayed with the deep-bosomed Hannah Munson and excited young Lyda while he went off to find the baggage. A gray-eyed girl whose burnished brown curls were pinned in a cluster at the nape of her neck smiled quietly on the fringe of the reunion until Lyda fondly pulled her into the family warmth.

"This is my dearest friend, Nona Keiser."

Jennie took her hand in her own cordially and said how many times her sister had spoken of her.

"But she never told me how pretty you are. Why, you are a lovely child!"

"She's no child, sis, she's engaged!" Lyda seized her friend's left hand and the small diamond on her finger flashed in the sun.

Nona was embarrassed but pleased, and her smile deepened. Jennie secretly marveled at the petal texture of her fair skin, tinted now by a rising blush. Then, in the midst of the flutter due the revelation of an engagement, Mac rejoined the women and Lyda introduced him.

"Nona's father owns the Webber House, where you are staying," she said.

As the happy, talkative group walked across the dusty plaza to John Keiser's hotel on Front Street, none could have guessed the part this girl would play in Mac's future—least of all, the two most concerned.

Through Keiser, who was justice of the peace as well as hotel man and real estate agent, they were able to rent a house on the western half of River Street. This was a noise-ridden location, but vacancies were scarce in the humming young town. They had to be content. Their kitchen windows opened on the clamorous hive of Schaffer's sawmill, their front faced a ragged row of scattered homes providing scant buffer between themselves and the railroad tracks. Just beyond the glistening rails stood the depot—a long yellow caterpillar of green-roofed ticket offices and waiting rooms, flanked by the Wells Fargo stage stop and a three-story hotel. A quarter-mile east was the roundhouse, squat and black as a sooty circus tent. Night and day the hiss, clang and roar of armored might stormed their beleaguered ears.

Not only that but, to Jennie's dismay, the Orientals occupied the other end of River Street, which was cut in two then as now by a bridge that spanned the river. Her spirits revived considerably when she found her immediate neighbors as refined (and Caucasian) as herself. In fact, Judge Keiser's oldest daughter, Ella

C. F. McGlashan at 25, when he first came to Truckee, in 1872.

Leonora G. (Nona) Keiser before her marriage to C. F. McGlashan, in 1878.

Webber, lived only a few doors down the street. The two young women slipped easily into the informality of sugar-borrowing neighbors.

Ella lived alone with her five-year-old daughter, Alice, and everyone presumed that her husband, Meritt D. Webber, was dead.

"I'm the only one who finds it hard to believe," she confided when they had passed the stage of superficial chitchat.

"Alice was a baby when Meritt disappeared—into thin air, it seemed. We were living then at Yankee Jim's. Like most men in the area, my husband had mining interests on the side, and every now and then he had to make a trip below to look after his investments. Well, this time he didn't come back. My father made every effort—even hired some men to look for him. But nothing. Not a trace could they ever find."

John Keiser believed that in all probability his son-in-law had been robbed, killed, and his body disposed of. After five years,

Ella supposed, she ought to accept this. But she wondered if her heart would ever stop listening for his footstep at the door.

Shortly after her marriage to Webber in 1866, the Keisers sold their hotel business at Yankee Jim's and moved over the summit to Coburn's Station.

"There was no town here at all then," she said. "Donner Lake had a store and a hotel for summer tourists. Some man was already planning another hotel for the foot of the lake, so Pa decided to build at Coburn's to meet the needs of travelers and men on the way to the mines. In fact, he turned the third floor into a free infirmary for sick and injured miners. 'I came back from hell, John,' one man told him, 'because I knew you'd take care of me.' Mother nursed them. Since we always had Chinese cooks and kitchen help, it wasn't too hard on her, she said."

That first hotel burned to the ground with the entire village in 1868, soon after the C. P. had chosen Coburn's, named it Truckee, and built the depot somewhat east of the original cluster of homes and stores. John and the other businessmen quickly rebuilt, parallel to and facing the depot.

Ella's alert blue eyes snapped with humor and intelligence while she talked and Jennie thought her far too attractive to stay single much longer. According to Lyda, in fact, a railroad man named John Greenleaf was hovering on the periphery of the young widow's orbit, waiting for the day she would declare herself free to look his way.

Meanwhile, Ella quickly brought her new friend into the genteel female society of which her mother, Elizabeth Keiser, was clearly a leader. It was from energetic, wiry Mrs. Keiser that Hannah, Jennie's mother, had already caught the determination of Truckee wives to help their men clean up the rowdy element in town.

While situations demanding immediate solutions, best handled with force, were left to the husbands, the women attacked the general problem of violence with massive good example. Resolutely set on creating as many proper institutions as they recalled from New England or midwestern backgrounds, they propelled into motion weekly whist clubs, church socials, amateur theatricals, reading groups, and sewing circles. As fast as the men

64

founded lodges, they formed sister lodges. Too, they planned a literary society open to either sex for the purpose of encouraging orations and debates. When this finally got off to a start in 1873, one of the first debates took the subject: "California should establish the public whipping post for the suppression of hudlumism [sic]."

This was no idle topic. Pushed to the limits of patience by boozing gamblers, vandals and trigger-happy toughs, Truckee wives could have stood around the whipping post as dry-eyed as Madame LaFarge at the guillotine.

With whale-boned formality they elevated Truckee's *tone*. Jennie was invited to teas which, for silver elegance and ceremony, might have graced a Boston parlor. When invitations summoned guests for Two Until Four, mobilization began about a quarter past one, depending on distance and mode of travel. Buggy-borne ladies came from Brickeltown, the western fringe where the town had begun as Coburn's Station. Walking guests, rustling in San Francisco fashions, plucked their skirts high from the snow-washed gritty dust and primly stepped along the hilly paths behind Front Street, or crossed the tracks from River Street and climbed.

When necessity forced a woman to walk the gauntlet of Front Street, she stiffened her spine, set nose and chin on course, and proceeded in full sail. The ruffians who lurched through swinging half-doors and those that leered, nudging their fellows who loafed against the store fronts, knew how searingly aware of them she was. She walked the interminable block with every sense perversely heightened, her unwilling nostrils drawing in the beery exhalations belched from saloon doors.

At the same time, out of these doors streamed ribbons of music, cut short here, interweaving there, released from piano keys, banjo, or fiddle strings by unseen fingers. Both repelled and fascinated, she sailed on. Front Street was the respectable woman's *via crucis*.

Men, on the other hand, found it the most exciting street in the world, as Mac discovered. Along its entire canopied length, the thin mountain air crackled with subliminal angers and tensions that gave depth to its attraction. A motley horde thronged its splintery boardwalk throughout the day. Boots of loggers, miners and ranch hands mingled with low-cut "citified" shoes of businessmen passing through or the denizens of the gambling rooms. Many an ankle-hugging "ground gripper" with cracked leather and obvious abandonment to Truckee dust revealed a local resident, like Dr. William Curless, the first C. P. physician-surgeon, who set up his home practice in Truckee—or attorney Ed Gaylord, who turned down a city partnership to live on the heights; and lumber men George Shaffer and Joe Gray, whose mill turned the timbers for the snowsheds when the railroad was toiling up the mountain. Others were Judge John Keiser, ex-miner, Forty-niner and veteran of two wars; Fred Burckhalter, owner of the leading mercantile store; Jake Teeter, Constable, who never used a gun, preferring a pick handle that "didn't misfire"; and editor Dave Frink, the Michigan man who was making *The Truckee Republican* a lively paper.

Always in and out among the heavier footgear, Mac noted the padded scurry of Chinese slippers.

Humor ran high along the street. Sometimes it was cruel, as on that winter day of knee-deep snow and keen wind when men left the bar rails to watch a coolie, pigtail flying, chase his gale-blown hat around the plaza. He sank to his thighs with every step and amid the guffaws of his delighted audience his slight form raged with shamed frustration.

Mac looked for and found that other kind of humor, typical of pioneer communities—the good laughter that turns back on one's self. Such humor, low-key as a wry chuckle, played through the pages of *The Republican* and spread along the street from reader to reader. The twice-weekly newspaper was read avidly and, next to the Magnolia Theater and the train depot, was prized as much for entertainment as for news.

All Truckee businessmen belonged to Masons, Oddfellows, Good Templars, or all three, and John Keiser offered to introduce the new schoolmaster at lodge meetings. The judge was obviously one of the town's highly respected founders and Mac was grateful for his sponsorship.

Over the next two years, he fell more and more in love with the evergreen forests, the lakes and trout-flashing streams, and in winter, the dazzling snow. His hobbies and even his work let him explore the region. As superintendent, he visited the school at the little town five miles down the river, called Boca. Often he caught a ride on the caboose of a freight train to the ice-plant town. In summer, he preferred to ride his horse instead, with his butterfly net held loosely across the saddlehorn in case he saw a pair of beautiful wings and cared to dismount and give chase.

To his surprise, he found in Boca the only library in the region. More astonishing yet, it was a law library. This struck him with the force of an omen. More and more of late, Ed Gaylord had offered to lend him his own law books, urging him to study for the bar examinations. Teacher that he was by instinct, he chafed at the confinement of a classroom. Moreover, he knew he lacked tolerance. The lazy and apathetic pupil infuriated him.

His sister Ann, who had known his strengths and weaknesses so well, had always steered him toward the courtroom. He decided now to let her counsels guide him as they had of old.

From this time on, Jennie often awoke in the night to find the oil lamp burning in the dining room and her husband deep in law books from the Boca library.

That first winter he gloried in the scenic splendor of the snow-transfigured landscape. He wanted to share it with the world. Editor Mills bought all the copy he could send the *Record-Union,* so he got out and experienced new angles on snow for readers "down below." He frequently rode a snow plow to the rescue of floundering trains. He shivered on the schoolhouse roof, noting the winter placement of the stars. At the Boca ice-plant he penciled his observations with frost-swollen fingers.

For editor Dave Frink he wrote local stories of a practical nature. These plunged him inevitably into the heart of Truckee issues, involving him totally—either to join a crusade or to initiate one. The first of his lone crusades resulted in the re-building of two burned-out churches, the Methodist Episcopal and the Roman Catholic.

Fires had leveled the town twice before his arrival. All places of business, including Jibboom Street, had risen immediately from their own ashes. Churches, however, languished in blackened rubble, waiting for public concern. Nothing happened. Then Mac became their champion and the persuasive powers destined for the courtroom proved more than equal to the barroom. He passed a hat in every saloon and the response was overwhelming. His appeals in *The Truckee Republican* brought lumber from the mills to the pastors' doors, free of cost, and parishioners did the rest, volunteering spare-time labor.

Of all his new friends, Charles Burckhalter became the enthusiastic partner of his scientific explorations. Twenty-two and at loose ends about his future, Charlie was clerking in his Uncle Fred's store when Mac and Jennie came to town. When he learned that Mac owned astronomy books and a five-inch telescope, he shyly hinted that if Mac started an adult night class, he'd like to be one of his pupils.

Mac forthwith advertised that he would meet with interested adult astronomy students. Soon he had a small class underway. Thus began for Charles Burckhalter a vocation that would eventually lead to his appointment as first director of Oakland's Chabot Observatory, a position he was to hold for thirty-eight years.

Increasingly, Mac's evenings were consumed by lodge commitments, rooftop astronomy classes, writing, and the study of law. There were nights, too, when he worked until dawn on an invention he had begun at Williston—a telegraph device to send and receive messages from moving trains. Onrushing trains all too often crashed head-on for lack of warning. No system of communication had yet been devised that would reach a man on a moving railroad car, and Mac had pondered the problem for five years.

In spite of absorbing interests apart from his wife, he cheerfully escorted Jennie when she calendared a social evening in advance. They rarely missed a new show at the Magnolia, where traveling troupes from back east played on their tours of the towns between Virginia City and San Francisco. Dancing, spelling bees, and amateur theatricals often took over this theater during winter months when stormy weather and deep snow kept people in town. Once Jennie took home the prize from a spelling bee, a soft-bound book of Longfellow's poems. Mac let himself be billed from time to time on amateur programs, usually rendering

Above: Southern Pacific depot at Truckee. Below: Southern Pacific roundhouse.

a reading that took none of his precious time in preparation.

Jennie wanted—legitimately enough, he admitted—a man whose interests see-sawed between job and home. He couldn't give her that. Life was too brief to satisfy the range of his restless energies and curiosity. Ann had tried to point him in a single direction, fearing that the variety of his talents might ironically defeat him.

"Scattering your forces," she had warned, "you will only be a jack-of-all-trades, and this must never be."

Well, he didn't intend it to be. When he came back to the west without the degree he'd yearned for, he returned purged of ambition for public life. He felt he had let Ann down, but how could she know what he had learned in "Lilliput?" The lessons were the same. Politics in a microcosm brought out the same jealousies, intrigues and, yes, corruptions as the real world. He wanted no part of it.

"Give me a mountain meadow and you can have the metropolises of the world," he told Charlie Burckhalter. "I would rather chase butterflies on the Truckee meadows than compete for position and fees and fame in any city. Big frog in a little pond? That suits me, Charlie, and I don't even care about being big. I love the pond."

The pond gave him freedom to be himself, competing with no man. Freedom, too, to go out of himself to nature, and to people. Freedom to learn from everyone who crossed his path. "I have never met a man in my life who couldn't teach me something I didn't know," he would tell his children and grandchildren in years to come.

More sensitive than he liked to admit, he was hurt and depressed when Jennie turned a dull eye on his intense enthusiasms. He loved her cute pouty prettiness, and he was jealous when other men looked at her.

Lonely, unaware of her own lacking contribution to the marriage, Jennie then made the worst possible mistake. She set out deliberately to ignite her husband's jealousy. Manifestly, she had no inkling of his Puritan heart. His father's lifelong fidelity to a dead wife had fostered an extreme ideal of fidelity to the living. Furthermore, Peter had seen to it that Fayette knew his Bible.

"He who looks on a woman to lust after her has already committed adultery with her . . . "

Jennie's flirtatious smiles and glances at other men shocked and infuriated him.

Matters in the home went from dull and cloudy to thunderously stormy.

From Lyda, Nona Keiser knew of the widening rift. It was characteristic that she kept her own counsel. Lyda blamed Mac for leaving her sister at home alone too many nights of every week. Nona listened and let her talk. For some time she had been silently aware of what she felt were Jennie's own mistakes. If Mac left his wife at night for work and meetings, she knew he never failed to ask her along in the daytime—to join him at butterflying and on jaunts in search of stories for the newspapers—for Lyda and Nona had gone with him sometimes when Jennie would not. Inseparable friends, the two girls had become like his younger sisters.

About this time, while Jennie was contriving to arouse Mac's imagined lagging interest, Nona and her betrothed, Ben Bacon, were having trouble. Radiantly in love, the pair seemed destined for a fairy-tale ending to their romance. As a telegrapher, Ben had a good job. He was handsome and Nona was lovely. When they waltzed or simply walked hand in hand, their friends smiled mistily. What could go wrong with this idyllic romance?

But something did. Ben drank. Nona didn't mind at first. Most men headed for a bar after work. However, he sometimes called on her with a whiskey-breath and slurred speech. When she protested, he vowed to cut down on hard liquor. However, soon after, he got roaring drunk and she learned of it. Sober, he came to her gate to plead with her penitently. She ran down the steps to meet him, but after a few moments of talk they quarreled. They made this up in due course, but more quarrels ensued, and more broken promises. Finally, Nona delivered an ultimatum: "Quit, or take back your ring."

Angry, Ben not only got sodden drunk, but he spent the night on Jibboom Street. That wasn't all. Whether a real or mock wedding took place, he married a Back Street girl.

Word sped along Front Street. Keiser, sick at heart for his

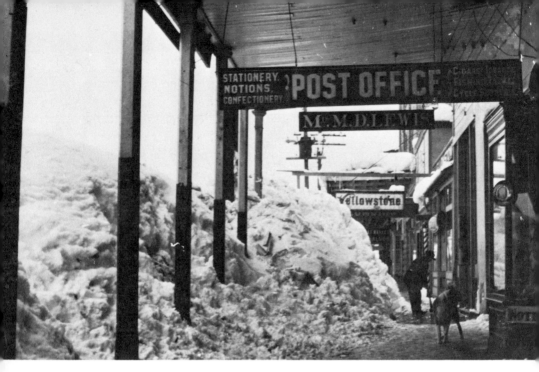

View of a section of Front Street snowed under, circa early 1900s. For many years C. F. McGlashan's office occupied the building between the Post Office and the Yellowstone sign above.

daughter, heard it. Nona could scarcely grasp its reality. Elizabeth, with the protective wrath of a tigress blazing in her blue eyes, spoke her mind without actually using the words "good riddance." Both John and she knew how much this was a tragedy for their middle daughter. She loved the man. Her ultimatum had only been uttered as a motivating force. It had worked otherwise.

When Nona was decades older, she would give a small yellow diamond, set in a gold and black enamel ring, to another Nona, myself.

"My father gave it to me so my finger wouldn't look bare and call attention to the fact my engagement ring was gone."

"Did you see Ben again?"

"Yes. He came one night to the gate and called me. He begged me to run away with him."

"Well, why didn't he leave that woman and marry you?"

I was a romantic thirteen. There were subjects one didn't discuss with children, and my grandmother adroitly diverted my attention to safer ground.

Nona was crushed in spirit, and her health demanded a change of scene and a lower altitude. As a child she had suffered rheumatism and had what the doctor called "a singing heart." The Keisers sent her to Santa Clara with Ella and little Alice.

John had built a house in Santa Clara on property he had traded for what was to become, if he had but known it, the corner of Montgomery Street in downtown San Francisco. Santa Clara's climate didn't agree with him, but he kept the property for his daughters' future use. They were well-acquainted in the town, since both had graduated from Reverend Tuthill's private school.

There, Nona had the good sense to throw herself into distracting work. She joined a guitar class at the Tuthill Institute and a watercolor class, as well.

Lyda wrote to her regularly and kept her abreast of Truckee gossip. She often mentioned Jennie and Mac. Then came a letter with shocking news: Swiftly and suddenly, Mac had resigned and left town. Jennie had moved into her mother's house, Lyda wrote. The couple had definitely separated.

The fact was, Jennie had said she loved another man.

Grimly perplexed, only half willing to see any side but his own in the shambles of his marriage, Mac had simply bowed out. In two short years he had built a life in Truckee. He dismantled it in an hour, beginning with his resignation of his position at the school.

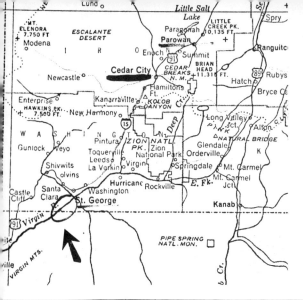

Left: Southwest corner of Utah showing approximate location of the Mountain Meadow Massacre (arrow). Below: Part of C. F. McGlashan's account of the massacre, published in the Sacramento Daily Record.

SACRAMENTO DAILY RECORD, FRIDAY, JANUARY 1, 1875

THE DAILY RECORD.

THE MOUNTAIN MEADOW MASSACRE.

Complete and Authentic History of the Horrible Slaughter.

Latest Developments and Confessions, Obtained Expressly for the "Record."

Mormon "Causes of Provocation"—Bloody Plot Emanated from Military Council of War—Sending Out a Forlorn Hope—Free Masons and Odd Fellows in the Train—Cutting Children's Throats.

Indians Torturing and Burning Captives—The Blood-Stained Spoils at Auction—A Ghastly Field—Mutilated by Wolves!

"Vengeance is Mine, I Will Repay, Saith The Lord."

BY C. F. McGLASHAN.

One cannot gain an intelligent idea of any great event without knowing the causes by which it was produced. Waterloo could never be understood if only the incidents of the battle were narrated. The causes which led to the Mountain Meadows massacre are interwoven with the fundamental principles of the strange religion of the Mormons. Place yourself in sympathy with those principles and you can obtain a faint conception of the motives ous ranks and classes, and in justice to myself I must emphatically deny that this great crime ought to rest upon the shoulders of the people. No denunciation can be too severe, no curses too deep or bitter for those who planned and urged on the crime, but do not infer that all this people are guilty. I am under a thousand obligations to my friends in southern Utah, and wish to state distinctly that the following pages are not intended as a tirade against Mormons or Mormonism, but as an outspoken charge against the murderers, thieves and assassins who committed or planned the massacre.

Israelitish Intolerance

Characterized the Mormon Church from the very beginning. The revelation of Joseph Smith made the Mormons the one chosen people of God. "Gentiles" and "Babylonians" are the terms which plainly indicate that outsiders have no rights which are to be respected. As the Israelites, the ancient people of God, dealt with the Egyptians, the Philistines, or the tribes that opposed them, so, if necessary, might the Mormons deal with "outsiders." This "cause" had much to do with the massacre. A prayerful assemblage were "counseled" to do the deed, and prayerful men led on the slaughter. From John D. Lee's conversation, I have no doubt but the story is true which says he waved his sword above his head, after the massacre, and shouted, "This day has the name of Israel's God been glorified!"

Avenging a Prophet's Blood.

Joseph Smith is regarded by the Mormons as the Savior is by other Christian denominations. The Mormons believe in Jesus Christ, but not more firmly than in this "Latter Day Prophet." Both suffered martyrdom at the hands of infuriated mobs. The murderers of Joseph Smith are regarded with the same intense hatred that would attach to those of our Savior had he been crucified in this age and day. One part of the great emigrant train came from the portion of Missouri from which the Mormons had been driven, and at least one person claimed to have been in Nauvoo when the Prophet was killed. It is currently believed that one of the emigrants swung a pistol above his head and swore that it helped kill "Joe Smith," and was then loaded for "Old Brigham." I have asked Mormons whether their religion would exonerate the man who should kill the desperado that boasted of murdering the prophet, and they bluntly answered, "yes."

Profanity —
Chick

There is, or was, a fanity. Some of the profane, and upon enter "Where is your da r: Their profanity at attempt to arrest the was made, and the abandon the attempt.

Again, it is told that the streets of Cedar suddenly down amo; killed two. Remem would kill the damn chickens, if they inte

Lee says that while town they tore dow fence, and turned grain.

It is rumored that beef, or a spring, Indians suffered fro have died, and the against the emigrant

A Bishop informe sent all over southe vengeance.

The

However, was that Utah, and the Mormon him with force and considered as an ene ed as foes. Practi martial law, and the larly each week. powerful company th route to California. stock alone amounto the costliest apparel citement prevailed, Driven from place to determined to fight accused of having the ern boundary of Ut entered at the nort minate the southern fell they would hang Kimball.

Bloo

Chapter Seven

Under the mysterious guidance he would acknowledge throughout his life, Mac went to see W. H. Mills in Sacramento. The editor had always received him warmly, and now Mac realized what a friend, almost another father, he had in Mills. He told him what had happened and why he had to get away to think matters through.

From Mills' point of view, Mac's unexpected severance of ties at Truckee came so opportunely he didn't waste time on sympathy. He did better.

He gave him the most exciting assignment of his life.

"Go to Utah, Mac, and get the story on the massacre at Mountain Meadows. Atrocity!"

He spat the word and chewed angrily on his cold and somewhat soggy cigar.

The massacre of an entire wagon train bound for California in 1857, seventeen years earlier, was just coming to light. The shocking crime was front-page news from coast to coast.

The emigrant train had been crossing Utah in a southerly direction when, apparently, it dropped from the earth. In a day of slow communication, years had passed before relatives and friends of missing families matched stories and realized that not a soul in the caravan ever reached California.

Unconfirmed rumors of an Indian massacre had drifted across the plains a year or two after the emigrants set out. But not until recently had chilling facts been uncovered that left no doubt of the slaughter and pointed to white men, not Indians, as the perpetrators. John D. Lee, Indian Agent and a major in the Nauvoo Legion at the time, was accused of masterminding a plot against the wagon train and ordering the final gunfire and butchery.

Public outrage demanded his head but he had fled to the hills. "Get him!"

The people said it, the federal government said it, and now Mills said it to Mac.

"Have yourself deputized and join the search. Get John Lee and get that story—however long it takes."

It took about two months.

—•—

Mountain Meadows, the scene of the massacre, he found, was a canyoned, hilly region some forty miles southwest of Cedar City in southern Utah. The emigrants, he saw, would logically have believed this to be their last encampment before crossing the border on the California trail.

As Mills had urged, Mac had himself deputized and was searching the hills surrounding Mountain Meadows when news came of Lee's capture. This freed him to pursue his story, a task that demanded all the tact of which he was capable. A gloom, either of sorrow or of shame, overlay the entire Mormon territory, and the communities he visited met his questions with stolid silence or a barbed evasion. He felt utterly shunned by a people who were known to be suspicious of outsiders anyway, and who were now humiliated by the blot on their name and culture, caused by the vicious act of a fanatical few. Many of these saintly people, he was sure, had known of the crime and buried their bitter knowledge in silence for nearly twenty years. How would he ever get them to talk?

The solution came more readily than he dreamed possible.

John Lee confessed in prison, and his admission of guilt seemed to release the people. Wherever Mac went thereafter, doors opened to him. Men brought him their stories as if to purge their souls of secrets endured so long. Soon he had the signed statements of eyewitnesses—those who had received the plundered goods of the murdered families, and those who had even killed, under Lee's command.

At the jail in Beaver he talked to Lee himself, who denied nothing. His attorney repeatedly warned the man not to talk, but he only seemed anxious to clear Brigham Young and other

76

superiors of complicity. This, he knew, would salvage his name among Mormons, at least to some degree.

Ready at last to write, Mac opened his story with the statement that Mormons themselves repudiated the crime. Then he wrote of possible motivations. Religious prejudice, he said, played a strong part, aggravated as it was by the inevitable few among the "gentile" emigrants who crudely ridiculed Mormon customs and beliefs even while they accepted Mormon hospitality.

The great cause, however, was that Johnston's army was entering Utah, and the Mormons were marshalling to oppose him with force and arms... Practically, the Territory was under martial law, and the Nauvoo Legion drilled regularly each week.

In short, although there were some strikes against the peaceful unsuspecting families in the caravan of emigrants, most of which had nothing to do with them personally, their chief misfortune lay in the fact that they crossed Utah at a bad time. They became aware of this quickly, for the Governor's orders had gone out that they were not to be sold food or grain "under pain of excommunication."

At American Fork, Battle Creek, Provo, Springville, Spanish Fork, Payson, Nephi and Fillmore they received the same harsh refusal to requests for trading or buying. They were ordered away from at least two places where they halted to rest and refresh their weary cattle.

Speeding on ahead of the caravan was Brigham Young's right-hand man, George A. Smith, warning every settlement of the edict. Mac had the story from a man who accompanied Smith on this mission.

The Apostle (Smith) traversed the entire length of the Territory and stopped to retrace his steps only after visiting the site selected for the butchery. The word he gave out was that their enemies (the U. S. government) were going to make things hard and they should save every morsel. No food or grain should be given emigrants or their animals.

'I never heard from George A. any idea or hint that we should molest or mistreat an emigrant,' the man said.

Smith even camped beside the emigrants finally. He advised them where to camp, in fact, before crossing the desert.

From the sworn affidavits of those who participated in the slaughter, it is conclusively established that Brigadier-General George A. Smith, Col. Wm. H. Dame, Lt. Col. I. C. Haight and Major John D. Lee held a council of war at Parowan. They determined on the place, the manner and all the minor details of the massacre. Where the California road crosses the Santa Clara canyon, the crime was to be perpetrated. Shut in between the perpendicular walls of rock, the very wagons were to be piled up as a blockade to prevent the escape of a single soul.

To make doubly sure, some men were delegated to a spot beyond the canyon to cut off stragglers. Guards were placed at other outposts, as well, to shoot down fugitives.

Arrived at the meadows, the unsuspecting and hungry train camped and rested the cattle. Soon, they thought, they would leave Utah.

Suddenly, unexpectedly, at daybreak on Monday morning, September 7, 1857 they were attacked by Indians.

At the very first fire seven were killed and fifteen wounded. . , . Had they possessed less bravery . . . they would all have been massacred on the spot. With a promptitude unparalleled in the history of Indian warfare, these emigrants wheeled their wagons into an oblong corral and with shovels and picks threw earth from the center of the corral against the wagon-wheels. . . . An eyewitness says it was done with such remarkable celerity that the plans of the painted assassins were completely frustrated.

The original plan had been to attack them at Santa Clara canyon, but the Indians became too impatient. These 'Battle-Axes of the Lord' had responded to the call of the Indian Agent, John D. Lee, and the liberal promises they had received caused the premature attack.

Play by play, Mac recounted the confirmed events of what became a prolonged eight-day siege. The starved people behind the barricade put up an astounding defense against repeated storms of whizzing arrows and bullets. Not once did they see a white man among the enemy. The only water source bubbled up beyond their reach. Unable to believe that even savages would kill a helpless woman, one young mother ventured to scoop a pail from the stream and was instantly shot. Lee may have counted on the weapons of starvation and thirst, but by the eighth day he could see they would hold until death.

He resorted to trickery therefore.

Suddenly all firing ceased. The emigrants saw a white flag appear—then the American flag. Officers of the Utah militia were carrying them down the meadows.

Surely the militia of the Territory of the United States was come to the rescue.

Witnesses said that the captives wept and danced and hugged each other, rushing out to meet their supposed friends.

Lee met them like a compassionate father, his eyes actually wet with tears. He assured them safe escort and helped them line up, each beside a soldier for presumable guard. When he asked the men to come unarmed, they unhesitatingly stripped themselves of belts and guns. Mac wrote:

John Lee is as smooth a talker as I ever heard. When I listened to him last week in Beaver jail, I kept thinking of how he talked those emigrants out of the entrenchments from which powder and ball could not dislodge them. Only fifteen had been killed in eight days. The corral was a bulwark of safety, but the honeyed words of a white man won their hearts.

The men marched out first, then the women, and lastly the children . . . There was the American flag, the dear old flag . . . they felt that the strong arms of the Union enfolded them.

And now, God help them! . . .

Suddenly, at a given signal, the troops halted, and down the line passed the fatal order, 'Fire!' It was given by John D. Lee . . . Sworn statements of participators say the militia fired volley after volley at the defenseless, unarmed men . . . But this was not all. The women were not all killed just yet.

The women were separated from the men for raping before they were shot. A bestial blood bath ensued, especially when a woman put up a fight. Lee assigned two men to cut the children's throats "unless too little to remember." Even so, babies were killed.

Oddly, it was Lee himself who "traveled up through the Territory and told everyone the Indians had massacred a train." At his report, men went to the scene and found naked bodies heaped on each other. Even though the wolves had eaten much, the half-hacked heads, the slit throats, the gun wounds were evident. One old man, alone, tried to bury the pieces, the bones, the putrifying flesh.

When notified, Brigham Young, aware that his men were at the heart of it, wept. Lee was cut off from the church.

Few believed the whisper that spread about white participation in the slaughter. But a few children had been spared and put with Mormon families. Some were not too young to recognize their mother's clothing, their father's tools, handed out like spoils. They were not too young, either, to remember the terror of that last day.

— • —

The story was done at last in Mac's flowing script, and he went out into the chill December night to mail it himself on the late westbound. He had no idea what kind of job he'd done. It had seemed vital to him that readers know the possible forces behind the crime as well as the sordid facts, and he had written in depth to the best of his ability. Mills could edit as he saw fit. Emotionally drained, he fell heavily onto his hotel bed fully clothed and slept around the clock.

When he awoke the next noon he lay still awhile, allowing his mind to approach here and there the outer edges of a personal life he had put aside the day he arrived in Utah. A letter from Jennie had come, thanking him for money sent. His thoughts lingered on the letter. Had he imagined its propitiatory tone? Suddenly he recalled another letter, still unopened and unread, buried in the clutter on his desk. He had recognized Lyda's round schoolgirlish hand on the thickly stuffed envelope and with an inward smile had tossed it aside to enjoy when his task was done.

He got up and doused his face with cold water. Taking his comb, he parted his hair with the high side part that controlled some of its curl and cowlick. He had begun to let his mustache flourish to cover his upper lip. Purest vanity, he told himself. It hid the two unsightly decayed teeth that no tooth surgeon was going to yank if *he* could help it. He and his sisters all had bad teeth. From poor food when they were children, Jennie said.

Jennie. He thought about her while the waitress went off to fill his order. Ham and eggs and three flapjacks. And coffee now, if you please? She was a cute little thing, this waitress, with something of Jennie about her. The cold thought that the "something" was the come-on look in her black eyes made him shift uneasily in his chair. He picked up Lyda's fat envelope.

Out of it tumbled a small folded note that he retrieved as it rolled to the table's edge. Curious, he opened it at once. It was a brief message, he saw to his surprise, from Nona Keiser.

"Jennie asks me to add my plea to her sister's," he read in Nona's rounded but slanting script. "Jennie truly wants you to come back, and she seems unconsolable without you, Mac."

Lyda's letter developed the same theme and he read it through before he unfolded the news clippings she had enclosed. His thoughts were mellow and he suppressed a chuckle of simple happiness while he read. He had heard so much of real tragedy over the past two months. His own troubles seemed ridiculously exaggerated. The huffings and puffings of a bloated pride must have made him walk out on Jennie. Of course he'd go back.

Then he opened the largest of the creased news clippings and pushed away his half-eaten meal. The shock of the headline was like a fist blow to his stomach, instantly sealing his decision to return to Truckee. It not only brought the totality of the town to the forefront of his memory, but in the intensity of his emotion, told him he belonged there.

Dave Frink was dead—tragically, accidentally killed, the item said, in a vigilante raid on the night of November 24, 1874. Truckee mourned the loss of a much-loved pioneer, as well as an editor who went far toward making *The Reublican* a unifying force in the community. Forty-three years old, David Belden Frink had worked up from printer's devil to journeyman on *The Marshall Statesman*, a Michigan paper. In 1861, he came to California and settled in Nevada City, where he worked for both the *Gazette* and *Journal*. After the death of his wife, he moved to Truckee in 1871, bringing his teenage daughter Carrie. Together with E. W. Hayden he built up the newspaper until he bought out Hayden and became its sole proprietor.

Another clipping showed the names of W. F. Edwards and Benjamin T. K. Preston on the masthead. Both were Mac's good friends, as Dave had been, and he was glad to know they had taken over the paper. Will Edwards, who was engaged to the youngest

Keiser daughter, Laura, shared his own enthusiasm for the scenic grandeur of the Sierra. In fact, they had talked of co-authoring a guidebook for tourists. Now that he was coming back, they could get on with it.

The circumstances of Frink's death concerned Mac deeply, for he had joined the vigilance committee himself in 1872, within weeks of coming to town. It was a secret organization, named and patterned after Virginia City's "Six Hundred and One". The citizens' solution to uncontained lawlessness, Truckee's "601," like Virginia City's, wore masks and issued warnings to undesirables in the form of red ribbons tacked up along Front Street. Apparently, the committee had posted red ribbons on November 19th, with the result that five men left town within hours. Conferring, the "601" decided to make a clean sweep, since several shoddy characters still remained.

On the night of the twenty-fourth, therefore, two dozen masked men filed quietly down Back Street. There in the obscure shadows of a saloon doorway, they saw a man lurking. Someone, a vigilante, fired. The man fell. Dead, his own mask in place, was Frink, who had left the group to follow a lead of his own.

—•—

Mac was back.

He was back with Jennie, apparently on his own terms. She had been the one to defect. He would take her back as she was, but she must accept him, too, as he was. They apparently agreed that the answer was a baby. Their marriage would be cemented by a living bond, and Jennie's time would be happily filled.

In the town, he was back as though he'd only meant to do the reporting job and return. But first and foremost he announced that he had passed the Bar examination.

On Wednesday, January 6th, *The Republican* announced in a neatly boxed ad:

C. F. McGlashan
Attorney and Counselor at Law
Office with the *Truckee Republican.*
Special attention given to collections and
all money collected promptly turned over.

On March 20th, however, a new ad appeared in its place:

Gaylord & McGlashan, Attorneys at Law
Office on Front Street, in Marzen's Building
Will practice all courts.

This was a flattering partnership for a new young lawyer. Gaylord, now District Attorney, had offices in Nevada City. His partner, therefore, would handle the mountain business. This meant that Mac would now begin to prosecute criminal cases before Judge Keiser.

He soon discovered that the courtroom gave him a stage on which all his elocutionary talents bloomed. He had earned honors in oratory at Williston. In his boyhood, his sister Ann had mercilessly corrected his posture, giving him a command over carriage and gesture that riveted eyes upon him when he wished it. His perceptions never came so clearly, or the words to express them, as when he stood before an audience. With this gift he possessed an intense, devoted interest in people. In the courtroom he knew he had found his forte. But not in prosecution. He wanted to defend.

"The boy's a go-getter, no doubt about it," John Keiser said, and the older businessmen smiled, recalling those first days when Mac had come, a stranger to them, with a butterfly net and a telescope.

"He was the first principal who stayed on, for all that," one said.

"The pistol on his desk. Remember?" said another, and the cronies slapped their knees and wiped away tears of mirth with large kerchiefs. For it had so transpired that one irate sire, hearing of the pistol displayed on the principal's desk for overgrown bully-boys to note, had waylaid him on the way to school one morning, waving a handgun of his own. No one witnessed what happened next, but that morning Mac laid two pistols on the desk, his own and the other's. It was after that incident that the solid citizens had taken him to their hearts.

"He had nerve," John said.

"It takes nerve to live in this town. Don't deny it." Another laugh made the rounds at this. But not one denied it in his heart, for they all had come when the town was born. They were its builders, the ones who loved every boulder, every pine tree on its hills.

The town was prospering now and some of these pioneers could take life a little easier. John was selling the Keiser House, the hotel his family had lived in for so many years, and building a home on High Street. He hoped to have it done for Laura's spring wedding to Will Edwards.

"How would you like to join me in real estate, Mac?" he suggested one day soon after Mac's return. "On the side, that is."

"I'd like that, John." As before, the two men, like father and son, were in orbit together.

Once again, Mac plunged into the heart of the problems of the unique and growing community. At this time, Attorney Hayden was urging the creation of a county called Donner, with Truckee as the county seat. In a Letter to the Editor, Hayden wrote:

Truckee has almost become a synonym for 'murder', 'robbery', and unlawful acts . . . Not a newspaper in the State but has chronicled some doings of Truckee roughs . . . These chronicles at present constitute the written history of the town and make it appear a veritable Pandemonium . . .

Our position is understood by few and appreciated by none of the denizens of the western slope. We are a community in ourselves. They (other towns) have no charity, no sympathy, no respect for us. Their papers have railed against Truckee because it filled their jails with its criminals and now howl with virtuous indignation at a measure which gives promise of benefiting the county (Nevada County) to an untold degree.

Spokesmen from other towns and counties of the region answered heatedly.

"Hoodlums would run the county," wrote the editor of the *Sierra Messenger*. Hayden retorted in the customary name-calling style of the day. Alluding to "the Messengerman," he opined that "nearly bankrupt Sierra County" didn't want to lose the rich valley.

The pollution controversy was also going strong early in 1875. The previous year, an attempt had been made to pass an Act in the State Legislature to prohibit lumber mills from discharging sawdust into the Truckee River. Sawdust not only formed bars impeding the migration of fish, but also polluted the waters and damaged grazing land.

Before the first January snowfall could prevent a visit to the Truckee Meadows where most of the sawdust backed up, Mac investigated for the paper and found the complaints exaggerated. With his contemporaries of the 1870s, he had little patience with those who counseled caution in the interests of ecology, with this difference: He believed such problems as pollutants should be met and overcome by, as he termed it, "the genius of man's inventive brain." He did not believe the responsible industry should be curtailed.

With his generation he used terms like "illimitable" forests—and believed, in truth, they were. Not until the Big Bonanza ended and the long logging flumes decayed, would they note uneasily the bald, stump-dotted hills where no tree would ever grow back.

To his joy, Charlie Burckhalter returned to Truckee from a stint in the Navy yards at Mare Island. He brought with him a submarine dredger, a ship's thermometer, and a salinometer, among other equipment, and he and Mac impatiently waited the winter out to make use of them. They planned to run tests on the waters of Lake Tahoe as soon as feasible, for a series of articles called "Scientific Fun on Lake Tahoe." These would appear under Mac's by-line in the *Record-Union*. His coverage of the Mountain Meadow massacre had established his journalistic reputation. The *New York Sun*, then a leading paper, had offered him a staff position almost as soon as the feature appeared. The story had gone far toward bringing about Lee's conviction, and with a glow of gratification that he kept to himself, he realized he would probably be welcomed by any paper in the country. However, something prompted him to be content with contentment.

As soon as the snow melted, the two men dredged up samples of sand and gravel from the lake bottom at different depths. With the thermometer, they compared temperatures at various depths. With the salinometer, they tested the purity of Tahoe and found that water taken from the middle of the lake was "very nearly as pure as distilled water."

With a champagne bottle they sounded Tahoe's "extremist depth" and found it was exactly 1,645 feet. Years later, the Coast and Geodetic Survey came up with the identical figure, using far more sophisticated equipment.

Before the end of 1875, Undine was born. Jennie recovered well, and Mac was transported with pride and dedication to what was now a *bona fide* family, complete, secure.

As usual, when filled with love, he took another job.

Will Edwards dissolved his partnership with Preston and asked Mac to be his editor. In a salutatory editorial, he wrote, " 'O, that mine enemy would write a book' is the expression that would be quite as appropriate if the last words were 'edit a newspaper' . . . I enter upon these duties with no undue confidence, yet I am not conscious of any particular fear. I shall do my level best; knuckle to no one; work with my might; and trust the rest to my friends."

For the next three months, the paper reflected his touch. His descriptions of snow scenes and winter sports foreshadowed his inauguration, in years to come, of winter sports in the Sierra. He began, too, a tactic he would use again and again. He promoted his advertisers. He made businessmen and merchants news-worthy. He told his reporters to interview in depth men known to everybody, praising the sacrifices and hard work that had built the community and continued to do so.

This was not only a shrewd business stroke—it was much more than that, as he was much more than a businessman. With these stories, he strengthened Truckee's community pride and forged another link in the fraternal bond uniting his fellow townsmen. He believed in the "pat on the back," the word of recognition. And he was determined to pass on to others all the encouragement he had received himself from Keiser and other Truckee pioneers.

However, in taking on the newspaper, he extended himself too far. He realized it almost at once. An editor's job should be full-time. It was too vital to the town, and he couldn't carry on a brisk law business and a biweekly paper.

Besides, his butterfly hobby, somewhat dormant in winter, had taken on new importance to him since the past summer when E. Henry Edwards, his entomologist correspondent, came to Truckee for the express purpose of hunting specimens with him on the meadows.

Edwards taught him to sugar for moths with a heady syrup of stale lager beer, dark brown sugar, and a strong jolt of Jamaica rum (one-half pint to a quart of beer). They painted the mixture on the trees and rocks along the banks of the Truckee River, returning at twilight to find the first rush of moths sipping happily at the edges.

At midnight they came back to the sugared route, darkening their lanterns not to attract the insects to them. Mac wrote in his notebook:

"One is thrilled with excitement at almost every step taken in the darkness amid the rustling bushes and trees along the river bank. There are surprises and half-adventures, such as the sudden whirr of a bird's wings or the crackling of a dead branch, and the gloom and solitude tend to make these harmless episodes almost tragic. The least noise...and prize specimens will be sailing safely above your head."

Edwards convinced him that his amateur work was valuable to the field. The science was in its infancy and would be so for decades to come. Scarcely anything was known of the Far West's insect life. He asked for as many specimens as Mac had time to find. He would classify them. All he asked in return was to keep the sample.

Thus after less than three months, Mac announced his resignation as editor of the paper, due to pressing commitments and a brisk law business. Will Edwards, now married to Laura Keiser, carried on the publication alone.

However, Will and Mac still pursued their mutual interest in promoting their beloved mountains, and by April, Will announced that they were preparing a *Guidebook to the Sierra*.

Meanwhile, a young man came to town and hung up his own Attorney-at-Law sign. He was Timothy J. Crowley, twenty-three, fresh from the Bar exam. He and Mac immediately liked each other. They had much in common—similar interests, avid curiosity, boundless energies, and a propensity for uninhibited laughter, preferably at themselves.

The Saturday, May 6th paper recounted the aftermath of a hunting trip enjoyed by Crowley, Mac, Yank Hammond, and a man named Gitchell:

Posted on Mac's bulletin board is the following:

Free Lunch by the Celebrated Caterers
McGlashan & Crowley
Bill of Fare

Boiled:	Bear Corned, Bear Ham, Bear Tongue, Bear Capered, Bear Giblets, Bear & Cabbage
Roast:	Bear Loin, Bear Rib, More Bear
Entrees:	Bear a la Mode, Bear Le Crowle, Bear McGlash, and Bear Cold
Relishes:	Bear Jelly, Bear Sour, Bear Warmed Over
Wines:	Bear Juice Hot, Bear Juice Cold, More Bear Juice.

The efficacy of the Bear Juice was evident. The outcome of this hunting trip was a new law partnership—McGlashan and Crowley.

Only a few months earlier, Mac had announced that he had left the District Attorney's office and was in business for himself. His very success in the courtroom had turned him against prosecuting. One case in particular led to his decision. He had prosecuted a Chinese of whose guilt he was never certain. He had won the case and the man had gone to jail. What if, he thought, an innocent man were hanged because I, doing my job, swayed the jury? He couldn't live with that; so he shouldn't risk it. He would be a defense lawyer.

However, he didn't like to work alone. He had always responded to the idea of partnership, of communal effort, and it was this that attracted him to the brotherhoods—Masonic, Knights Templar, and in due time, the lodge he would love best, the Knights of Pythias. He was delighted, therefore, to be in partnership again and in an atmosphere of rich mutual understanding. They made, their colleagues said, "a lively firm."

If ever a man was entrenched in his life work and his community, it was himself in May, 1877.

As for Jennie, *The Republican* recorded the fact that "the McGlashans attended Joe Marzen's wedding and gave the bride a gold thimble." They were seen, as before, at socials, spelling bees, the theatre. Simultaneously, Mac's name appeared in every issue as officer of this lodge or that, announcing meetings for "the first Thursday after the Full Moon."

Jennie's mother had died the year before, leaving a gap in her daughter's life. However, Ella, now married to John Greenleaf, still lived on the same street. Moreover, Jennie had little Undine to occupy her. Still, she was lonely. Mac had forgiven her, but the scar of their former rift still festered.

Believing all was stable, Mac invested in plush office furniture and carpeting to be shipped from San Francisco. This was known about town, making incredible the announcement that appeared in a May issue of *The Republican*. McGlashan, it said, was considering an overseas assignment on one of the leading newspapers, and would depart soon if he took it.

No one who knew him well believed it. But within weeks his ads were deleted entirely from the paper.

On the street, townsmen knew the truth—or a version of it sufficient to let them guess what they wished. One night at a Masonic meeting he surprised a smirk on some man's face and overheard him speak the name of the man who had so nearly broken up his marriage. Could the fellow be back in town? Uneasiness changed to alarm; then to black foreboding. At the first chance, he left the hall inconspicuously and went home. The front door was unlocked. He pushed it open quickly. Jennie and his rival sat decorously, the table between them. Their faces were grave and pale in the lamplight.

"Get out," Mac said, "before I kill you."

—•—

Full circle. He had proposed on a sweet May morning in 1871. Six years later, on a May morning no sunshine could brighten, he and Jennie agreed to divorce.

Before June was out, Jennie and Undine were on the train, bound for the home of relatives below; the house was up for rent; and Mac remained only to wind up his affairs. As Tim's partner, he would continue on with the cases handled through the County Court at Nevada City. For his own sake as well as Jennie's he wanted to get out of town. Loyal as their close friends were and undisposed to malicious gossip, he still found it hard to face them. Divorce was a scandalous word. He felt branded and besmirched by it.

Lyda and Nona, still unmarried and close friends, sympathized deeply with the couple. Tearfully, they saw Jennie and toddling brown-eyed Undine off on the morning train. Mac had joined them to take care of tickets and baggage. Then he held Undine close for a long moment, gave Jennie a white-faced nod, and abruptly left the station platform for his office.

When the train pulled out, the two young women turned away with a sense of vacuum, like mourners who leave the burial ground to resume a life that must go on.

"Why don't we see if poor Mac needs help," Lyda suggested, and Nona agreed.

They crossed the plaza to Front Street and turned left to Marzen's on the corner. When he didn't answer Lyda's light tap on his office door, they pushed it open and went in.

He sat alone. Crumpled paper overflowed the wastebasket beside his chair. He was packing some of his books and these were stacked on the floor. The shelves showed gaping spaces. Everything within his radius spoke of the shambles in which he saw his life. He looked up and Nona caught dark woe in his eyes. Impulsively, she crossed the room and put her hands on his shoulders.

"Oh, Mac, don't grieve so," she said, and kissed his cheek.

With that kiss of self-forgetful sympathy, his brotherly feeling for this calm, beautiful girl quickened into something much more. With instant recall, he remembered her penetrating questions about his hobbies. No one else had shown such intelligent interest, for instance, in his "bugs." He had liked her quick, retentive mind and gravely listening face. This was the kind of woman he had known before Jennie, a woman with a mind for conversation beyond the whist table and sewing circle. How I need a woman to be friend and companion, as well as my love, he thought.

A woman? Why, by now she must be twenty-three or so. He

had known that Charlie Burckhalter was in love with her and had been her escort constantly since the broken engagement. Charlie had confided to him with mournful acceptance that she loved him like a sister. He had wondered then if Charlie would ever love so wholeheartedly again. And now he understood why.

Stunned by this unexpected rush of thoughts and their insights, he gradually realized that Lyda was asking him a question. Would he promise to write? They were asking for an exchange of addresses.

"I will be in Santa Clara for the fall and winter," Nona was saying. "You can write to me in care of my sister. That would be the John Greenleafs."

In confusion, he found pencil and paper and wrote down the addresses. As the girls were leaving, he regained his wits enough to follow them through the door and ask Nona if he might call on her in Santa Clara.

"I'll be in San Francisco frequently, and that's not far away."

"Why, yes, Mac. I'd like that very much."

He finished his packing rapidly but automatically, as if someone not himself were doing it. He felt drained of all emotion, much as he'd felt after the Mountain Meadow massacre story. He must get away quickly from the scenes of his personal disaster. Then, once more, he must shape the course of his life.

Gently as a current of spring air, the thought came to him that he had just now glimpsed, perhaps, his promised land in the profound depths of a pair of gray-blue eyes.

—•—

They walked under the shaggy pepper trees, took buggy rides into the countryside with its brown, oak-studded hills, so different from their forested mountain home, and Mac courted her with the reserve dictated a century ago by a divorce not yet final.

In March, 1878 he came to her, heralded by a bouquet of fresh violets. In the center of the fragrant purple gleamed a golden wedding ring with a tiny scroll attached. He waited in the foyer while she read it.

"If you will wear this ring, it is yours. If not, I will understand."

She pinned the flowers to her small waist and slipped the ring on her right hand. It would be for him to put it on her left.

She wrote to her parents. So did he.

Elizabeth's eyes blazed. "A divorced man!"

John didn't like it either. He had sponsored Mac, loaned him money, taken him into partnership. He liked the man, but . . . Did Nona realize the gossip this would cause? A divorced man . . . And less than a year ago, he'd had another wife, whom everyone knew right here in Truckee. Distressed, John shook his head. He didn't want Nona hurt by tongues.

Elizabeth wrote. Was she in her right mind? No, they would not consent.

Saddened, but firm, Nona replied. She would "run away, then, with Mac."

Perhaps John and Elizabeth remembered then their own elopement, for John thundered in the next mail:

"Come home and be married like a lady."

They were married on April 7, 1878 at the Keiser home.

It took courage to face the town. For both of them it took courage. They mulled it all over between them and talked it out. If gossips were unkind, they could move away. But Mac wanted the mountains, the meadows, the friendships. So did she. Why not try living here first? The novelty would wear off as a sewing club topic. And Mac believed it was important, for every kind of growth, to stay put.

They stayed. And for the Keisers' sake, for Nona's, Mac's and Jennie's too, the whisperers were disposed to be kind. Elizabeth urged them to move into her extra rooms, emptied when Laura married, and until Mac could find a suitable house to lease, they agreed. He knew his mother-in-law's acute sensitivity to impropriety, which their marriage on the heels of divorce was, in her eyes. "She doesn't see me, only some spectre called A Divorced Man," he told Nona.

Hostility on John Keiser's part was somewhat checked by his respect for Mac's character and achievement. But an obvious coolness reduced his former cordiality to a polite gravity that pained his daughter as much as her husband. Only time could heal the relationship, they both realized.

92

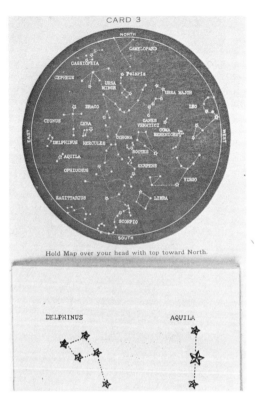

CARD 3

Hold Map over your head with top toward North.

DELPHINUS   AQUILA

Among his other hobbies, McGlashan enjoyed astronomy. He mapped the stars in each season, then had the charts printed for his students. The individual constellations at the bottom are on the first page of a fold-out booklet attached to each card.

Ten days after the wedding, Mac and Crowley resumed their law partnership.

The Truckee Republican's editor, George O. Ford, announced the fact. George and his brother, Tom, were also attorneys and although Tom was on very good terms with Mac and Tim, George made no pretense of friendliness. Under his editorship, references to the firm were vinegary and belittling.

"General Growleyowskie and McGlashan Pasha fought the legal battle," he wrote in the case of the People vs one Carmen, who got off too lightly, in Ford's opinion. The jury was "bamboozled by the antics of" the defense men, he said.

True, under McGlashan's lead, the young lawyers were dramatic. Mac introduced demonstration whenever his imagination supplied the effective, spellbinding "trick," as Ford called it. And in the verbal summary and pleading of his case, his powers gathered in the intensity of his piercing, almost hypnotic eyes.

In midsummer, Mac borrowed the money from John Keiser to buy the newspaper from Crowley, who had bought it from Ford. T. S. (Tom) Ford agreed to be his editor.

93

Thus, for the third time Mac immersed himself in the Sierra town's life. Appointed deputy Fish Commissioner, he watched over the unlawful catching of trout. And he was back to the rooftops with his telescope and star mapping, out to the meadows with his butterfly net. More seriously, the Chinese question was in the foreground throughout the state, and he joined the local version of Caucasian leagues that were starting up and down the coast.

In short, he was in love again. His energies were unlimited, his mind overflowing with projects.

With Nona's marriage, two former suitors bowed out. Ben Bacon, who had moved to Boca and had unsuccessfully contended for office in the State Assembly, moved now to Reno, the newspaper said. Charlie Burckhalter married in September and moved to Oakland.

As for Nona herself, she was happy and pregnant, expecting around the first of the new year, 1879. Her sister Ella too was pregnant and their mother's strong efficiency operated back and forth between them. From Nona she walked down the hill and across the tracks to Ella's house several times a day, as their time drew near.

Chapter Eight

Since I cared little for hard facts, I never asked questions about the Donner party. Others did in my hearing, however, and I came to believe I knew all about the sad story which, after all, was a constant of our environment.

We lived only three miles east of Donner Lake, the scene of the disaster which every wild winter snowstorm brought naturally to mind. When a heavy storm was brewing, my grandfather would settle into his springy black armchair facing the western windows and light up a cigar. Mama then took her place near him, and the three of us, with Brownie at Papa's feet, watched the clouds gather thickly over Donner until the summit peaks were lost in the murky gloom.

With no words spoken, I knew Papa's thoughts were on the long-ago despair of a snowbound wagon train. My own thoughts turned to those doomed people whenever blizzards struck at night and witches danced on the whistling winds that rattled our many windows. And when I woke on sub-zero mornings to a deaf white world muffled in twenty-foot snow drifts, I pictured the frozen cattle of the Donner party—buried standing.

In the Rocking Stone Tower I saw the relics found where the starving families had huddled for shelter near the foot of the lake. The toe bone picked up from a fireplace reminded that cannibalism had been part of the tragedy and most of the horror. We often visited the wooded sites of the vanished shelters, long rotted away, for my grandfather had marked and preserved the locations since 1879. (In 1910 the Native Sons of the Golden West relieved him of this solitary vigilance by installing permanent markers.)

The spot he guarded jealously was that of the Breen cabin. In the spring of 1879, while he was writing the history of the Donner party, James and John Breen and other survivors came to the lake for the express purpose of identifying the sites. At the Breen site, they found the fireplace and prints of the foundation logs still clearly visible. Digging, they turned up fragments of painted china, corroded silver spoons and forks, and other household items immediately recognized and claimed by the Breens. Beyond possibility of doubt, this was their cabin.

This was the spot Papa chose for a future monument and memorial to the Donner pioneers.

He based his choice on three facts. First, not only was the Breen site visible from the railroad along the southern cliffs, it was both accessible and visible from the most traveled wagon road. Second, this cabin had been central to the theatre of the tragedy. Third, it was enriched by previous history.

In the autumn of 1844, two years before the Donner party's arrival at the lake, a group of young men reached the same spot at the base of the summit pass. Fearing the sudden onset of winter and sensing the need for haste, they agreed to lighten their oxen's load by building a cabin to store the supplies they carried. Ahead, the peaks rose two thousand feet straight up from the level of the lake. They must tackle the ascent quickly. Moses Schallenberger, just turned eighteen, built the cabin with two of his companions and these three volunteered to stay and guard the goods.

"There's plenty of game around," they said, "Don't worry. We'll make out all right. You come for us when the snow melts."

But soon after the others left, a violent storm struck. Snow fell without stopping and all deer, bear and fowl fled over the mountain. Starvation was certain. They must strike out for the summit without delay, or be lost. Rapidly, they nailed the house shut and set out.

On reaching the summit, however, young Schallenberger doubled over with cramps so severe he could not walk.

"Take me back to the cabin," he begged. "Let me take my chances there."

Reluctantly, they brought him back and settled him as comfortably as they could. For fully three months he remained alone. Fortunately, he found steel traps among the supplies. He was able to catch a skinny fox from time to time, his only food. His friends returned for him in March, 1845. In November, 1846, the Donner train reached the lake. The cabin was in good shape and the Breens moved in.

The loneliness of the boy's long vigil can be imagined. Even today, with a Donner Memorial State Park filled with happy tourists, somber loneliness pervades the area. My grandfather often referred to Donner's "frowning cliffs." The solemn trees, the ponderous crags, the moody rippling lake—these have no smile. A hushed solemnity prevails. This place, so saturated with memories of human desolation and despair, seems aware. Not hostile, but remembering, as if it holds an eternal wake.

Only thirty-one when he wrote the Donner history, my grandfather often went alone to the scenes of the tragedy to reconstruct them in his mind. Leaning against the rough-barked pine, he would listen to the silence and reach for the past. Finding it, he wrote; and writing, he wept.

He finished the book in a white-hot concentration of only four months. When it was done, he wrote to Eliza Donner Houghton, youngest of George and Tamsen Donner's daughters:

A great winged spirit seems to have caught me up four months ago, swept me through realms of thought where mortal never trod before, showed me the lives and hearts and promptings of people who are dead and people who are living, brought me in contact with friends I never before saw, but whose friendship takes hold of my very soul—and now dashes me to earth again. How lonesome it is! How I miss the snow, and the storms and the misery!

The survivors, of whom twenty-six were living at the time he wrote their story, loved him as he loved them. He had done more than scrape away the fungi of legend to discover the most powerful drama in the opening of the Far West. He had written as both historian and defense attorney, to restore these people to their place of dignity in human society.

For they had survived the ordeal by hunger only to face an ordeal-by-pointed-finger. The emaciated adults who staggered down to the valley settlements carrying the children their self-denying sacrifices had saved, heard themselves accused of devouring children. Heard, or read in irresponsible published accounts, that they had murdered for human flesh. Heard or read.. until family by family they went underground.

Their true story had been so quickly superseded by the tales of sensation-mongers, it seemed hopeless to refute them. Some tried, to no avail, to present the truth in magazine articles. It seemed best, finally, to move where their connection with the Donner party was not known. Thus they spared the children the schoolyard cruelty of being stoned with the word "cannibal." Never close friends among themselves, Donner party survivors lost touch, and preferred it that way.

When word got about that the editor of *The Truckee Republican* intended to exhume their story and had already begun to publish it in his newspaper, one of the daughters of Captain George Donner brought immediate suit for libel, prompted simply by past experience. Another daughter, Eliza Poor Donner (Mrs. S. O. Houghton), welcomed the publication of the truthful account and had taken pains to assure herself that McGlashan's motives were consonant with the best interests of the survivors. She upheld him in court, therefore, and the case was summarily dismissed. From then on, through Eliza's persuasion and his own native tact, all survivors gave him their full confidence and cooperation.

The whole thing had come about in November, 1878, when a tall stranger, fortyish and well-dressed, walked into the newspaper office at Truckee and asked the price of a year's subscription. "Six dollars," he was told, and having paid it, he jotted down his name and address on a piece of notepaper. Mac read, "James F. Breen, South San Juan, San Benito County, California."

The new young editors and law partners, McGlashan and Crowley, had lately been hard put to build up the newspaper's circulation. Mac had written an article on the attractions of Donner Lake, with the tentative notion to run a series on mountain vacation spots. Now Breen was saying:

"I came by a copy of your paper with the story on Donner Lake. Thought I'd come up and look around. I was with the Donner party long ago, and I was curious to see if anything was left of the cabin we used."

"*You* were *with* the Donner party?" His reporter's antennae quivering, Mac offered a cigar and a chair. "Please sit down and talk, Mr. Breen. I've lived here seven years and as teacher, lawyer and editor I've never been able to learn a thing about the Donner party," he said. "As far as I can tell there were four people— Donner, his wife, a Dutchman and . . . somebody else. And the Dutchman ate the others up."

James Breen smiled broadly. "That's about as truthful as most tales floating around the country. Actually, eighty or ninety people, counting children, were in the party. Only half survived, I'd say."

The firm of McGlashan and Crowley exchanged glances. Here, dropped from heaven, sat a *bona fide* survivor of the Donner party. The golden potential for the paper struck them both, and Tim joined the conversation with an inquiry about other survivors.

"I can't give you a single address of anyone outside my own family," Breen said. "My brother John might help. He can tell you much more than I about the whole story. He was twenty at the time it happened and I was only four. He and our father both kept diaries."

Diaries! What more could they ask? Breen left that day with the promise he would write to brother John, who was presently somewhere "in the mountains above Yosemite with some cattle," and the promise that John would send them the true history.

The following account was written by my grandfather:

The next issue of the paper contained an account of Judge Breen's visit and that he would send the history of the Donner party for publication at an early date. This item was copied far and wide, and I began to receive letters from all over America, even from Europe and the Orient, containing money and asking for the history. Very foolishly, I liked this, and wrote other things . . . which brought more letters and more money for subscriptions. *The Republican* soon had a subscription list of six hundred people who lived outside the Truckee Basin. But John stayed in the mountains, and the history did not come! I was prospering financially, but week after week passed without my knowing one word about the history. Each day I grew more desperate—furious is the better word,—but John was still in the mountains, letters containing money still flowed in, and I was absolutely helpless.

At last, a single sheet of legal-cap arrived. It contained about sixty names, above which was the heading, "Fatal List." After each name was a single word, "survived", or "perished." That was all! After all the glowing promises I had made, this was the promised history! I published the list. Three days later a letter came from William G. Murphy, city attorney of Marysville, saying that he had read in a San Francisco daily, copied from *The Republican*, what purported to be a fatal list of the Donner Party. He wrote: "You say I perished; I am very much alive, and have a wife and seven children. You state that my sister, Mrs. Foster, perished; she is alive in San Francisco, or was alive last week. You say my mother survived; I regret to say she perished at Donner Lake. If your statements regarding other families are as reliable as in the case of ours, I advise you to correct your list..."

The next day I was in Marysville, the guest of William G. Murphy at his beautiful home.

Each clue led to another survivor. He finally had the addresses of twenty-six. He was to interview and correspond intensively with twenty-four of the twenty-six—all then living who had been old enough to remember.

Continuing his account:

Many showed great reluctance to having their stories made public by a stranger, and I had to vigorously cultivate their acquaintance, and convince them I was seeking the plain truth, not a mess of sensational horrors, before they would even consent to correspond with me.

In her first letter, Mrs. Houghton (Eliza Donner) stated a truth irresistibly impressed on my mind. She wrote: "I am satisfied no individual could give anything like a history of the party after arriving at Donner Lake. There were three camps—(and two tents, and all were buried in ten feet of snow)—and each family occupied separate cabins. Some remained at the camps a shorter time, some went on to Sutter's Fort with different relief parties. The knowledge of each individual, therefore, is confined exclusively to his or her family." For instance, who but a member of the Forlorn Hope could describe the sufferings endured by that heroic group? Who but Keseberg could tell what occurred after he was left alone in the mountains? The history must be compiled, rather than written, and every survivor who was old enough to have taken any important part must contribute the facts within his knowledge. It was perfectly plain that the task of gathering, compiling, and harmonizing the statements was to devolve upon me,

100

Donner Lake. This lithograph was the frontispiece in C. F. McGlashan's History of the Donner Party. (From a photograph by H. K. Gage, June 12, 1879.)

101

and the more I knew of the story and its mournful, heartbreaking details, the less I wanted the job.

On more than one occasion I was ready to quit, but some unexpected thing happened to spur me on in the work. A detective agency spent some weeks in trying to locate Keseberg, but could not find a single trace of the man. By merest accident I learned that the Catholic Bishop at Sacramento knew him, and through him I found Keseberg's secluded cabin in Brighton, near Sacramento, got his story, and became satisfied he did not murder Tamsen Donner...

Reed, Graves, Pike, Snyder, Donner and his wife Tamsen—these and many more were faceless names, jotted into his notebook. These were the unknown characters, without size or weight as yet, in a story he saw only through mists of myth. One name on his list drew him, mainly because of the Donner name—Eliza Poor Donner Houghton. Murphy said she was the youngest, he believed, of George and Tamsen Donner's daughters and was now living in San Jose. Five Donner children had been with the train, two girls by Donner's two former wives and three by Tamsen. All had been rescued.

Mac wrote to Eliza first, then to five other survivors, all of San Jose.

Eliza Houghton answered four days later—intelligently and decisively. She was not about to release any information until she knew who wanted it and for what purpose *exactly*.

"I feel a deep interest in having the truth told," she wrote, "and in such shape that it will be accepted as such, so that false impressions will be corrected."

But she would not waste her time, and certainly not information, if he planned another "sentimental story." If he really wanted to give the world the truth, she would cooperate to the limit.

He replied immediately, assuring her he wanted to publish only the truth, without sensationalism. He then received, in token of her trust, copies of letters written by Tamsen Donner, her mother.

"All the information you give me comes to me fresh and new and unheard of," he wrote, thanking her. He included more questions, which she answered promptly.

However, by March fourth he had received no response whatever to his letter mailed a month earlier to the five others.

"Please use your influence to gain their cooperation, for I sorely need it!" he begged Eliza.

Meanwhile, six hundred scowling out-of-town subscribers, all paid up, marched at his back. The Donner Party was foundering all over again—this time, in the columns of *The Republican*.

"Crowley, take over. The law business, the newspaper, everything! Do the best you can without killing yourself. I've got to get out and get this story."

Tim grinned. They both saw the same vision. *The Republican* had bitten off a pebble and started an avalanche. The two men could communicate with a look—and then burst into shouting laughter, comprehensible to no one but themselves. This they did now.

"Go." That was the only word Mac needed and he got it.

But Nona? Would she accept this? Every one of those names on the list had to be found, interviewed with infinite tact, stories compared and sifted—and damn it all, at least one issue of the paper each week had to carry the serialized story.

Why had he taken it on? No, he didn't mean that. He wanted tremendously to do it. But could he? He knew how the railroaders must have felt when they started laying the rails over the Sierra. To tackle his own mountain he had, as yet, only the statements of two or three people.

"Do what you have to do, dear," Nona said.

He caught the next train for San Jose.

—•—

The Houghton home was set back from the street, inside a white picket fence. It was a two-story frame house whose main glory was a semi-tropical garden that almost hid it from sight.

Mac took this all in while he opened the gate. He hoped the palms and pepper trees, interspersed among a haphazardly gracious abundance of floral growth, promised informality and generosity in the owners.

He was not disappointed.

The pretty woman in her mid-thirties who opened the door fully embodied the spirit of her garden. Her dark blue eyes welcomed him warmly as she led him inside. Her husband, too, was cordial. Mac was glad to meet a handshake as firm and dry and, he sensed, as wholehearted as his own. Sherman O. Houghton, as well as his wife, trusted him and would help. In the face of frozen silence from the others, he had only begun to realize how important this trust was.

He left well after midnight that night.

—•—

Eliza Poor Donner was four, when rescued. Rescued with her were thirty-two children—not all at the same time. But this was the stunning truth and the refutation of the calumnies spread about. Of eighty-one souls who ascended the Sierra the last day of October, 1846, forty-five would live to reach the settlements below. Of these, five were men, eight were women. *All the rest were children.*

Surviving with Eliza were her sisters Frances and Georgia, and her half-sisters, Leanna and Elitha.

Mrs. Houghton told all she remembered or had learned from her older sisters of their rescue. Her father had pitched camp nearly ten miles behind the rest of the party. He had accidentally hurt his hand with a chisel and the wound became infected. His brother, Jacob, was not physically strong, so the two Donner families (Jacob and his wife Elizabeth had five small children and two older boys by a former marriage) stopped at Prosser Creek.

"Uncle Jacob was the first to die," Eliza said. "His death shocked everyone terribly, even those encamped at the lake, for now one of us had actually starved to death."

Mac sat back, his notebook idle on his lap, not writing lest he inhibit her thought and flow of speech. He felt a strong rapport with the Houghtons, and Eliza was giving him her complete, unstinting confidence. With the collaboration of a Donner daughter, how could he fail?

Tamsen Donner, she said, had chosen to send the children to safety with the third relief party. She remembered how her mother hugged her tightly, kissing her and her sisters again and again. Then Tamsen was walking away, not looking back, into the frozen forest. She went to their father, whose infected hand had never healed. He died that same day, Eliza was sure.

"Keseberg is supposed to have murdered Mrs. Donner," Houghton said. "My wife doesn't want to accuse him of it, but he was the last person to see her mother alive. It would comfort her and all the Donner girls to learn something of her last hours. Assuming he didn't cause her death, of course."

Houghton was "a distinguished looking man," according to his wife's description, and Mac thought it apt. He had been mayor of San Jose at twenty-six, and Representative to Congress in its 42nd and 43rd sessions. Now he was one of the city's prominent attorneys. He had espoused the Donner cause as his own thirty years before. His first wife was Eliza's cousin Mary (daughter of Jacob Donner), who had died in childbirth. When he married Eliza, Mary's daughter was the first of what would be a large family of their own.

"Do you think Keseberg murdered your mother?" Mac asked bluntly.

"My mother's body was never found."

They were standing at the door, just prior to his leaving, and he looked down into her face, searching for her meaning.

"All the published accounts accuse him of it, Mrs. Houghton. Do I understand correctly—you don't?"

"I only know there is no proof. Can I judge the man without it?"

He left that night convinced that this Donner survivor, at least, was on his side. And he knew enough facts to keep his readers happy for another week.

From the interview he took with him a vivid insight into the bickerings, dissensions, back-biting and snarling quarrels among the Donner train that had led to the fatal delays along the trail. He gathered, too, that the survivors had not only gone their separate ways, for the most part, but were inclined to blame each other for exaggerated tales.

What would this mean for his research? Would any two agree?

Meanwhile, he'd get up to San Francisco and read old issues of the *California Star*, said to contain valuable information, mixed with a supply of utter nonsense. He wouldn't waste much time reading what he now understood were largely falsifications. He'd go to Marysville and see Murphy again. He needed the facts on the Reed-Snyder quarrel, ending in Snyder's death and Reed's expulsion from the train.

At the same time, he would hire a detective to find Lewis Keseberg. He keenly wished to confront Keseberg with Eliza, then hear him tell his story. The man would probably hang if the full truth were known, he thought. Could a man be so universally maligned without cause? Even Eliza had been frightened of him, as children are frightened by bogey-man stories. She said he'd been limping around, miserable with an infected heel. That made him frowning and cross, she supposed. But Philippine, his wife, was nice. And Keseberg loved their little girl tenderly.

Why he'd become the villain of the horror stories, she couldn't really be sure.

Two days later Mac wrote Eliza from the Cosmopolitan Hotel in Sacramento. It was midnight when he took up his pen.

Late as it is, I feel I ought to tell you I have spent the evening with Lewis Keisberg [sic]. I have just left him. And return early tomorrow morning to complete my interview. By merest accident, I found a clue to his whereabouts. After dark I obtained this clue, hired a carriage, drove six miles, found him, and have just returned.

At first he declined to tell me anything but somehow I melted the man's reserve and he talked freely.

He swears he did not kill your mother. He declares it so earnestly I cannot doubt his veracity. Tomorrow I intend plying him with questions and by a rigid system of cross-examination will detect the falsehood if there is one in his statement. He gives chapter after chapter that others never knew. He tells me incidents that make my blood curdle. His life has been a succession of incredible disappointments and failures ever since he reached California.

I cannot say more tonight, but desire that you write me any questions you might wish me to ask Keisberg. If I have not already asked them, I will do so upon my return from San Francisco.

The following day, he wrote again. He had received a good letter from Eliza's half-sister, Leanna Donner App, and husband. The Apps would extend his friendship and cooperation.

In pursuit of his interview with Keseberg, Mac wrote:

I was with Lewis Keisburg this morning at seven o'clock and only left

106

him in time to catch the 3:20 train for San Francisco. He is poverty-stricken and most miserable. One daughter is an idiot, subject to spasms, and another suffers from epileptic fits. They are his constant and unceasing care. His wife is dead and he is a prisoner in his own house on account of his helpless stricken children. The County gives him $18 per month, but no asylum or hospital will receive his daughters because they are *idiots*, not lunatics.

I cannot believe he killed your mother, nor that he succeeded in appropriating any considerable amount of your father's money. He is, Mrs. Houghton, one of the most forlorn, pitiable, accursed beings I ever saw.

One of his sentences, copied verbatim in my notebook reads:

'I often think God Almighty has singled me out in order to see how much hardship, misfortune and misery a human being can bear.'

Fire and flood and nameless disasters have constantly followed in his footsteps and swept away his property and accumulations.

I have a thousand incidents in his life which are at once tragic, tearful and marvelous. He is the most remarkable monster my eyes ever beheld.

Again he wrote, only two days later. He had seen Graves, and was elated. The Graves cabin site was in his pocket, sketched by the man himself on Mac's note pad. He itched to get back to Donner Lake and search it out in the slush and mud of April's melting snows—if another snowfall didn't blank the area out.

He apologized for writing informally and with such frequency.

Of Keseberg, whose name he now spelled correctly, he wrote:

Keseberg spoke in terms of greatest praise of your parents, although he keenly feels that their names have been the one great curse of his life.

Keseberg's interview was full and complete. I asked every question I could devise, read Thornton and Bryant to him, told him what Graves had said about Wolfinger, and what Mrs. Farnham stated regarding Hardcoop. In short, I tested the man's veracity in every conceivable way.

I wish you could see him.

Here he merely suggested, without urging her. His sensitivity told him what such an interview meant to Eliza. And yet, her husband had said that an encounter with Keseberg would comfort all the daughters if it gave certainty that their mother died of natural causes.

If I send word for him to come to Sacramento, he will come. If you and your husband could be in Sacramento on Thursday or Friday of this week, I could arrange an interview at the hotel...

Your mother was not murdered. Your father died, Keseberg thinks, about two weeks after you left. Your mother remained with him until the last, and laid him out tenderly, as you know.

The days—to Keseberg—were perfect blanks. Mrs. Murphy died soon after your departure, and he was left alone. Alone in his cabin. Alone with the dead bodies which he could not have lifted from the floor because of his weakness, even had he desired. The man sighs and shudders, and great drops of agony gather upon his brow as he endeavors to relate the details of those terrible days, or recall their horrors. Loneliness, desolation, was the chief element of horror.

Alone with the mutilated dead! One night he sprang up in affright at the sound of something moving or scratching at a log outside his door. It was some moments before he could understand, in the darkness, that wolves were trying to get into his cabin.

One night, about two weeks after you left, a knock came at his door, and your mother entered. To this lonely wretch her visit seemed like an angel's. She was cold and wet and freezing, yet her first words were that she must see her children. Keseberg understood she intended to start out that very night, and he soon found she was slightly demented, perhaps on account of the agony and desolation, the hunger and the feeble condition of her body.

She kept saying: "My God, I must see my children. I must go to my children." She finally consented to wait until morning, but was determined nothing should prevent her lonely journey. She told of your father's death; she told where her money was concealed; she made Keseberg promise solemnly he would get the money and take it to her children.

She would not eat his accursed food, she had not tasted human flesh, and she would hardly consent to remain in his foul and hideous den. Too weak and chilled to move, however, she finally consented to lie down on the floor and he covered her as best he could. He made a fire to warm her. But it was of no avail. She had received her death chill, and in the morning her spirit had passed heavenward.

I believe Keseberg tells the truth...

The story told by Mrs. Farnham and others, about the finding of your mother's remains, and that by Thornton concerning the pail of blood, is unquestionably false. She had been dead six weeks, and as Keseberg confessed to me, no portion of her body was found by the relief party.

My dear friend, I have attempted to comply with your request. More than once during this evening, I have burst into tears. I am sorry, almost, that I attempted so mournful a task. I am conscious of my inability to write the details of this sad interview in such a manner a daughter's eyes may read it...

Keseberg is a powerful man, six feet in height, with full bushy beard, high forehead, and thin brown locks. He has blue eyes that look squarely at you while he talks. He is sometimes absent minded, and at times seems almost carried away with the intensity of his misery and desolation.

— • —

Meanwhile, Nona...

Although she was busy with the baby and had the company of her sisters and parents, Nona chafed at the absence of her husband. She had known he'd not be sitting around the house. Nevertheless, she was beginning to understand Jennie more and more.

She realized the pressure he worked under. Letters were beseiging him now. He meticulously sent each completed chapter to every survivor of the Donner party for corrections and criticism. He got both, in abundance. At the same time he had to keep up with installments in the paper. When he was at home, he was madly writing. As soon as a chapter was done for *The Republican*, he caught the westbound train again to talk to Donner people.

Between trips, he came home later and later to dinner.

They were still living with the Keisers and Nona felt humiliated before her parents when Mac failed to join her for the evening meal. His empty plate enlarged before her eyes until it filled the whole table.

As winter months turned into spring and she could make her way down the slushy, muddy hill to the news office, she would walk down to remind him that dinner was only an hour away.

"Thank you, love. I'll finish this page and come."

Hours later, she warmed his portion of the meal he'd missed again. She would sit listening, biting her tongue not to talk about her own day, while he glowingly recounted the progress of the Donner story.

"If you want to know the truth," she quipped in later years, "*I* was the chief sufferer of the Donner Party."

Mac would then add his favorite anecdote, laughing until tears brimmed his eyes.

One night he had been late again and it was already dark. Not for the first time that evening, Nona came to call him. She found him still writing in the lamplight, his cheeks shining with tears.

"Mac, your supper's cold. Come home."

He added a final word before he turned to answer.

"My dear," he said, "sit down. Let me read you this last page."

Choked with emotion, he read aloud the heartbreaking scene of Tamsen Donner's decision to let her children go to safety without her. She turns from them to walk back fourteen miles to the Donner cabin and to her own certain death, for she has elected to remain beside her dying husband to the end.

At the end of the reading, Mac blew his nose and wiped his wet face. "Such heroism! What a woman! What wifely devotion!"

Nona said nothing.

"Well? What do you think?" If he referred to the literary merit of the page, she preferred to misinterpret the question.

"What do I think? *I think she was a damned fool!*"

Instantly she turned, for she had refused to sit, and was gone. He heard her footsteps running down the stairs. Hatless, he went after her. With his long-legged strides she couldn't get far ahead of him up the steep grade. And, fuel to the fire, she heard his chuckling laughter.

It was so funny, comical, witty, appropriate. He laughed for all these things. And he laughed for joy. A light had risen in Israel and he had seen—seen his mistake, his fatal mistake with Jennie, the threat to this marriage if he repeated it.

From then on, he drew her into all that he did, shared with her all that he did. Unless she were ill, or indispensable at home, Nona went with him on all his trips.

Thus she was with him when he met the Houghtons in Sacramento for the confrontation with Keseberg. From the

Golden Eagle Hotel they drove to Brighton where the man had arranged to meet them. Shy of public places and unwilling to have them see his depressing household, he had tidied up a room in a brewery near his home. Since it was Sunday, he said, they would not be interrupted there.

Eliza, in her own book, described the dignity of the meeting. The two did not shake hands. Keseberg came straight to the point.

"Mr. McGlashan has told me you have questions about what happened in the mountain cabin and you want to ask me yourself."

"Yes, for the eye of God and your eyes witnessed my mother's last hours, and I have come to ask you, in the presence of that Other Witness, when, where, and how she died."

They sat down, facing each other, and Keseberg quietly began to tell his story as he had told it to Mac. Suddenly, with a swift movement, he knelt before her.

"On my knees before you, and in the sight of God, I want to assert my innocence."

Eliza got up quickly and drew the man to his feet. She put out her hand, palm upward, and asked him to lay his right hand on it. She then covered his hand with her left palm.

"Now speak, Mr. Keseberg, with your hand in mine."

He spoke unfalteringly, and looked into her eyes.

"I did not kill your mother or harm her in any way."

"Lewis Keseberg passed the ordeal which would have made a guilty man quake," Eliza stated later. Whatever slander accrued to Keseberg's name, Tamsen Donner's youngest daughter was convinced he did not murder her mother.

Mac, too, was convinced of the man's innocence. The matter of money, some of which was recovered and some not, he felt was better forgotten. Keseberg's honesty on that score didn't concern him as deeply as the accusation of murder. He would have taken his defense confidently in a courtroom. Before the world, as best he could, he would clear the man's name in his book.

Without today's rapid means of communication, without libraries organized to assist researchers, his task was enormous and under utmost pressure. Bancroft had collected clippings and articles on the Donner story with the intention of writing it himself. He now made all his files available. My grandfather read every published account written by Breen, Graves, Mrs. Farnham, the Reeds, Dunbar. He closely followed the records of the relief parties, the transcript of Fallon's diary and Patrick Breen's, as well as records, reports and letters that have since been incorporated in the Fort Sutter collection. He supplemented these with conversations and correspondence with survivors of both the Donner party and the relief parties. McCutcheon, Cady and Clark talked with him freely and wrote to him. Eliza used her name and influence to gain him the full confidence and cooperation of her sisters.

It was Elitha Donner Wilder and her husband, Benjamin, who brought suit to stop the publication of the history. Eliza wrote a letter to her brother-in-law that only a woman could write who had suffered like his wife from sensation-mongers.

Years ago I resolved, if ever an opportunity occurred when the survivors could give their version to a writer who would take the trouble to compare and reconcile conflicting statements . . . I would not only tell what I know, but would use what little influence I had to lead others to do likewise. I do not think it respectful or kind to the memories of those who lost their lives at that time, for us to silently permit their sufferings to be brought before the public every twelve months in a new form . . .

Elitha is the oldest survivor of the Donners in the party, and doubt-less remembers much that would be of interest to the history as well as add to its correctness . . . The entire vote of the survivors could not stop the publication of the History even if we should desire it, so would it not be better for us to try and make it a book to which we can point and say This is as near true as it ever will be written, and by this means silence future attempts and failure?

Mr. McGlashan has spared neither time, trouble or expense in his endeavor to obtain the true statements, and has succeeded in getting the material for a very full history . . . What little assistance I have been able to render him has been freely given . . . to place a subject which has been so frequently and unkindly handled beyond the reach of those who would again bring it into unpleasant notice in the future.

My grandfather brought to the task talents and skills so personal that he wondered if he had been destined to it. He had known hunger much of his life. Its pains, fantasies, and fears were among his earliest memories. For another thing, he knew the Sierra's wild winter storms, and he had intensively studied the region during his six years in Truckee.

Most important, he was a lawyer, practiced in eliciting answers and in sifting truth from falsehood; he was above all, vitally attuned to people. He conveyed to every person, "You have my rapt attention." Irresistibly flattering, this gift of total listening won him the confidences of people too wary, cynical or guilty to open up to anyone else. He was courteous, sensitive, gentlemanly—old fashioned virtues by today's standards, but essential in his own day to obtaining information that would otherwise have been buried forever.

He had to publish his first draft as it was, with little or no polishing. By the second writing, a revision of factual material only, there was no question of changing the style. The book was already out.

He wrote under emotional pressure, as well. He wrote with tears streaming down his face. After visiting the Donner's camp at Prosser Creek, he told Eliza in a letter:

Your mother was everywhere the central figure in the thoughts passing through my mind. I saw her at her husband's side—going to the creek for water—looking every now and then for the prayed-for relief—sighing in her loneliness, yet thanking God for her children's safety. Ever and always I kept thinking of that long night walk to Keseberg's cabin. I drove along the very route over which she must have hurried. Gaunt gray wolves and famished bears surrounded her in her lonely tent, and on this memorable night. Yet her love for her children... overcame all fear.

His tears for the frozen tears of thirty years before gave his book its enduring quality.

C. F. McGLASHAN, Editor.

The Daily Press.

TUESDAY, OCTOBER 12, 1880.

SALUTATORY.

Work, in this nineteenth century, is generally more acceptable than promises. I come to the good people of Santa Barbara, filled with the idea that I am to work for their interests. I shall work zealously, faithfully; firmly believing that the success of a local paper is identical with the growth, development and prosperity of the community in which it is published.

Santa Barbara, with its beautiful

REPUBLICAN NOMINATIONS.

Election, Tuesday, Nov. 2.

For President:
JAMES A. GARFIELD,
OF OHIO.

For Vice-President:
CHESTER A. ARTHUR,
OF NEW YORK.

For Presidential Electors:

JOHN F. MILLER,	HENRY EDGERTON,
JOHN A. BAUER,	CHARLES N. FOX,
W. W. McKAIG,	THOMAS R. BARD.

For Member of Congress—Fourth District:
ROMUALDO PACHECO,

For Member of the Assembly,
MILTON WASON.

For Superior Judge,
D. P. HATCH.

For Justice of the Peace—2d Judicial Township,
H. G. CRANE.

The Daily Press.

Entered at the Postoffice at Santa Barbara as second-class matter.

C. F. McGLASHAN, Editor.

Santa Barbara County Official Paper.

FRIDAY, DECEMBER 24, 1880.

⁎⁎⁎ THE PRESS invites correspondence from all quarters on live topics. Local affairs and news given the preference. Brevity, clearness, force and timeliness should be kept in view. Correspondents held responsible for their own statements. Use one side of the sheet only, write plainly and send real name.

ANNOUNCEMENT.

I have purchased the DAILY and WEEKLY PRESS. I will assume control on Monday next. In order to accommodate the increase in advertising patronage, and induce extra additions to the subscription lists, I will enlarge both daily and weekly during the first week in January. The subscription price will remain unchanged.   C. F. McGLASHAN.

The first months of C. F. McGlashan's short career with the Santa Barbara Daily Press *are chronicled in some of its headlines. His "Salutatory" (upper left) was his first editorial, October 12, 1880. Later that month, he made recommendations for the 1880 presidential campaign. On December 24, 1880 he announced his purchase of the* Daily *and* Weekly Press *and the first issue with his masthead was published on December 28, 1880.*

The Daily Press.

SUPPLEMENT.

Entered at the Postoffice at Santa Barbara as second-class matter.

C. F. McGLASHAN, Publisher and Proprietor

Santa Barbara County Official Paper.

TUESDAY, DECEMBER 28, 1880.

An Awful Record of Crime.
From the S. F. Chronicle.

Chapter Nine

Seven years to the day since his arrival in Truckee, his book came out—on July 12, 1879. He received the first shipment of copies that morning and immediately sent one to each of the Donner people for comment and corrections. He would start work on the revised edition at once and hoped to have it ready by Christmas.

Acclaim was immediate and widespread. All leading newspapers commended the history. A. L. Bancroft praised it unequivocally. The California State Board of Education unanimously voted to adopt it for school libraries. The University of California at Berkeley stocked it as the definitive history of the Donner Party.

By Christmas, Nona was again pregnant, expecting in June. As before, Ella was pregnant too, but this time Nona would not have to rely on her sisters for company. Mac was all hers once more.

She saw how tired he was. Enthusiasm hurtled him along, but he had worked nights on the revision while he still shouldered his full share of legal business and newspaper work. He was bone-thin, too, both from overwork and a severe bout with tonsilitis in the fall. She wished she could persuade him to break off in midyear and take a long rest.

For his part, he observed shadows under his wife's gray eyes and he tried tenderly to massage her swollen ankles. "Doc" Curless blamed the swelling on heart as much as on pregnancy. Was he doing her harm by remaining in this high altitude? He'd always known why the Keisers sent her to Santa Clara for months at a time. Doc called it "a singing heart," a term Mac thought appropriate for her, but he dreaded its significance. For the sake of that heart, he decided, he must adjust his mind to the idea of living "below."

It therefore seemed providential when his sister Martinette wrote to him from the pretty coastal town of Santa Cruz. She was teaching in the high school there. A widow at thirty-four, Nette was very happy to be teaching again. She sang the charms of Santa Cruz, mentioning its nearness to San Francisco where their sister Laura lived.

Santa Cruz. Why not? he thought. He could devote a year to the Donner history and nothing else, and the Lord knew he needed a vacation. Santa Cruz would put him in a town neighboring San Jose, where most of his Donner party friends lived. He still needed their help with the book. Additional engravings, for one thing, would be easier to come by.

When he told Nona the trend of his thoughts, she agreed wholeheartedly with the entire plan.

"We don't need to call it more than a vacation," he said. "We can stay a lifetime, or a year. But in a year I think we'll know what we want to do."

John Keiser and Will Edwards took over the newspaper, and by May the McGlashans were ready to leave. On the eve of departure he wrote a letter to Eliza that indicated he believed the move would be permanent. If so, he said, "it seems as if I lived in Truckee for the express purpose of being fitted for the work which was so strangely undertaken." He referred to the Donner history, of course. "At Santa Cruz, I shall do nothing but complete my second edition. We will pass through San Jose Friday afternoon so you may write me in the future at our new home. Nona and myself are glad we are going to live so near you, and hope for an interchange of visits." He signed, "Your grateful friend, Fayette McGlashan."

They left by train the following day. Nona looked heavily due to bring forth at any moment, although she had a month to go, and Elizabeth Keiser insisted on accompanying her daughter to Santa Cruz. This was a great comfort to Mac as well as Nona. The resilience and moral strength of her slight mother flowed about them—a deep current that buoyed them up even while it swept them along in its practical channel.

June Laura was born on June 24, 1880. The delivery was made memorable by an astonishing action on the part of the attending

116

doctor. He was a stranger to them, recommended by a friend of Nette's. Nona and her mother had liked him immediately. However, to their surprise, he demanded soap and a basin of hot water before he approached the bed where Nona lay. Without explaining, he proceeded to roll up his sleeves and wash his hands, wrists, even his forearms.

"I'd like you to do the same, Mrs. Keiser," he said quietly. And in that hour of travail and birthing, mother and daughter knew they had witnessed a breakthrough in the history of childbirth care.

Mac announced his new daughter far and wide in letters to their relatives and friends. His sister Adelia sent the baby a gift from Red Bluff, with a chatty epistle that brought them up to date on her own large family. George Balis was nearing fifty and taking life easier now, for health's sake. Their wheat and sheep ranch had prospered beyond their dreams. She begged her brother to bring his wife and babies for a visit.

Lib wrote from Healdsburg. Jimmy had grown so tall his uncle Fayette wouldn't know him. Like Adelia, she longed for a reunion with Nette, Laura, 'Delia and himself. Couldn't it be arranged for the following summer?

Laura visited them, delighted to have inspired the baby's middle name. Nona's sister Laura took the honor to herself too, so both sides of the family were content with the choice. Nette, who was able to drop in frequently to chuck the infant under the chin and argue politics with her brother, caused a flurry by announcing her engagement to a suitor of long standing, George Kinsell, owner of a music store in San Jose.

"We're setting the date for Christmas or near it," she said. From a slim girl she had become a handsome woman who carried an aura of height and breadth beyond her actual dimensions. Alongside of her, Nona usually felt reduced in all her own measurements, both in size and intelligence. She sensed condescension in the older woman and had to remind herself that, understandably, Nette would always think of her as the schoolgirl chum of Jennie's little sister.

Early in September, the assassination of an editor changed their lives. Theodore Glancey, editor of *The Santa Barbara Press*, was shot and killed by Clarence Gray, a nominee for District Attorney. In a day when editorial gunning was not only commonplace but expected, Glancy's offense seemed too innocuous to bring on his execution. He had simply mentioned in print that Gray had used many aliases in the past—a past which he commended to "a charitable silence." Outraged, Gray had sought him out and shot him publicly.

In need of a new editor, publisher John P. Stearns wrote to colleagues in Sacramento and learned that McGlashan might be available. Stearns quickly tracked him down and offered the job.

It sounded good. He had gained back lost pounds, felt fit... and restless. But he accepted cautiously. It was the year of the Garfield-Arthur campaign and he committed himself to the partisan (Republican) daily for the election interim only. He left Nona and the babies at home, sailed by steamer to Santa Barbara, and checked into the comfortable Morris House in mid-October. Within the week his name appeared on *The Press* masthead.

At his new desk he found political hatreds much inflamed by the murder—and himself a prime target for unknown enemies who tended to chastise editors for editorial opinions. One had been cowhided. Midnight arsonists had tried to burn the news office more than once. And now an editor had been killed. On the other hand, his predecessors had kept feuds going with rival newspapers until Santa Barbarans might well believe that vindictive abuse was the mark of proper journalism.

From 1876 until February, 1880, Harrison J. Otis had been editor of *The Press*. Brilliant and vitriolic, Otis had carried on an entertaining war of insults exchanged with the town's rival daily, *The Independent*. To seek a larger arena, Otis had sold *The Press* and left town. In due time, he would build up *The Los Angeles Times* and his fortune. Meanwhile, *The Press* had limped along until Stearns, a prominent lumberman and former mayor of Santa Barbara, bought it in August and hired Glancey. A month later, Glancey was shot.

"There's a bandit hiding out in the hills who calls himself Joaquin Murrieta," well-wishers told Mac. "He brags he can call the tune for any paper in town. Keep your gun handy."

"I'm out of practice, I fear, but . . . " He strolled to a fencepost

118

and inserted a match upright in a crack. The old stunt never failed to impress and, smiling to himself, he thought of his first day at Williston. If there did lurk a Murrieta in the hills, he hoped this shot would keep him there.

He wrote to Nona, "Pack up, darling, and come down here. I think we can plan to stay."

He knew she would delight, as he did, in the Spanish architecture, the plumed palms, the crimson hibiscus, the mild southern California climate. In an editorial tribute, he had mused:

Santa Barbara is in many respects a New England town. There is a calmness, a serenity, a peacefulness brooding over it which is essentially New England. There is none of the bustle and strife and confusion so frequently found on the Pacific Coast. There is a silent, invisible strength and energy of character about the citizens . . . There is no blare of trumpets, no great display of enthusiasm or excitement, but in the most silent, unostentatious manner, the labor is done, the result obtained. Yet the people are intensely enthused and every nerve is being strained.

He was to find he missed the fanfare of uncontained enthusiasm; for that was his own kind and he spoke its dialect. But in the beginning, he was charmed by the town's sleepy temperament and pace and he determined to give his best to it.

He wrote to his sister, asking Nette to help Nona pack up their household goods. Somehow he would get away in time to make the final arrangements and to bring his family down to Santa Barbara.

He outlined in detail the newspaper task he faced—restoration of lapsed circulation, pressures of a daily press, and the like. He hoped he was equal to it, he said, and he rather liked the novelty of his challenges here. But when would he find time for butterflies again, or for anything else?

Whatever his misgivings, if any, two months later his name appeared on the masthead as publisher and owner. Just before Christmas he had bought the paper from Stearns.

In his salutatory editorial he asked support of the businessmen and promised to increase the staff, enlarge the columns, and "give more complete telegraphic world news." He further promised never to "deal in personalities or abuse, never to be controlled by any power save principle." He would do his "level best" to prove that a newspaper could attract readers without flinging epithets at the rival daily.

Tactfully, he set out to convince the businessmen they needed the paper as much as he needed their advertising. But for a few months he did it with his pistol on his desk.

Nona, meanwhile, went straight to Santa Barbara's fiesta-loving heart with her guitar. She played and sang with fire and flair. She was often asked to do both at the festivals and parties Mac and she enjoyed together. She played, too, for concerts. Her nimble, slim fingers had mastered formidable chords, and she had brought along her portfolio of music when she left Truckee. At twenty-six, she looked eighteen. Those who heard her were as charmed by her pictorial beauty as by her music.

This she would never have believed. Elizabeth had eyed the budding comeliness of her daughters with single-minded resolution. She brooked no vanity in them and therefore never commented favorably on their looks.

"Laura, tell me," Nona might ask when, as girls, they stood before the mirror, curled and dressed for a party. "Do I look just awful?"

"To me you look all right," her sister would answer, unsure that she was fit to judge. "How about me?"

"You look fine. To me, anyway."

"Now *be ladies*," their mother admonished on every such occasion, after a touch here and a tug there to ensure absolute tidiness. "You have little *else* to speak for you, you know."

As Mac had foreseen, Nona was enthralled by the early Spanish history of Santa Barbara and the picturesque architecture that gave the past continuity with the present. She never tired of the tales of half a century ago when one way of life revolved around the Presidio near the ocean and an entirely different life around the rambling adobe mission at the base of the green hills. The thick pinkish walls of the Casa de la Guerra sparked her fancy and she could imagine the household of aristocratic Don Jose, Commandant of the Presidio, abustle with preparations for the wedding of his daughter Teresa to handsome William E. P. Hartnell of Monterey. She could visualize the colorful fiesta in

120

the Playa del Armas, where every resident of the pueblo gathered to celebrate the linking of the most important de la Guerra family with one of California's most distinguished organizers and executive planners.

She never dreamed that the strong kinship she felt with the beautiful town and its past and people would assume a new reality years later when a daughter of hers would marry the grandson of the couple feted on that long-ago wedding day.

By June, 1881 the fourth printing of the Donner history was out in hardcover, and a paperbound railroad copy as well, with Bancroft the publisher. Nona was expecting again, this time in early spring of 1882. George and Nette Kinsell, married six months, paid them a visit and fell in love with the town's climate, the view over the sparkling ocean and out to the islands, the rugged green backdrop of the Los Padres mountains. Moreover, they enjoyed the newspaper office and presses.

Blue lights danced in his sister's eyes as she watched the printing operation. Mac said impulsively, when they were alone together, "Sis, be my associate editor. You're every bit as capable as I am, and believe me, I could use the help."

"You really think I could do it? I'd love to, you know."

"If you mean that, Nette, I'll talk to George about it tonight."

"I mean it with all my heart, Fay. I'm restless to work again at something. Schools won't hire married women if they can get a single girl."

That night over their after-dinner cigars the men talked long and earnestly. When they joined the ladies, Mac announced the decision: George had agreed to be his business manager and, if Nette would like to try it, she had George's consent to be associate editor.

The evening ended in high optimism for the future. George said it might take him a year to settle his affairs up north. For one thing, he'd have to sell the music store. After that, they would be free to move down the coast.

Although Mac didn't say it, the fact was that one job was not enough for him. He had turned to the train telegraph again before he left Truckee and had patented some of its parts in April, 1880. Still no other means existed for communication with moving trains and he knew his invention would work. Every catastrophic collision spurred him on and he spent entire nights working on it.

Whether or not he admitted it to himself at this point, the agreement with the Kinsells laid the groundwork for his future release from the daily.

On February 4, 1882 their third daughter was born. They gave her Nona's full name, Leonora Gertrude.

From the first hour something was terribly wrong. The baby wailed incessantly and refused to nurse. Frightened, Nona held her, night and day. Mother and infant fought together for the newborn life. But within two days, Gertie, as they called her, died in Nona's arms. In the belief that Santa Barbara would be their permanent home, Mac took out a deed on a large family plot in the cemetery and marked the tiny grave with a marble head-stone.

Nona's sorrow was fathomless. And Mac wept with her. His tears, shed for her loss as much as for his own, told her that here was a first for them to share—the only first in marriage left for him, she was ruefully aware—this grief in the death of a baby. Ever since the day that she missed seeing a wondering awe in his face when he beheld her first baby, Nonette, she realized nothing would be a first time for him. Now she saw she had been wrong. They had sorrow to share. Was this her portion?

Her recovery from the difficult birth (and death) was slow, aggravated by a homesickness she didn't want him to guess.

A month after the baby's death, the Southern Pacific railroad publicly demonstrated his telegraph at San Francisco, "with entire success," the newspapers said. The first message ever sent or received by a moving train was dedicated to Nona.

Almost overnight the invention demanded all his time and he begged the Kinsells to come quickly. The Pennsylvania Central had offered him their shops and personnel to develop the last missing parts. He must go east as soon as Nette could relieve him at the desk.

In July he took out another patent on the device. It was late August when the Kinsells finally arrived. On September 9, 1882 his readers learned that "a half-interest in *The Santa Barbara Press* has been sold to W. G. Kinsell, late of San Jose." The publisher's sister, Martinette Kinsell, would be associate editor. The paper would follow the same policies under her guidance while he took a three-month's vacation in the east.

Back east, he found bitter disappointment. He had talked too openly, to anyone and everyone. Someone had already patented the essential parts to complete his telegraph.

Returned to Santa Barbara, his hopes dashed, he now felt extremely restless. He loved the town and had made staunch friends, but now he found the climate enervating. The relaxed pace had intrigued him as a novelty. Now it only irritated him. He felt he must rouse himself to action or sink into a quicksand of inertia.

As if to intensify his dissatisfaction, an old pair of galoshes spoke to him from a closet. There they lay when he reached for his hat and coat—the crumpled "overshoes" he had hauled over his black groundgrippers so many times in snowbound Truckee. Their tarnished buckles flopped forlornly to the floor on either side. He picked them up tenderly with shining eyes, drawing deeply into his lungs the rubbery smell.

"Look, Nona!" he shouted. When she came to the door, her eyes widely inquiring, he said, "I'm homesick. For the snow and the cold and the mountains. For Truckee! How about you?"

He waved the overshoes under her nose to sniff.

Pregnant again, expecting in May, oh, yes, she was very homesick. She blinked back her glad tears against his 'shoulder while he danced her around the room.

The Kinsells bought the newspaper and he bowed out in January, 1883. He left it in good shape and they, in turn, sold it back to Stearns within a few months.

Mac and Nona were free to go home.

Main Street, Truckee, circa 1900.

Chapter Ten

1883.

They returned to the heights on the melting edge of spring, when winter storms were past but snow still lay, chunkily packed, on Truckee roads and hillsides. Under a lemon-pale sun, not even the pussy willows along Trout Creek had ventured a bud. Only the plum-pudding brown mud, now and then richly turned by the cut of a sled runner, assured winter's end.

John Keiser stood among the crowd on the depot platform when their afternoon train pulled in. Nona saw him through the vestibule window just before the red-capped porter opened the door. He wore the familiar weatherworn mackinaw and ear-muffed cap; the same black overshoes buckled over his trouser legs to the calf. Never a tall man, he looked shorter for the middle-aged plumpening of his compact frame. Suddenly his homesick daughter saw him revealed in essence for what he was to her—the personification of enduring strength and love and home. A rush of tenderness flooded her eyes with tears that her husband saw and understood.

To the joy of the two little girls, their grandfather had a team and sleigh waiting on the plaza side of the depot, ready to transport them all up the big hill to High Street. Elizabeth had written, "You must come straight home to us, Nonie, until the baby is born and you are on your feet again. It's the only sensible thing."

Mac had agreed that it was. Although his mother-in-law still maintained little more than a prim civility toward himself— would she never forget his divorced status?—he knew he needed her competent presence in the coming ordeal. Nona still mourned the baby buried the year before. One of their last goodbyes had been to the small grave in the Santa Barbara cemetery. And he knew the infant's death had unnerved them both for the birth that lay less than two months ahead.

"Tell your mother I thank her and accept with all my heart," he said when Nona sat down at the walnut secretary to answer the command-invitation.

"I will, dear." She gave him an appreciative smile, her eyes darkening with warm sympathy. For her sake he was letting himself in for two or three months of an uncomfortable situation, long familiar to them. But she'd be bearing it with him. Her mother's posture of armed truce put her squarely in the middle.

"I'm the saw-horse that balances the teeter-totter for their ups and downs," she had told Ella, alluding to the other aspect of the strained relationship. Although Elizabeth's unrelenting politeness was matched by unflagging gallantries on her son-in-law's part (he had dedicated his book to her, for one thing), it struck Nona that every controversial subject possible cropped up when the two were together. No matter the topic, they chose opposite banks of the stream. Buckle by buckle, they undid the constraints of high-flown courtesy, chose weapons, and had at it. Eyes glittered, voices rose, nostrils flared.

Listening on the sidelines, her stomach knotted in dismay, Nona surmised they both enjoyed these verbal clashes. Her own anxiety, however, reverberated only to the ringing swords of joined combat.

"Oh, Ma, why?" she asked once when they sat alone together, mending by the light of the front windows.

John had built directly overlooking the rooftops of Front Street and the plaza. It had been Elizabeth's idea to line the front with windows, putting porch and steps on the side, thus permitting a view of the southern rim of the saucer from Mt. Rose to Donner summit. Directly down the hill, they also beheld the bustle of the depot, especially colorful when the emigrant trains steamed in from the east. These disgorged clumps of disheveled humanity that fanned out in scurrying strings of hungry people seeking cafes or saloons. Then, when the monster engine itself had drunk, fed and summoned the passengers with a scream of its whistle, the train departed majestically for the valleys and cities

126

below. Truckeeites wondered about those who came west not in ox-wagons but thus, on mighty wheels. They called the emigrant trains "Zulu cars" and were inclined to joke about the new breed of pioneer.

"Sometimes, Mother, it seems to me you take issue with every word Mac says."

Elizabeth shrugged a neatly shawled shoulder and bit off the end of a silk thread with a toss of her silvering groomed head.

"Nothing for you to worry over, child. Maybe I like a rousing good discussion with the boy."

"But those are hardly discussions, Ma. They sound more like . . ."

"Never mind! Now, there . . ." she gentled her tone. "I have never, never said I don't have a high regard for Mac's mind. I do. If you think I pick at him deliberately, well, you're wrong. I simply like to get at his thinking. With which I don't always agree, nevertheless."

"*That's* the truth, for sure!" Exasperation sent Nona's voice up the scale to end on a squeak.

Her mother threaded a needle in silence and then said, "Just leave us alone, child. Why we argue, I'm not sure. But don't worry about it. Leave it alone."

Nona's father, on the other hand, had long since abandoned his own distaste for her marriage to a divorced man. "What's done is done," he decided characteristically. "He's still the same man I liked before, and he's good to my girl. So what's the fuss about, Elizabeth?"

Of four Keiser brothers who came west together in 1849, John was the only one who remained in California. His favorite brother, David, returned to Iowa with another brother to resume the business they had left, the importing of Arabian horses.

John Keiser's forebears were among those who crossed the Atlantic with William Penn, receiving from him parcels of land in what became Pennsylvania. John's father sold most of his estates, keeping only a large farm and the road that led to it. "I like the idea of driving up my own road to my house," he said.

John, who was born March 24, 1824, grew up to reject farming and at twenty left home to learn a trade. He apprenticed himself to a carpenter until, in 1846, the Mexican War broke out. He then joined the army and fought in Texas.

Mustered out a year later with the rank of lieutenant, he went to see David who, like himself, refused to farm and had gone to Indiana. Since David's Arabian horse enterprise had its start there, no doubt he was already engaged in it and hoped John would join him. At nearby La Gro, Indiana John met and fell in love with nineteen-year-old Elizabeth Alice Bedsaul, a society belle descended from an aristocratic plantation-owning First Family of Virginia. Two uncles cited for valor in the Revolutionary War made her a D. A. R. Mindful of these glories, the Bedsauls looked down their English noses at "the farmer boy from Pennsylvania" and forbade Elizabeth to see him.

"So we eloped," John liked to say.

"It was a perfectly proper wedding, nonetheless," Elizabeth usually added, depending on the look in John's eye. Given an inch, he'd spice the tale every time. The wedding certificate, an ornately colorful document, hung framed on the bedroom wall and attested to their marriage at La Gro on December 16, 1847. On Christmas day that year, Elizabeth turned twenty.

Nona and her sisters loved to hear the story of their romance. The Bedsauls had literally closed the door on the couple. Not until Ella's birth, two years later, did they forgive their daughter. John's family had move to Burlington, Iowa in his absence and there he took his bride. The elder Keisers welcomed her warmly and insisted on keeping the newlyweds until John got on his financial feet.

"Not a soul in that house spoke English," Elizabeth told her daughters, who relived with her the memories of a lonely young wife in a strange big house where the books and even newspapers were in German.

"One day soon after we came to the Keiser home, I saw a big red family Bible on a table in the parlor. Why, of course! I thought. Here is something I can read—the Bible! But when I opened it and saw the strange lettering, my heart sank. Even God spoke German in that house."

Sewing and mending in the circle of her female in-laws, she passed dreary hours. An incomprehensible chatter swirled about

128

her ears until evening brought John home. When the weather was good she sometimes took a pencil and a pad to the fields to sketch a bridge or flowers beside a stream; or else she walked to the hill overlooking the Mississippi and brought home a sheaf of sketches.

In 1848, reports of gold in California electrified the country—and the Keisers. The four brothers burned to join the caravans that began to assemble and roll. Even their father caught the excitement. Since he couldn't go himself, he outfitted wagons for his sons, who began to plan for the spring of 1849.

None was more anxious to go than John. Elizabeth, pregnant and expecting in March, could have stopped him, but she wouldn't.

"How can I do this?" John groaned. "How can I leave you with a newborn baby? Months will go by before I can hear from you and know you're all right."

"I'll be all right, John. You can just know I am, for I'll go to my family. I'm the one who will worry, with you out there in the wilds and I not knowing if you've been tomahawked or whatever. But you have to find out what's out there for you, and us. I know that. And I know you'll never stop wishing you'd gone if you don't go now."

She was right. Conviction gripped him. He had to go to the far frontier. Perhaps, he thought, it was for this that his restlessness had kept him from finding a niche in the world. He would root in a land where his back and heart and head were needed to help build it.

The baby, named Sara Ella, arrived on March 25th, 1849 the day before John's own twenty-fourth birthday, and in ample time for Elizabeth to recover and journey to the Bedsauls before John and his brothers set out. Mercifully, she did not know she would have to wait four years for his return.

Arrived in California, the brothers immediately prospected with great success near Hangtown, then at Yankee Jim's, a camp named for a lynched horsethief. They made rich strikes at nearby Georgetown, as well. With another prospector, John was hailed for the discovery of a gold-bearing site they called, for some forgotten reason, Mameluke Hill, a region still mentioned in Mother Lode lore.

Then, among the oaks and pines of Yankee Jim's, John built a log cabin for Elizabeth, a house with many windows and a fireplace.

"I'll be home in early June," he wrote her, and since it was nearly Christmas 1852 then, knew that the letter would reach her most likely in late spring. He told her he had made her an easy chair out of a barrel. A second barrel had turned into a center table with a polished round top. They could bring from home the additional touches so dear to a woman's heart—carpets and curtains, and yes, the sewing machine he promised her for the one big present, to cover all the birthdays and Christmases and anniversaries they had missed.

Eastbound trains could leave on the overland journey as early as weather permitted, so John caught a Wells Fargo stagecoach to Carson City before the snow fell.

However, heavy rains soon began slashing the coach. The struggling horses were hard put to make time in the slick mud of the road.

Suddenly the coach halted. John opened the door to find out the trouble and looked into the barrel of a long rifle. A man with a blue bandana tied around the lower part of his face waved the gun in a gesture that said, "Get out." Other masked men leveled guns at the passengers from the backs of rain-beleaguered horses.

It was soon over. In silence, the few passengers let themselves be stripped of purses, money-belts, watches and jewelry. They watched stolidly while the bandits dumped the contents of their luggage into rivulets of red mud. They counted it bargain enough, the cost of survival.

All but John. While he submitted with the others as the only course of good sense, he fumed with inner fury, a rage that didn't explode until the robbers rode off and the coach moved on. What caused him the most acute dismay, a suppressed protest like a burning fuse that reached the powder of full-blown anger only when the coach started up again, was this: He had taken gold from his first mine to San Francisco and bought Elizabeth an oval locket and chain as the first fruits of his strike. Inside the locket was his photograph.

The bandits could have everything else. Not this.

"Stop, driver!" he shouted and, before the coach wheels could halt, leaped to the ground and swung himself up to the driver's seat. "Go back! Go back! On the chance they dropped something. I've got to look."

The driver could see he'd waste more time arguing than giving in to this wild dreamer. There was no turning on that narrow road in the rain, but he promised to hold the coach while John ran back to the scene of the holdup.

There, in the mud, glimmered the locket on its long chain. Nothing else. But it was all he needed to find. His photograph had been touched by the seepage of water and he quickly dried it. Otherwise, the gift was undamaged. The coach could go on.

Elizabeth and Ella, who was now four, came west via Panama, for Elizabeth was pregnant by the autumn of 1853. John wouldn't expose her to the rigors of wagon travel. Ella would always remember crossing the Isthmus on mule-back, and her fright when natives carried her into deep water to meet the ship waiting on the Pacific side.

Elizabeth found it hard to leave the east. Her sister, however, reconciled her to the move by migrating herself. With her husband and three small girls she had embarked on the overland route in early May, and Elizabeth looked forward to a reunion in California. This was never to be. When the Keisers reached Georgetown, only her brother-in-law and the three children were there. Elizabeth's sister had died along the trail.

"We buried her at a spot called Ragtown," the bereaved husband said.

Staggered by the loss of a companionship she had counted on, overwhelmed with sorrow, Elizabeth gave herself a dose of the cure-all—work.

"Let us take the children," she said. "They'll be like our own until you make a home for them."

Expecting in February, she found herself with five children to care for, all under seven years old, and not a minute left for the homesickness devil.

Leonora Gertrude was born February 18, 1854 on a day of heavy downpour that John and David utilized for ground-sluicing on John's claim. The men were digging a ditch to carry off the

John Keiser   Elizabeth Keiser

Leonora Gertrude Keiser, as a child at Yankee Jim's.

132

water when suddenly they pulled over a rotted stump and found, clinging to its spidery roots, a wealth of nuggets.

"But this was the biggest lump of gold that day," John would say, giving Nona a special hug.

"And that was *my* production, if you'll recall," her mother would put in, just to pepper the give-and-take.

The story didn't end there. Elizabeth had pleaded, "Oh, John, let's sell the mine and go home. It's just too hard, raising all these children in this rough land."

John had agreed and, selling the new mine, pocketed a sizable fortune. When all his affairs were in order and Nona was big enough to crawl, he took the family to San Francisco to book passage on the first eastbound steamer. No ship was due for several days, however. So, for the interim, he deposited the bulk of his money in the Adams & Co. Bank.

Within three days, the bank closed its doors, reducing him to the money on his person and his remaining interests at Yankee Jim's. Back they went to the timbered foothills and to Yankee Jim's. There John built a boarding house, a livery stable, and a theatre. Two years later, in 1856, Laura was born to the Keisers, Elizabeth's brother-in-law reclaimed his daughters, and John's enterprises were prospering.

"Little Lotta Crabtree, the child actress, wanted Ella to be her dancing partner during those days," Elizabeth said. "Of course that was out of the question. Neither your father nor I would hear of it."

By the look in John Keiser's eye and the unvoiced messages they often flashed each other, Nona understood he had not been consulted. His heart would have prompted, Why not let her have a fling at it? But he would have said, she knew, "It's up to you, love. You have the say in bringing up the girls."

Ella learned a few of Lotta's song and dance routines and the two children, near the same age, were playmates when Lotta entertained at Yankee Jim's. The child longed for normal family life. She often slept on muleback while trekking with her father from camp to camp along the Mother Lode. Her performances enchanted the cheering, stomping miners. But when she played at Yankee Jim's, she could hardly wait to nestle into the Keiser household, a child among children, secure in the momentary relief of being ordinary.

When the Civil War broke out, John served as a Union army captain. On his return, another daughter was born. The tragic death of this infant led directly to the family's move to Coburn's Station in the high Sierra.

"I sent the girls to the drugstore for a medicine I favored for croup," Elizabeth said of this sad time. "By mistake, the pharmacist gave us the wrong bottle—a poison. When our baby died the man couldn't forgive himself. Everytime he saw us or one of the girls he plunged into a terrible despondency."

Compassionately, the Keisers decided to move away. If they waited for the druggist to leave town, they feared guilt and remorse would drive him to suicide first. Moreover, Ella had recently married Merritt Webber, who could and would ably take over the hotel, freeing them to locate elsewhere.

For a man to build a three-story hotel at Coburn's Station, a mere stage-stop on the Dutch Flat Wagon Road in 1866, he had to have uncommon foresight or uncommon luck. In John Keiser's case, it must have been luck, for he expressed small faith in the railroad's advance up the mountain, despite the fact that the rails had already reached Dutch Flat.

"You young folks will see the railroad reach across the nation," he told Ella and her new husband, "but I doubt if it will happen in my time."

He watched the Central Pacific's toil with the respect due a gargantuan undertaking. But he would not have believed that within two years the steel tracks would crest the summit and swoop to the basin like a benevolent fairy godmother, creating a town from Coburn's scant village and, with a magical swiftness, gilding John's own investment there.

"Only George Schaffer and Joe Gray had cabins here when we came," Elizabeth said. "Joe's was the stage-stop. His wife managed it when her husband joined Schaffer in the lumber business. Then our hotel became the station."

Schaffer held the C.P. contract for beams to timber the long galleries of snowsheds. With Gray for partner, he built the first lumber mill across the river.

Unusual and rare view of inside the snow sheds. These sheds were built up against the mountainside over the tracks to keep the snow from covering them.

"We didn't need all three floors for guests," John said of his hotel. "We used the middle floor for our own living quarters and the top floor for sick miners. Doc Curless was C.P. physician and surgeon full-time then. My wife nursed the men but we sent word for Doc to come when a badly injured man was brought in."

The girls remembered those days well. Nona and Ella were never allowed on the infirmary floor. However, their mother used their young legs to run up and down the three flights on innumerable errands to the kitchen, where they relayed her orders to the Chinese cook in fluent "pidgin" English.

—•—

After the past three years of new beginnings in strange places, years of childbearing and one baby's death, Nona sank gratefully into the healing restfulness of simply being with her own family. More than once she thought, If only Ella were here it would be almost like old times. Then she smiled at the enormous content of that *almost*. It held her own two girls and the new baby coming; Ella's young Carl and small Augusta; Laura's dark-eyed six-year-old, Lizzie.

She had been staring across the river into the timbered hills and now she turned to watch her mother fit tall candles into crystal holders for the dinner table.

"Ma, I'm twenty-nine. Is that . . . old?"

"Why, hardly, child. It's not old at all."

"But it's not young, either, is it? Still, it can't be as old as I feel sometimes."

"I know," Elizabeth said, thinking, At twenty-nine I'd lived six years in a mining camp and had my own third baby, so I do know.

Her mother's murmured response drew her into her thoughts and, quickly appreciative, Nona said, "Of course you do. I don't mean to sound complaining. Being home rejuvenates me anyway."

"All right, if you feel young enough, sit down and fold these napkins. That Chinaman will be the death of me. Every single one has to be refolded. Like this. Your father says they are easier to shake open if they're three-cornered."

Thus Elizabeth rallied her ponderously pregnant daughter

136

from what she diagnosed as "the blues" and gave her the sure antidote—busy work.

Dr. Curless, who had delivered Nona's first baby, found something to puzzle him in her present confinement. That she was a month overdue was neither unnatural nor new to his experience. But this other matter was both. This is what it was: When labor finally started in earnest, the lady wouldn't let him approach her until he washed his hands.

"But..." He had tossed away a well-chewed cigar at the outer door and now he spread all ten fingers as if to assure himself none were missing. "My hands are perfectly clean. I washed them before lunch, not an hour ago."

"Best do as she says, doctor."

Mrs. Keiser confronted him with a folded white towel on her shoulder, a bar of yellow soap in one hand and a pitcher of steaming water in the other. This could only be conspiracy, which he chalked up to the whims of pregnancy and womankind in general. Notions like this could spread from female to female in a small town, and he sighed. In prophetic vision he saw himself bound to scrub before future Truckee babies were allowed, bawling, into this world.

The birth was a hard one; for the boy born on the twenty-seventh of May weighed eleven and one-half pounds. Nona recovered well, however, and Mac's jubilation sped far and wide in announcements to his sisters, and to friends "below." The fact of a son fulfilled him, and without a thought to the old curse on the name for a first-born McGlashan male, he agreed to call the child Charles Fayette, Jr.

John Keiser's joy in his new grandson amused everyone. He quickly staked his claim in Fayette Jr. by declaring him "all Keiser."

"Look at those black eyes. See that curly hair? That's my brother Dave all over again."

It was no use to tell him the baby's eyes were blue. "Oh, they'll turn black. You'll see. Or dark brown."

Nona winked at her mother, but Elizabeth backed John up.

"He's right. I saw your uncle David's baby pictures in the old album back in Burlington. Even now, without the mustache..."

She tipped her head to the side, bird-like, squinting her blue eyes to visualize a miniature mustache on the tiny face.

John chuckled happily.

And looking into her newborn's face, Nona realized that her parents weren't joking. An ageless being gazed back at her. Almost an ancient being, she thought, so timeless the soul in his eyes. A sudden little shiver contracted her shoulder muscles and she held him tighter.

"I remember Uncle Dave," she said aloud. "Isn't that the Arabian he gave us out in the stable?"

"Yes, and skittish as ever. Old age hasn't taught him a thing. Retired race horses! He won't let another horse pass him you know. I won't let John hitch him to the buggy any more. He's wonderful to ride, but I could never hold him from a buggy seat if he bolted. And he will, mind you, if another horse comes alongside."

David had given her the Arabian when he brought his large family west for a visit. Nona had been in her teens then, and remembered her cousins well. Samuel was nearest her own age. Now he was his father's partner in the importing business at Keota, Iowa. Their firm was internationally known for fine horses.

"It's Keiser and Sons now," David had recently written to John. "When I retire it will Keiser Brothers, I trust, with two of my boys carrying on." (Sam replaced his father as executive until his own premature death in 1907.)

Beside that bed and in that idle conversation above the infant head of Charles Fayette, Jr., one might have believed, using hindsight later, that destiny brooded. Nona's involuntary little shiver of prescience could be called exactly that, although she did not "foreknow" a single fact of what was to come. All she knew was a chill of fear which she quickly dismissed.

Mac had gone to the office and so was present only implicitly, as inseparable from wife and child. But he was fully included in the cloud hovering above the little group in that room. In fact, he would be drastically affected by what it portended, even brought to a direct crossroads. His choice then would determine the tenor of the rest of his life.

138

Chapter Eleven

Thirty-five and graying, Mac returned to Truckee in 1883 in an aura of widespread fame. Not only was the Donner history in its fourth printing and still selling rapidly. Civic groups with a bias for western lore had discovered his ability to enthrall an audience and he was much in demand as guest speaker in cities and towns "down below." In short, old-timers could see, the "go-getter" had gone and got.

Truckee too had come of age. He found it brisk and flourishing. With scarcely a ripple of the surface he slipped back into its vital stream. Where this would take him he didn't ask. He only knew that here was the final home of his energies and he surrendered to the daily thrust of its invigorating current in a spirit of glad dedication.

His first move was to notify his friends by an ad in the newspaper that he was re-opening his law office. John Keiser and Will Edwards were putting out the paper these days. Edwards had gone ahead with the guidebook he had begun in collaboration with Mac. He called it simply "Edwards' Tourist Guide and Directory of the Truckee Basin."

Will Edwards was a shy man, tall and fine-boned, with dark hair that fell like shadow over a forehead too pale. The day that he showed Mac the guidebook his thoughtful eyes glowed with pleasure at their reunion; for they had been friends and now were brothers-in-law and both were glad of it.

"I've used your description of the town, Mac, and your synopsis of the Donner story, of course."

Leafing through the little book, smiling and nodding approval, Mac sensed that the other had something else on his mind and wasn't surprised when he came out with it.

"Look, old man. Why don't you take back this editor's desk? I'm doing well enough with the Sun Insurance agency, you know. Accident and fire policies sell like hotcakes up here. And to tell the truth, deadlines twice a week eat up all my time."

He didn't say that his health had been failing over the past two years. Laura's round rosy face puckered with worry when he coughed. "You've got to see the doctor," she'd scold. But he was always putting it off.

"I'm on vacation from deadlines myself right now, Will," Mac said. "I may want to get back into the traces later on. When that happens, I'll let you know. And thanks for the offer anyway. I'll keep it in mind."

Meanwhile, he renewed acquaintance with every aspect of the town. Not much had changed. John Keiser was still justice of the peace. Newlywed Jake Teeter still wielded a deadly pick handle in lieu of a lawman's gun. Bawdy Jibboom Street was in fine fettle, supplying Truckee people with piquant anecdotes for the pages of *The Republican*. According to the reporter, a madam named Epimenia Anaya had brought one Hallett, a "fancy man," to court for disturbing the peace of her dance house. Hallet cursed, disrupted proceedings in the courtroom at every chance, and finally yanked the judge by his iron-gray hair.

"Fire the son-of-a-sawbuck into the Bastille!" roared Judge Keiser.

Jake and two of the girls took the prisoner off to jail—a one-story cube of brick and steel built in 1875. With practicality and common sense, the citizens had erected this necessary structure on the west corner of Back Street. Jake needed only to shove the culprit out of a saloon's rear exit, cross the alley, and lock him up. The town contemplated a second floor for the accommodation of female prisoners. Teeter's journal chronicled frequent tooth-and-claw, hair-yanking skirmishes among the Back Street women, with stabbbings and gun-play when jealousies reached a deadly pitch. The second story was added in due course, with an outside staircase to its only door. (This access route was eventually replaced by an inside flight of steps that may still be seen today.)

Although Mac relished the brisk vitality of Front Street after the sleepy southland, he longed to get out into the woods once more. His legs craved exercise. More, the whispering conifers called him; the meadows, crisped and greened by hidden waters from alpine streams, beckoned; even the granite boulders—multitudinous, coarse-grained, peppered with black, sparkling mica—summoned him.

He used the Donner cabin sites for an excuse to hike, with thick meat sandwiches and a canteen of water put together by the Chinese cook under Nona's eye. At Prosser Creek, northwest of town, he found the last vestiges of George Donner's camp sunken into rot. Here he sat down to rest on Indian carpet, a rubbery spined growth that spreads at the base of evergreens. All about him stood tall dead stumps like broken Greek columns—monuments to the snow depth of the winter of 1846. The stumps made the flat meadow look like an ancient Doric shrine. For him this was a shrine—to the Donner party. Here he relived the tragic drama and his own vivid experience in writing its story.

Munching his sandwich appreciatively, he drew into his lungs the pungent woodland scents mingled by a silken breeze. Automatically he reached for the pencil and notepad he usually kept in his breast pocket. He'd forgotten them. Well, he would try to remember what had just struck him. It was the forest odors, scents of pine, sage, cedar, willow. All these interplay, he told himself. They don't erase each other or blend, but intertwine like strands of colored thread. He'd write that down when he got home.

Another day he found that the seasons had severely gnawed the markers at Donner Lake. Before snowfall, he determined, he must put up the large durable cross-beams he had planned for markers. A white cross at each site would be appropriate.

He had never forgotten his dream of a monument on the Breen cabin site. From this day onward he began scheming toward that end. He saw small hope of raising sufficient funds by private donations. His best chance, he saw, lay in State legislation, if he could get it.

To celebrate the birth of a son unforgettably and to introduce Nona and the children to his sisters, he wrote Adelia Balis that he thought it was time for a gathering of the clan. She concurred enthusiastically. Invitations sent to Lib, Nette and Laura called them and their families to a reunion in August. The Balis ranch at

Red Bluff could accommodate the crowd. It would be the first reunion since Ann's death in 1868, she reminded. With the multiplication of McGlashan progeny, it might well be the last. So come!

Adelia was right. The happy week, highlighted by a hunting trip for the men, proved to be the last time the sisters and brother would thus convene. Healdsburg's *Russian River Flag* reported that thirty McGlashan relatives attended.

From this occasion on, until the summer of 1887, Mac's public life accelerated to such a degree it seemed Ann had been prophetic in steering him toward politics. But again, as at Williston, his passionate response to personal values was to intervene. This time it would propel him on his final course and cast him in his ultimate role—a role emanating from his inmost core.

—•—

"Lucky Truckee—
Chinatown Holocausted"

So rejoiced *The Republican* when, in 1883, the shanties burned, not for the first time in the colony's history. As before, the long-suffering Orientals rebuilt, this time entirely across the river.

The high Sierra's anti-Chinese sentiment was matched state-wide in the 1880s by fear of Japanese interests in California's agriculture. As editor of the *Santa Barbara Press*, Mac had been acutely aware of the rancher-farmer's concern. Now, committed to Truckee's economy, he plunged headlong into its quarrel with yellow labor. And it was this cause that led directly to his election in 1884 to California's 26th legislature, as Assemblyman from Nevada County's 15th precinct.

For more than a decade Caucasian leagues had formed like bubbles on a scalding brew. Most of them had been dissolved and were in disrepute with federal authorities for alleged brutalities. Californians now felt the time had come to settle the problem with maximum legality. Localized anti-Chinese committees, not affiliated with so-called Caucasian leagues, were solely bent on securing protective laws against "the yellow peril." The majority believed that only absolute exclusion from all rights of citizenship would effect this, and in those days Mac was among them. (Much

C. F. McGlashan when he served in the California State Assembly. Picture taken in 1885 or 1886.

Below: Melataea macglashani, *discovered by C. F. McGlashan on June 9, 1885. This well-preserved specimen was about 60 years old when this photograph was made by McGlashan's daughter Ximena.*

Charles Fayette McGlashan, Jr., born May 27, 1883, died December 2, 1886.

later, when the Exclusion Act was passed [largely written by himself], he would tell his daughter June that he had "come to regret it bitterly.")

He realized very quickly that the twenty-sixth legislature was not ready for the Oriental issue. Despite his campaign promise to work for anti-Chinese legislation, he must labor outside for the cause. The struggle for control of hydraulic mining was a fiery issue that the session considered more immediately pressing. He found himself assigned to the mining committee.

He had long since relieved Will Edwards and joined his father-in-law on *The Republican* staff as editor. But after his election he was able to do scant work at the desk. In fact, the paper began announcing "McGlashan was in town" as a newsworthy item. Edwards good-naturedly filled in for him. Mac faithfully penned editorials for Will to use and sent home reports on the Legislature.

Nona, meanwhile, was preoccupied with the children—and with one on the way. On June ninth, 1885 she gave birth to Mary Elizabeth. Mac had canceled every appointment in order to be home for her confinement and, during her hours of labor, took June for a walk along the railroad track—a favorite pastime of Truckee children, who walked the rail like a tightrope or hopped from tie to tie.

Suddenly the five-year-old squatted, her dark curls tumbling about her face while she gazed at a butterfly poised on a leaf beside the track. Instantly, the collector in Mac came alert. He saw brown checkered wings like none he'd seen before. Was this a new find? Even a new species? With eyes shining, he matched the leaf from which the butterfly had circumspectly departed with the bush it came from. This was the food plant. If he found eggs on it, he could raise the insect's progeny. Sure enough, there were the newly deposited eggs on the underside of the leaf he held in his hand.

In high jubilation, the two discoverers sped home and learned that a new baby girl had arrived. Mac kissed his wife's forehead and lips gently, holding aloft from harm the precious egg-bearing leaf.

"I've always suspected," Nona liked to aver with only a partial smile, "that he was more excited about the new butterfly than about the new baby."

It was in fact a new discovery. J. J. Rivers classified it for him, calling it the *Melataea macglashani*.

The butterfly drew him back to his old beloved hobby. On the train to and from Sacramento, he used odd moments to design an air-proof, bug-proof case for his specimens. He took out a patent on this design the following spring, 1886. During that summer, Albert Koebele, a renowned entomologist, came to Truckee for the express purpose of netting with him on the Truckee meadows.

A special session of the legislature had been called in February, 1886. In the same month, Mac was elected chairman of the Anti-Chinese League, formed at San Jose by delegates from nine counties. Another such league was organized, with George B. Katzenstein as chairman, at Sacramento where the two groups met in joint session.

Since the anti-Chinese question was essentially a labor issue, more and more of his time was given to labor disputes. He espoused unionization wholeheartedly and whenever angry railroad strikers met at Bill Hurd's hall in Truckee, Mac was there.

In September, the young Labor Party in San Francisco nominated him for governor—a touching expression of esteem and affection that went to his heart. He had not run again for assemblyman. His name had come up for senator instead, but he had lost the nomination to another candidate.

"I'm glad you lost it, Mac," Nona said. "You're tired, dear. You can't keep up this pace."

He had to agree. He was suddenly very tired. Once on the merry-go-round, he mused, how do you get off?

Then, in late November, scarlet fever terrified the mothers of Truckee. Fayette, now three years old, came down with it. Night and day Nona and her mother watched over him. Mac dropped everything to be home.

The bond between John Keiser and his grandson had grown stronger each day since the boy's birth. Toddler and aging man flew together like iron to magnet when John came home from work. With his father away so much of the time, Grandpa became the one male figure he could count on.

145

This was never glaringly apparent. Fayette acknowledged his father shyly, but sufficiently, when Mac was home. But in the terrible days of December 1886, an unnerving situation unfolded. When the child opened his feverishly brilliant dark eyes and saw his father at the foot of the bed, he screamed.

"He's delirious, dear," Nona said. "He doesn't know you. Don't take it to heart."

But he did take it to heart.

Fayette's condition worsened drastically, hourly.

"I fear he has diphtheria as well as scarlet fever, Mrs. McGlashan," the doctor said.

What hope could there be? Once more pregnant, Nona knelt by the boy, crooning to him, bathing his hot, flushed forehead with cool damp cloths. Elizabeth could not pry her from the bedside. John and Mac hovered in the shadows outside the sickroom door, or took turns to walk, scowling, around the block and back.

When all hope was gone and death seemed to delay only from pity, Nona found herself sustained in a transcendent calm. I am in the eye of the hurricane, she told herself.

But for Mac there was no refuge from those stormy eyes that accused, "I know you not." He fled down the back hill to Hurd's saloon and ordered a whiskey at the bar. Friends who started toward him saw his haggard face and turned away in tactful silence. One or two touched his shoulder briefly in that kind, wordless way men have with each other. He didn't stay long. His glass emptied, he strode out into the night and up the hill. Halfway to the house, he turned his face to the shrill winter stars in time to see two meteors fall. They seemed to disengage willfully from their clustered peers and he stood still to watch the long, leisurely, flaming curve of their descent.

"Angels of death," he whispered. "Why two, I wonder?"

He went on to the house thoughtfully and entering, expected to hear that his son was already gone. Not yet. Another day or two Fayette lingered. Unable to bear another rejection, Mac only dared to look at him when he slept.

He died five days before Christmas.

"Cry, Nonie, try to cry," Elizabeth urged. But she could not.

She only rocked back and forth, back and forth, in the low chair she used for guitar practice. She would answer if spoken to; otherwise deep silence claimed her.

Once when her father came in from town she put out a hand to touch him, for his face was a mask of sorrow. He went to the window then and stood gazing at the hills. She knew he wept by the way he blew his nose.

"Oh Pa, don't grieve so," she said. "You'll be next to see him." Then she heard what she'd said. "Don't listen to me, Pa. I don't know what I'm saying. I didn't mean that."

But her father turned and met her eyes thoughtfully. In command of himself, he kissed the top of her head, stuffed his handkerchief into a back pocket, and went out to the kitchen to find Elizabeth.

At her child's funeral Nona sang in a clear contralto that did not waver or break. Her grief remained locked beyond relief. Mac hovered near her constantly, for his own comfort as much as hers. His own tears came freely. The legitimate business that had kept him from home haunted him, distorted and blackened by remorse into spectres of utmost neglect on his part. Nothing Nona said could console him, for in truth he had lost forever the chance to know his only son intimately. Even the old superstition concerning the name Charles Fayette, Jr. gave him cause for self-condemnation.

"I should never have allowed that name! My father said in infancy or early childhood a first-born male McGlashan . . . "

"Nonsense." Nona broke in before he could use the self-punishing word "dies." "Don't add that to your guilt feelings, dear. Whatever his name, he had scarlet fever and diphtheria. Face facts, Mac, for they're comforting sometimes. Whatever his name, God wanted him *now*. We must see it that way."

He knew it would take him a few months to sort out the lessons of the stupendous heart-blow of his son's death. He would work out the details in time, but already his mind framed a major premise for the future. He knew he was an extremist, constitutionally incapable of doing anything halfway; therefore he had better make a choice. Public Servant or Family Man—which would it be? Big frog in little pond, he could still serve and devote himself to Nona and the children. Out in the larger lake, the currents took him from their shore.

"Anyway, I would rather chase butterflies on the Truckee meadows than be a tycoon in any metropolis of the world," he had said lightly, but meaning it, more than once.

His choice was clear.

His hair, threaded with gray, now rapidly turned snow white.

The months moved along with a healing uneventfulness, and Nona's seventh month of pregnancy drew near completion. May 27th would have been Fayette's fourth birthday and that morning she woke up with a sense of dread. This day—could she get through it? Could she handle the clamorous memories, each one a child's treble vying with the other to tell of last year's birthday, and those before it?

When Mac left for work that morning she pinned a small blossom to his lapel, the ritual "buttonhole bouquet" he wore for his lady each day of their life, and the words she had suppressed at breakfast spilled out. "It's Fayette's birthday, Mac." She could have bitten her tongue for the slip, but he simply kissed her gravely and turned away to walk down the hill to his office.

At lunch, her father himself, the last one she wanted to remind of it, said, "This is the twenty-seventh of May. Fayette's birthday, isn't it?"

"Yes, Pa."

"He would have been four," Elizabeth said. Then they went on sipping Wong's chicken soup, to fill in the collapse of small talk.

"I'm going to the lake," John said when they rose from the table. "You won't need the buggy, I hope, Elizabeth."

"No, but John, the mare's being shod this afternoon you told me. You aren't taking the Arabian, are you?"

He was. And no amount of wifely admonition was going to change his mind. "Skittish? I know he's skittish, but I can manage him. He's used to the buggy now. I had him out the other day."

"You didn't!"

John laughed and tweaked her cheek with a caressing thumb and knuckle. "Don't think I'd tell you, love! But he wasn't a whit of trouble."

"Oh, these retired race horses! Now be careful, John, or I'll die of worry."

"I'll be home around five," he said, meeting her kiss and reaching for his battered brown hat. Truckee's seasonal dust, rain, wind and snow gave men's hats short shrift, and most of the older men, including John, had long since abandoned fashion for longevity in headgear.

That afternoon passed slowly and restfully. Elizabeth got out the sewing machine to stitch and mend her grandchildren's clothing while Nona napped on the sofa. Under her mother's foot the treadle made a soothingly muffled sound that combined with the needle's staccato click to put her to sleep.

About four o'clock the sewing was done and Nona awoke. The two women joined each other in the alcove by the windows where they could watch the scene below until the men came home.

Suddenly, about half past four, they heard a crash and loud commotion on the plaza. Rooftops hid whatever had happened, but the shouts of a gathering crowd reached their ears.

"It's John!" Elizabeth cried out. "I know it's John."

"Oh, Ma, no, it can't be ... "

But Elizabeth was already out of the house and running down the crooked dirt path to Front Street. Nona, enormous with child, followed heavily.

Arrived at the plaza, Elizabeth pushed her way through a cluster of men who fell silent as they recognized John's wife. Immediately she saw him, stretched motionless on the ground. Doc Curless knelt beside him, his long fingers exploring the limp wrist. Later, the doctor said he found no pulse or heartbeat and was on the point of covering John's face when Elizabeth fell on her knees at his side.

She slipped her arms under the bloodied head calling, "John! John! John!" In pity, most of the men moved away, for they knew he must be dead or very near it. Then suddenly, he opened his eyes and looked directly into her frightened face.

"Why did you wake me, love?" he said. "I was sleeping so sweetly."

His head dropped back. He was gone. He was sixty-three.

"I will always believe he came back from death to give me

those words for comfort," she said later.

As she had so feared, the Arabian had been "spooked" by an old nag pulling a milk wagon. The old racer would never allow another horse to pass him, and when the rattling tin milk cans sounded just behind the buggy, that alone had made him nervous. John pulled on the reins to slow him down at the plaza. It was then the milk wagon drew up alongside. The Arabian bolted and reared, overturning the buggy and throwing John violently against a telegraph pole.

Elizabeth wanted Nona and Mac to remain with her in the Keiser house, which they did. Five years later, early in April of 1891, she announced at breakfast one morning, "Today I am going to die."

"Nonsense, mother, don't talk like that." Nona was sure that until that minute her mother had been perfectly healthy.

That evening Elizabeth went to bed early and asked for June, who was eleven, to sit beside her and hold her hand until she fell asleep.

"How I'd love to have John's arms around me and hear him say once more, 'Elizabeth, I love you.' What difference does anything else in the world make?"

That night she quietly died in her sleep. She was sixty-four. They buried her next to John, over whose grave in the pine-shaded cemetery on the hill the Veterans of Foreign Wars and his beloved brethren of the Oddfellows Lodge had erected a tall marble monument. Fayette's small grave, first to bloom in the family plot, nestled at his grandparents' feet.

Chapter Twelve

My grandfather's decision to forego the public arena for the home front may or may not have made a difference to California statecraft. But oh, the difference to the home front!

He now knew what he was giving up. Before he had tested the lake he claimed to prefer the small pond. Like a man who rises abruptly from a good meal in mid-course, he felt the wrench of sacrifice. And since it was for home and family he curtailed the range of his energies, that institution would receive the full battery of his time and creative effort.

Reasonable as this sounds and was, an understandable apprehension may well have lurked behind the children's enthusiasm over "having Papa home more now." Their life would never lack color and spark, for he encouraged celebrations, games, storytelling and all manner of family entertainment. At the same time, his 19th Century convictions on child-rearing came straight from his own father's stern disciplinarian example.

Moreover, his sister Ann once reminded him that "at one time or another, a McGlashan must conceal or confess to a fiery temper." She had written him thus while he was teaching at Cold Spring mining camp, aged eighteen. Two pranksters had goaded him beyond endurance and, in a red blaze of anger, he'd chastized the pair with a severity their parents considered undue. Called on the carpet by his principal, he had stated his case and was let off with a fatherly admonition.

But conscience had troubled him. He wrote the whole incident to Ann, confessing that impatience was his besetting sin, a sin he wrestled with mightily.

Now the old teaching days were far behind. He had lived a lifetime since Cold Spring. All through his young adult years, so crowded with events and interests, he had rarely been irascible, let alone angry. But as he approached the forties and what he believed should be his prime, he recognized the old family trait (if so it was) uncoiling as from a long sleep.

He was no youth straining for perfection now. Pondering his sudden intolerances, he wondered if anger weren't more an ally than an enemy. He considered the varieties of anger and tried to analyze his own. If anger weren't the snarl of self-love's defensiveness or the destructive rage of willfulness run amok, then it had its place in a man's make-up. Hadn't the Lord angrily whipped the money-changers out of the temple? No, he told himself, the man whose gorge won't rise in burning disgust, whose blood never boils in instant defense or rejection of a principle, that man is a bystander, uninvolved and unconcerned— a beachcomber on the shores of his own life. This he could never be. He would thank God for anger. Of course, he'd have to harness it.

From the point of view of his three oldest—Nonette, nine, June, seven, and Elizabeth, two (Earl Leo had just been born that July, 1887)—the trait operated within a perspective of their own. Their father's prematurely white hair and mustache enhanced the piercing brown of his gaze and dramatized the regularity of his straight nose, even jaw, and high forehead. He had gained an actor's command of gesture, carriage and stance from courtroom and speaker's platform and had early discovered that fashionable dress gives self-assurance. For himself, he had adopted the cutaway coat, celluloid collar and string tie of that day's gentleman.

All this he put to use in the bosom of his family when, ringed about with small solemn faces, he presided—head and father, prototype forever in those young minds, as in my own a generation later, of God, the Father eternal.

Loving dispenser of wonders (lavish Christmases, surprise outings, spontaneous entertainments) and revelations (candy or toys tucked for finding in his greatcoat pockets on his return from the City), he was likewise the implacable dispenser of justice. He was capable of enormous Jovian thunders and lightnings over broken house rules or lagging obedience. Small hearts thrilled even while they trembled at resounding doomsday warnings, rendered with incomparable theatricality. This was living—vivid, intense, unmistakable!

Only their mother knew, only she had the gift to discern where wrath ended and sheer histrionics began. She never revealed such secrets, but watched silently until such time as her comforting bosom might restore a small pariah to full citizenship in the kingdom of family love.

Whatever his mood, angry or benign, their father's presence always electrified the house with a mysterious crackling current of excitement. Lights brightened, furniture took on burnished substantiality, colors sparkled, clear and true.

In 1893, the year he built the Rocking Stone Tower, Maqueda and Lotus were the toddlers, with Ximena (pronounced Zimena) on the way.

"Maqueda. What an odd name," people said.

"It's the name of the queen of Sheba," Mama replied.

"I see." Clearly, they didn't.

After Ximena, she gave out the only really simple explanation for the unusual names she chose for her girls: "In case," she said, "they marry men named Smith."

Few outside the immediate family ever knew how my mother, Ann Maqueda, really came by her name. Born roughly two years after Fayette's death and Earl's birth, she came into the family during Papa's earnest inquiry into the occult.

A fad for spiritualism and attendant cults had rippled across the country throughout the 1880s, titillating only the outer fringes of my grandfather's curiosity until Fayette died. The child's rejection, so sealed by death, sent him reeling to the comfort of his Christian belief in the soul's immortality. Strong as he thought his faith was, he now felt the need of absolute certainty that Fayette understood those absences from home and forgave him. He longed for a message from beyond, and yearned to get a message through to his son.

One day he brought home a book on spiritualism, a "how to" manual of sorts, filled with table tipping, ouija board operation, numerology, automatic writing, and the like. Nonette and June were ready accomplices, scarcely able to wait to join him in these "games." But their mother would have none of the book.

"It's of the devil, Mac. Not everything *spiritual* is *good*, you know that as well as I do. And I don't know that I like the girls fooling with that *fol de rol*."

"Oh, come now, dear. Just for the fun of it, there can't be any harm . . . " he went right on setting up a small table for tipping. "Now it says here . . . read it to us, Nettie, while I put the chairs around."

Nonette read brightly in a breathless semi-lisp. They were to lightly drop their fingertips on the table, shut their eyes and concentrate.

"All right, then. If you are set on doing it, go ahead, but mind you, I don't like it." Mama said. She wasn't expecting until September, six months off, so she still had ample lap to hold Earl, who had her large gray eyes. Swinging him aboard, she rocked in her low rocker as if the gathering momentum could waft them both out of sight and sound of this dark sortie into the nether world.

She need not have worried. Nothing happened. No matter how hard her family blanked their minds and concentrated, the table remained still. At last Papa gave it up.

"Well, let's try the automatic writing, girls. Nona, won't you join us, just this once? For the fun of it, that's all."

At the word "fun," Mama scathed him with a look that only brought on his special laughter, an irrepressible chortle that convulsed him when he thought her comical, cute, or as now, his match in a battle of wills. Finally, with affectionate wheedling he won a reluctant assent.

"Bring the table here, girls, in front of your mother. Now, take this pencil, Nona, and sit relaxed, the book says, in a position for writing." He positioned a tablet of long legalcap paper under her hand and stepped away to leave her undistracted by his presence.

"Now hush, everybody. Sit on the floor, girls, and don't say a word."

After a moment, she began to write. And write. Without a single interval for thought, she filled page after page of the long sheets with her flowing rounded script. When at last she was done, Papa wonderingly read aloud what she had written. It was a complete adventure-romance, entitled "Maqueda." Until then

154

they had not heard the name or known that, as her story explained, it was a name of the queen of Sheba. They later corroborated this. The story was fully plotted, with masterly characterizations. Astonishing touches like "she threw herself onto a manzanita bush and found it held her up like a rocking chair" proved true when the children tried it out.

"If the new baby is a girl, Nona, I suggest we name her Maqueda," Papa said when her confinement drew near. She agreed and they chose Ann for her first name. His sister Ann had been much in his thoughts since Fayette's death.

Mama's repudiation of spiritualism steered him back to the solid shores of his sturdy Protestant faith. But he never lost a restive desire for more direct, burning knowledge of God. Fayette's death turned him into a pilgrim seeker of Truth, glad for golden crumbs he begged at various tables—theosophy, Christian Science, the mystic symbolism of Masonry. Twenty years later, my own mother's death would bring him back home to the Scriptures in which he found, to the end, the fullness of the feast for his hunger, and his own place at the banquet.

"I am a student of the Bible," he would say simply then, when asked. But he left himself room to be eclectic and brought along from his theosophical pilgrimage a stubborn belief in reincarnation.

"I don't find anything against it in the Bible," he'd say. The idea of coming back for another round pleased him. "I think I'll be a mother next time," he said, "for I can't think of anything nobler than the self-giving of a mother's love."

Those were thoughts he voiced in his latter years, when only Mama, Brownie and I were around to hear.

Mama had one more go at automatic writing. In her mother's footsteps she had become the right-hand assistant of the doctor. Young Dr. Shoemaker took over Doc Curless' practice in the Nineties, and she was on call when he needed her. Since girlhood she had accompanied Elizabeth and Doc Curless to the rescue of train wreck victims in the snow sheds. She had gone into the night many times to watch at sickbeds. With her own children running barefoot throughout the long summers (she endorsed such liberation of feet), she worried over the problem of rusty

155

nails. In the case of a deep puncture, the doctor would cauterize it with a swab dipped in carbolic acid—an agonizing procedure for the young patient, comparable to red-hot knives twisted into the flesh.

"If we only had a strong antiseptic," she mused inwardly. The problem was constantly in her mind as snow melted and Truckee earth dried to dust in the sun.

"Maybe you have an answer inside yourself and don't know it," Papa said one day when she spoke of her wish. "Why not sit down with a pencil and paper and see what flows from the unconscious?"

"Well, all right, Mac. Put *that* way I don't mind so much."

Before the words were out he had her seated at a table, pencil in hand, tablet in place.

She soon began to write swiftly. Under her firm hand a formula that incorporated carbolic acid with beeswax, glycerine, honey, olive oil and camphor filled a quarter page. "Beat on a marble slab for two to three hours," she wrote, "using wire egg beaters."

Papa removed the marble top of the bathroom table for the beating. Utilizing all available right arms, in the third hour of whipping the mixture turned from beige-yellow to a white creamy salve, light textured and pleasantly scented.

The carbolic gave the ointment its strength while the other ingredients, with the addition of home-made attar of roses, produced a hand cream. For years she supplied the doctor and her neighbors with this cream gratis, as if it were a boon from heaven she had no right to price.

Chapter Thirteen

The 1890s

On May 14, 1891 the country's interest in the Donner party was reawakened by two prospectors who discovered the cache of coins Elizabeth Graves had buried on the north shore of the lake. The discovery, with the attendant flurry of identifying and then restoring the coins to the Graves family, also reawakened my grandfather's determination to put a monument on the Breen site. A Donner Monument bill was introduced into the 1892 Legislature through his efforts, and all his Sacramento friends assured him it would be passed. It was—only to be vetoed by the Governor "to retrench expenses of the session and keep the tax levy within bounds."

Stunned with disappointment, he would not let go.

"All right, then. So help me, if I must, I'll raise the money myself. The day is almost here," he told Nona, "when California will need its history recorded in markers and monuments. For its own posterity, let alone for tourists. And a monument here, at the foot of the summit pass is so appropriate. Not only the Donner party but all the emigrants who suffered the hardships of those days would be honored."

"How much would it cost, dear?"

"Oh, five, ten thousand. Maybe more. But there has to be some way to raise it."

It was time to go down the hill to the office and he plucked his gray felt hat from the antlered hatrack in the corner. Nona lifted her face to his goodbye kiss. He wore the blue bachelor's-button she had pinned that morning to his lapel. "Put on your thinking cap," he smiled. "Between us we'll come up with something."

As he walked down the dirt footpath to Front Street, he had no illusions about the audacity of taking on, single-handed, the task of raising thousands for a monument. Until the 1890s money had been "easy come, easy go." However, by early 1893 he could feel the chill breath of a full-blown economic depression. More and more, he was hard put to maintain the fiction of plenitude in which he had sworn to raise his children.

"I will not have them burdened beyond their years with anxiety over money, Nona. I was penny-conscious from the cradle, and I don't want that for our children."

Not only his own children concerned him. His hand was always ready at his pocket when he walked down Front Street.

"Mr. McGlashan sure hates nickels and dimes," Truckee children decided among themselves. "Look how he gives them away."

"Go buy a horse," he would say, pressing a coin into a grimy palm. "How I used to look at those glass jars full of candies when I was a boy," he told anyone who might wonder at this habit. "I always hoped someone would think to buy me a piece." But nobody ever did.

And then, there were the hoboes.

"Spring..." wrote *The Republican*'s editor as early as 1886, "and with it comes the usual horde of tramps. Year by year, tramps have increased from squads to companies, from companies to regiments... and on to an army."

Once the trains entered the snow sheds, hoboes went unmolested by trainmen, who feared the sure retaliation of arson in the timbered galleries. With the hard times of the nineties, the numbers swelled—and Truckee got them, coming and going. Ridiculed, despised, denounced as lazy beggars, they wandered over the land, outside the bounds of sympathy—except for one immediacy my grandfather could never withstand. They were hungry.

He could not resist a hungry man. He had known hunger too intimately. Hunger was something as real to him as a cut artery— an emergency, a bleeding that had to be stopped. He therefore instituted the daily pot o' beans, slab of bacon, and slice of red onion with bread and coffee for any tramp that knocked on our kitchen door.

Right: One of the vials of wood from the foundation log of the Murphy cabin. These were sold as part of McGlashan's campaign to build a monument to the Donner Party. Actual length of the vial was about two inches. Below: The labels attached to each bottle certified authenticity of the wood and stated the purpose of the sale.

MURPHY + CABIN,
DONNER LAKE.

August 12, 1893.

We this day assisted in taking up the foundation log, or last remnant, of the Murphy Cabin, of the Donner Party.
C. F. McGLASHAN,
NONA McGLASHAN
A. E. BAUGH,
HATTIE A. BAUGH,
E. K. DOWNER.

NO.............

PRICE $1.00.
Sent by Mail Prepaid.

I hereby pledge that the net receipts from the sale of 5000 of these relics shall be devoted to the erection of a monument to the Donner Party.
C. F. McGLASHAN.

I hereby certify that this vial contains a portion of the foundation log of the Murphy Cabin of the Donner Party.
C. F. McGLASHAN.
Subscribed and sworn to before me this 12th day of August, 1893.
W. H. HILL,
Justice of the Peace.

"If he asks to chop wood in payment, let him. But don't demand it. Just feed him."

"But hundreds take advantage of you, Mac," friends said. "They've got your house marked."

"If I feed a hundred men and only one of them is really hungry, it's worth it to me for that one," he told them. And if any "hired help objects to cooking and serving the food, fire him or her," he told Nona.

Thus it was, even unto my time, years later.

The family was still living at the Keiser house, which Elizabeth left in her will to Nona. Then, in 1893, Papa built the Rocking Stone Tower on top of the huge, flat-topped parent rock and

159

The Rocking Stone Tower in 1893, when first completed. White picket fence was removed then house was built.

there housed the Donner relics, his butterfly collection, and a growing number of curios, including Indian baskets and beaded headbands.

In July of that year he set out on horseback to check the Donner cabin sites and their markers with the thought that he should search for any log or partial timber that might be extant from one of the disintegrated shelters. Such a relic should certainly be rescued and preserved in the Tower.

The Breen site showed nothing, but when he followed the pine-shaded trail to the high rock that had served for the north wall of the Murphy cabin, he saw one lone decayed log. Imbedded in the damp earth, it had somehow been preserved by the earth. He could not have wished for a more satisfactory relic, for this was a foundation log, a doorway beam. He would need help to remove it, and most importantly, witnesses.

Suddenly, he knew what he could do to raise money for the monument. He wouldn't store this beautiful Murphy timber. He would . . . bottle it? Yes, bottle it. In tiny vials to be sold, a dollar each, for the cause. His forty-sixth birthday lay ahead, on August twelfth. On his birthday he would make a party of removing the log—a picnic for family and friends, to vouch for the authenticity of the rotting tamarack wood. The Donner party was famous. Who wouldn't like a splinter from one of the cabins "that witnessed more horror and death than any of the others?" Bodies of the starved victims lay beneath its floor. Already the words of

160

an advertising brochure were forming in his mind. He spurred his horse homeward. He felt he flew through the warm summer air on the wings of new hopes and plans.

Nona invited their good friends the Baughs. A. E. Baugh was principal of the Truckee schools and his name would carry weight as a witness. Another old friend, E. K. Downer, owner of the Downieville *Messenger*, happened to be in town and accepted an invitation with alacrity. His name, well-known beyond Truckee, would speak to multitudes of non-residents. Moreover, he promised a good write-up in his paper.

A few months later, in a four-page tract describing the relics and the reason for their sale, my grandfather told what happened next.

On August twelfth, "the log was taken up in the presence of witnesses and conveyed to Truckee. Hundreds...attest to seeing the log and to the fact that it is the last portion of the cabins of the Donner Party. This log was cut in small pieces and placed in vials which were sealed, labeled, and certified to under oath. Among the many who assisted in the task of filling the vials, and who bear witness to the authenticity of the contents...are the following:..." Nearly a hundred local names were followed by more than a hundred names of out-of-towners, including Mrs. V. E. Murphy (Virginia Reed of the Donner party). This indicates that the log was displayed during most of the following year, while "bottling bees" employed helping hands to fill five thousand tiny vials. The remnant "could provide twenty thousand more" if they ran out of them through sales.

Of course, he gave out his dream for the monument which, he stated then as he always did, would rise on the Breen cabin site, a spot that the Breens had confirmed as the exact location of their house. Work on the monument, he said, would begin "immediately and proceed as rapidly as funds permit."

He visualized dollars flowing in. The work would be under his direct supervision, he promised, and he offered a fifty percent commission to salesmen, while he called for agents from every parlor of the Native Sons of the Golden West. He saw dedicated agents selling in every "newspaper office and in every school on the Pacific Coast."

However, after the first spurt of interest, led by fellow townsmen and loyal Lodge brothers, the sales lagged. People were careful of dollars in the mid-'90s. Unemployment, coupled with labor disputes had increased. Violent clashes between railroad strikers and police, widespread and frequent, paralyzed freight and hurt the economy all along the line. Truckee people, wholly dependent on the railroad for food during winter snow, often had to hoard provisions.

Sold-out grocery stores were not the worst that Truckee suffered during a railroad strike. Terminus that it was, hundreds of sullen idled men were let out in town to drink, gamble and turn ugly when their pay ran out. As days dragged by without settlement, men who were reliable husbands and fathers under normal conditions became dangerously soured. When scabs stealthily moved the trains in the black of the night, the first hiss of steam emptied the saloons of a hornet-mad horde, sober enough to know it was being tricked and drunk enough to be deadly.

One of the favorite family stories of these hard times concerns my grandfather's varied schemes to supplement his own vanishing income. Since it revolves around a railroad strike, this is the place to tell it. We call it How Papa Got the Railroad Pass, or (in today's parlance) the Frog Pond Connection.

By the mid-nineties, he had seven young mouths to fill. (Bliss Isabel, the eighth and last, was not born until 1896.) At the same time, and of great importance to him, Nonette and June were nearly through high school and ready for college. And to college they would go, he promised himself, although he wasn't sure how he'd manage it. He said nothing to Nona this time, but bent his wits to the problem. However he tried to hide it from her, he knew *she* knew the paper and his law practice were not bringing in enough when both subscribers and clients were counting pennies.

In recent years frog legs had been in demand at gourmet restaurants in San Francisco. Virginia City and Truckee residents too would pay good prices for such delicacies. It occurred to him that production of frog legs might be profitable if frogs could survive the sub-zero winters.

162

There was one way to find out. He sent for two dozen French frogs, which he received by express from San Francisco. Then he hired a man to carry the frogs on horseback in two milk cans slung across the saddlehorn to a little lake he had named for Nona. (It is now called, one might guess, Frog Lake—but only because a boulder shaped like a frog sits on its shore.)

With the first snows the French frogs perished, unfortunately. Tiny mountain frogs flourished in a nearby swamp, but these were too diminutive to furnish so much as an *hors d'oevre*. However, if he caught these small creatures and put them in the lake where he could control their fate (at least there he could see them!) perhaps with luck they could be interbred or otherwise induced to grow larger. It was a long shot but worth a try, he decided.

Meanwhile, the Southern Pacific (no longer the Central Pacific) offered him a retainer's fee to be a company attorney. Much as he sympathized with the railroad workers and their complaints, he was in no position to turn it down. Accepting, he stated clearly that he believed in the justice of the men's demands when they called a strike; but the officials who retained him didn't seem concerned. They shook hands and left, happy to have him bound in conscience to their side.

Inevitably, he found himself faced with a strike—an embarrassment he managed to evade for several days by locking the office and looking after his frogs, several miles north of town.

The officials, however, lay in wait and caught him at the office door just as he returned from the lake one afternoon.

"Now, Mac..." (He had let them in, for what else could he do?) "Now, Mac, we know you have influence with these men and we want you to..."

"Stop right there. I told you from the start that my sympathies are with the men and their demands. I will not have anything to do with their backing down on a single point."

"We hired you to work for our interests, McGlashan."

"Your interests be damned, gentlemen." He walked to the door and held it open. "You can leave my office now."

They hatted themselves huffily and departed muttering.

A day or two later, the angry, bored strikers who lounged in

and around The Last Chance on one corner or The Bucket o'
Blood at the other end of the street found large signs that said in a
giant scrawl:

Anyone who Would like a Day in the Country
With Free Food (All you can Eat), Meet Teams
Tomorrow at Last Chance Saloon—8:00 A.M.
Signed: C. F. McGlashan

Every man was glad to go, glad to get out of town, glad to catch
tiny frogs in the swamp and dump them in the little lake all that
sunny day. Not a striker remained in town.

They took their time coming home, for the horses were tired
and what was the hurry? It was after dusk when they reached the
point where the road bends down to Truckee—and there they
saw: The trains were moving. Scabs had taken over.

"But weren't they angry? Didn't they blame you, Papa?"

"Did you do it on purpose, really? To break the strike?"

All the answer we ever received was the muffled eruption of
his chuckle between teeth clamped on a cigar.

"Great work, Mac," said the S. P. officials, returning to shake
his hand and slap him on the back. "We knew you wouldn't let us
down."

"Gentlemen, I refuse to shake hands on what you infer I did for
your interests." According to Papa, he showed the men out as
perfunctorily this time as before. But they persisted in believing
he was bluffing and they left in good spirits.

Within the week, a lifetime pass for himself and family arrived
in the mail from the Southern Pacific, his grateful client.

Whatever his intentions other than catching frogs that day, he
was undyingly grateful for the pass. "It helped educate every one
of you," he said many times. I know that it paid for innumerable
trips to and from college, made by nine children, including
myself.

He knew that for the time being he must shelve the monument
project. He put the majority of the bits of bottled history in the
Rocking Stone Tower for visitors to the museum to buy. A daily
trickle of people climbed the hill from the railway station, usually
passengers waiting between trains, grateful for something to help

164

kill time. But collectors they were not, and the vials of Murphy wood moved slowly.

When the first snow fell in the winter of 1894, he used the editorial column to rally his own and the town's spirits. Trains were running, but they faced winter now, the long white season when business fell off for everybody.

"Dear old Truckee," he wrote, "home of warm-hearted, honest men, beautiful women and bright, healthful children. How many have slandered you, how few understand your virtues. Where on earth have friendships been truer or less selfish, where are people more united..." he continued in this vein, reminding his fellow-townsmen how they had worked together, built together, and above all, how they had valued each other and loved this little town. Pointing out the community's assets—railroad, sawmills, the ice industry, factories, dairies, plus all the opportunities "for carpenters, masons, builders, and all classes of skilled workmen"—he knew, even as he wrote, that morale-boosting words were not enough. Something had to be done, and quickly.

But what? The snow was here, the months of short money and marking-time-until-June stretched ahead. Apprehension lay like a lead pellet in many hearts. Snow. Snow? Why, snow was their answer! Suddenly he remembered he had always known it. He had visualized special trains pulling into Truckee from east and west in winter months, scattering hundreds of ecstatic, joyously shouting people over dazzling hills packed with snow.

"Think of the business a well-advertised carnival would bring Truckee," he had enthused to anyone who would listen. He had written it all in his column, as well. But no one would take the notion seriously.

"Sure, Mac, but...Wouldn't it take a lot of...uh, doing? Where would you begin to get a thing like that going?"

And so now the winter of 1894 was coming on, and the merchants and hotelmen and restaurant men simply tightened their lips, and belts, to wait it out.

But my grandfather began doing an odd thing on the hill beside the Rocking Stone Tower. He didn't begin until February, 1895, for then he could count on sub-zero temperatures—at night at least, and that was when he needed them.

Within a few days of his hilltop activity the town saw a tall conical frame covered with chicken-wire standing beside the white tower on the rock.

"What's going on up there, Mac?" friends asked.

"What's it going to be, Pa?" asked the children.

"You'll see."

And then they did begin to see. Every night he sprayed the sixty-foot frame-and-wire cone from top to bottom. In the morning, his children trailed him up the hill to see the result. Just as he hoped, the frozen frame retained more ice each day. Even when the wintry sun gazed on it, the ice did not entirely melt weepingly away. Little by little, the cone took on the thickness of a bona-fide icicle, higher than the little tower itself.

To crown his creation, he fastened an arc light to the tower's centered flag pole and, as the icicle grew in size and substance, a phantom glow played over the scene every night.

(From this spot, the 1960 Olympics torch blazed more than a half century later for the Squaw Valley Olympics.)

His icicle had worked. It worked! Now he knew exactly how to build an Ice Palace. If he could convince the town to let him...

He presented his idea at lodge meetings and met with full response. It had been a hard winter, and Truckee men were now willing to try the solution he proposed—winter sports. He told them his dream—a spacious ice palace, illuminated during the day by a transparent roof of thin ice, but supported by thick walls of ice surrounding a large skating rink. Music, concessions, everything to draw a crowd and bring it back for more—these they must plan while the summer months gave them time. Special excursion trains would be arranged with the Southern Pacific. He had already seen to that.

The finished Ice Palace covered an acre of the plaza. Its proximity to hotels and restaurants was for the convenience of female excursionists. The oblong structure had rounded corners and enclosed an oval rink a fifth of a mile around. The solid walls, three feet thick, withstood sunny days, and every night they were hosed inside and out. Cedars and pines ten feet tall ornamented the outer rim of the roof. At night, twenty arc lamps illumined

Above: Front of the first Truckee Ice Palace, built in 1895. Below left: Toboggan slide in back of the Ice Palace. It descended 150 feet from a 75-foot tower. Below right: Souvenir medallion of the Truckee Ice Carnival, featuring the toboggan slide.

the rink. A toboggan slide was added to the western end of the palace. Tobogganers would climb to a tower on the roof, then "whoop and shriek as they slid down" one hundred and fifty feet to street level.

The first ice carnival of the West, for such it was to be, did not lack advertising. All the newspapers and journals on the coast carried the story of it and announced the date the first excursion trains would bring the excited happy crowds for the gala opening.

Local hotels and eating places stood ready. Reservations poured in, and even the snowstorms obliged. The town was assured a record depth, for the snow began falling steadily on Monday. The opening was set for the weekend.

Wednesday, the snow stopped coming down.

Thursday, the sun came out.

Friday, temperatures touched a record high for that time of year. The excursion trains were canceled.

Saturday, the snow fainted away to soggy clumps of dirty drifts lining the roads of mud.

When Papa was momentarily dejected, depressed or disappointed, he sat forward and somewhat sideways on a chair, staring into space or at the floor. With his left hand on his thigh, the fingers of his right drummed on the chair arm or, at times, rubbed his brow.

"Well, that's it," he said to the silent, gathered family, at some time after breakfast.

"Well, Mac, if it wasn't so awful, I guess it would be ... "

He stopped her with a wave of his hand.

"No, no, no, don't say it. I know what you are going to say and I'm not sure I'm ready for it. You want to say that it would be funny if it wasn't so ... "

And suddenly it *was* funny—terribly. The comical side of disaster always came through. This was the humor of pioneers, Truckee, of my grandparents. Short of disease, death and maiming, however calamitous the happening, it would flip over to reveal an antic aspect. Those who felt victimized suddenly floated out of themselves, looked down, and saw they were victims of a cosmic practical joke to which the only normal response was laughter.

Papa began to laugh until tears bedewed his mustache. With his kerchief he wiped them away and still they came. Mama joined in, her shoulders shaking with merriment. Such laughter infected the children, who laughed if only for laughter's sake.

When he went down to the office that day he found that the laugh had already spread around the town and everybody was braced for the next snow, the next "go round."

For the next six years, thousands of tourists enjoyed the ice palace and Truckee's winter sports. When the palace began to sag and was declared unsafe, the snow carnivals didn't stop. Another and yet another ice palace was built, but none to match the original. Donner Lake itself was skating rink enough. Six and eight-horse sleighs shuttled hotel guests three miles to the lake and back many times a day. Burgeoning crowds rode the excursion trains to Truckee for nearly thirty years to come. For the 1890s, certainly, the town's economy was saved, and the jingling of sleighbells mingled joyously with the jangling of cash registers.

One serious problem plagued Truckee's winter sports: Snow melted rapidly in its immediate environs. Many excursion trains had to be cancelled for sudden lack of snow, although the surrounding hillsides a few miles out of town retained an abundance.

My grandfather urged the town to buy these outlying snow-fields. His last letter, written in November 1930, just before his death, warned the Chamber of Commerce that individuals or organizations were considering potential resort areas and the town stood to lose winter sports to rivals if it didn't secure hillsides of long-lasting snow. However, by then it was too late. The stock market had crashed the year before. Nevertheless, Truckee was to benefit, and still does, from the resorts that later blossomed near it, such as Soda Springs and Squaw Valley.

From the Ice Palace of 1895 to the Squaw Valley Olympics of 1960—it all began with a sixty-foot icicle and one man who loved his town.

—•—

Perhaps a chapter on the robustly colorful nineties should not close with so tidy a concept as that above. An anecdotal collage has come down to me from family versions of it. A vignette or two may serve.

Although Papa owned the water company, possibly an inheritance from his father-in-law, John Keiser, he gained little from it. As for the newspaper, he rejoiced if it broke even. In fact, it was during the business panic of the nineties that *The Republican* is said to have changed hands over the poker table more than once. With the consent of their practical wives, most of the solid men in town, including my grandfather, bolstered their weak financial positions with serious sessions of poker from time to time.

While Papa enjoyed the challenge to his wits, at the same time he chafed under the shortage of money. He longed to give his children more than absolute security. They must have color and music in their lives.

Toward this end, in addition to daily reading aloud and listening to music *en famille*, he instituted the annual Trip to the City. Ostensibly a shopping trip, each year they brought home a piece of furniture for the home he would one day build beside the Tower. Each child was allowed to pick out her and his own chair, which gave zest to the hours of traipsing from Doan's to the Emporium's third floor.

Always they stayed at the famed Palace Hotel. This was memorable mainly because of the restraints they suffered.

"Oh, Ma, do we have to dress up every night for dinner?"

"Yes, we do. Now let June comb your hair. Get in there, Earl, and take your bath."

"Why do we have to dress for dinner, Ma? Why?"

"Well, to tell you the truth, girls, I think we dress for the hired help. They expect it of us."

After dining in grandeur, they strolled under the painted lanterns of Chinatown. From store to exotic store they inhaled the blue incense that swirled around porcelain dolls and other fragile wares as if a smiling genie were about to appear. Most unforgettable of all, they peered into eerily dim and dingy rooms below street level where men with parchment pale skin smoked and dreamed on board bunks tiered against the walls.

—•—

Early in his children's lives, when it became noticeable that the majority of the family would be female, he decreed that "every one of you girls is going to learn how to earn your own living—in case you ever have to." Mindful of his own sharp-witted, valiant, tough-fibred sisters and other pioneer women he had known, his respect for women's intelligence and resourcefulness induced him

McGlashan children in 1896. Left to right, back row: Nonette, holding Bliss, June; middle row: Maqueda, Earl, Elizabeth; front: Lotus, Ximena.

to put the same demands on his daughters that he did on his son. In short, he gave them ambition to use their brains and talents to the fullest, while holding up before them wife-and-motherhood as the supreme ideal. Such orientation, so far ahead of its time, was apt to have painful consequences for one or two. But at the hour of growing-up, each girl stretched a sword-arm high and felt like Joan of Arc.

The year 1896, therefore, was memorable for the family, not only because Bliss was born on June sixth, but because Nonette and June left for college. That is, June, now sixteen, entered the University of California at Berkeley, and Nonette, seventeen and a half, enrolled at Hopkins Institute of Art in San Francisco (named for Mark Hopkins of railroad fame).

Nonette's talent had driven rather than led her toward art school from the time she could hold a crayon in chubby three-year-old fingers. When other children were still at the mud-pie stage, she was molding wet earth into cows, sheep and kittens. At school her chewing-gum dolls (figures wrought of well-chewed gum) brought her such a steady income of candy and cookies from classmate customers, she never doubted that art would support her.

Her mother, whose eyes she had inherited in a gray-green version and whom she shadowed everywhere, taught her her first art lessons and championed her when, on graduation from high school, she begged to go to art school instead of college.

"But can she ever earn her living at it? I mean, if she has to. I will not have our daughters dependent on a man to support them." Ann, Nette, Lib, all of his sisters had been able and willing to earn, and he had determined to put some grit in his daughters, too. He had kept in close touch with Undine, Jennie's child, who was very dear to him. He counted her always among those he would send to college. But she, too, chose art school.

"Can a girl earn a living at art? What do you think, Nona? I'm serious. Would she teach it—or what?" The possibility of selling or of receiving commissions seemed too dim to mention.

"Of course she could teach it when she's through school. But that doesn't matter, Mac, so much as letting her learn all she can. Nettie has genius, Mac. I believe it. True genius. She wants with all her heart to enroll at Hopkins. She and June can find a boarding house in San Francisco and June can commute to Berkeley. Why not?"

"Well, I suppose you're right. College won't do her much good if her mind is on paints and clay. I'll enroll Undine too, if she insists on art." It would always mystify him that anyone, no matter who or for what reason, might not care to go to college.

The birth of Bliss, so named for her happy disposition, was perilous for Mama. A few weeks before confinement, a sharp pain in her side alarmed young Dr. Shoemaker, who diagnosed appendicitis. Nothing could be done, he said with tears in his eyes, for he loved her, as everyone did, and she had often worked with silent strength beside him when trains crashed in the sheds.

"We can only wait. If it ruptures . . . If it ruptures, we have one hope—the poison could drain through the bladder."

"And if not . . . ?"

"Sir, we do have that hope. You are a praying man. Pray for that, and so will I, very much."

Mama told me that the hope he gave sounded like none at all, especially as the day of confinement drew near. She lay on the big bed waiting for the scissoring pain (as she imagined it) of rupture and the end of two lives, her own and the baby's. Papa could never bear to have her ill. The depth of his worry and fear for her manifested in irritability, and from her hushed bedroom she smiled somewhat tenderly when she heard him roundly scold the children for one thing or another.

"Your mother is sick, can't you be quiet?" he'd shout. Or, "No, I won't help you with arithmetic. It's time you stood on your own two feet." He, whose greatest joy was to hear a young voice ask for help with studies, just for the chance to stuff a small head with knowledge.

Then, one night, Mama knew the baby could wait no longer. With the violence of her labor surely must come the dreaded explosion. Between pains she sank into a kind of stupor. She had made her peace, accepted from God's hands and given back to Him everything He asked of her—Mac, the children, the new life that would go out with her. She rested without thought or prayer.

"I don't know when it was, but something made me open my

173

eyes," she told me, "and there at the foot of my bed I saw a man, an old man with a long white beard, dressed like a monk in a long black robe with a cowl. I stared at him for a long time. His eyes were in shadow from the hood that covered his head, but I felt that he was returning my gaze. I didn't feel frightened. I was very peaceful. Almost like I rested in that long look we exchanged. Suddenly he was gone, like a flame blown out."

She lapsed into silence, as if remembering. Impatiently, I called her back. "Then what, Mama?"

"Well, dear, then I fell asleep. When I woke up, I found that the pus and poison had been running out of me—draining, just as Dr. Shoemaker said. Bliss was born a day or so later, perfectly normal. I have always thought that God sent some great soul, perhaps an angel, to me that night."

"To cure you?"

"Yes."

Her convalescence was slow. When Nonette and June could no longer delay finding a boarding house in the City before schools opened, she still couldn't go with them.

"Don't worry, mother, we'll be fine," Nonette said, "and yes, we'll be careful of friendly strangers, I promise you."

Like most Truckee teenagers, the two oldest had gone to high school "down below" and were long past homesickness and timidity. Their mother knew the vast difference between sophisticated San Francisco and the country-town life they'd known in Grass Valley. She trembled for her daughters. But she had no choice. She could only follow them with her prayers—and almost at once these went to work.

From Nonette's account, she and her sister followed no pattern or guideline in their search, but set out early on the first morning of their arrival in the City. As if they were in a rural town, they simply climbed the steps of large, high-storied, frame fronts at random and rang a bell or clacked a knocker, as the case might be.

After receiving several negatives to their polite, "Do you have rooms to rent?" they thought they had finally struck pay dirt. A young woman they would always call "the princess" answered their knock at one door. She was dazzlingly dressed in what they

174

later learned was a satin and boa-feathered negligee. To mountain-bred innocence she looked "elegant." They noticed her odd frown and hesitation when she heard their question, but she only shrugged and said, "Follow me."

Behind the shining fabric of her gown they mounted a carpeted, narrow, dark staircase to a hallway lit only by the gray light from a window neither the sun nor sky would ever know existed. Here, the princess led them to a door that opened on a bedroom. A fat, fifty-ish woman, clad only in a laced corset, sat before a dressing table mirror in which she looked them up and down.

June was the first to find words. Nonette was too busy taking in impressions of color, texture, and generally tumbled form in the lavish disorder of the room, which reminded her of pictures she had seen called Backstage at the Opera.

"D-d-do you happen to have any rooms you care to rent?" June's embarrassment at the woman's state of undress made her voice quaver with apology for the intrusion.

For a long moment no answer came from the puffy white-powdered face in the mirror. It continued to regard them in thoughtful silence until, finally, in a bass pitched like a man's, hard and gravelly, she said, "Wait in the other room."

To their guide she gave an eyebrow-and-head-toss signal which the princess seemed to understand. She beckoned and they followed. As soon as they were out in the hall she closed the door on the corseted woman and pushed the girls ahead of her in a rapid descent down the stairs.

"For the love of God," she hissed, "get out of here and run like the devil is after you."

Which they did.

Papa soon realized that Nonette burned with exceptional talent. Reports of her student work during the three-year course at Hopkins Institute of Art, praised her highly. In her last year she was one of the students chosen to work on the Donohue fountain that has stood for decades on a corner of San Francisco's Market Street. This tribute to Mechanics was commissioned by the much-loved mayor, James Phelan, who asked Douglas Tilden to be the sculptor.

Nonette, sculptress, (Mrs. J. S. Hennessy) graduated from Hopkins Art Institute in San Francisco and then studied under the American sculptor George Gray Barnard in New York.

Tilden, a handsome man with thick dark red hair, was a deaf-mute. Nonette learned sign language in order to communicate with him. With all others he used a pad and pencil to write his directions and thoughts. His design of the sculpture, to be cast in bronze, showed a group of men hammering on an anvil and constructing a wheel, among other devices. Nonette was assigned to model the figure of an old workman and to lend a hand on the anvil, shaft, and large wagon wheel.

When the sculpture was done, Mayor Phelan asked to see it before the casting. Tension gripped the apprentices. Minutes before his arrival, Nonette climbed a nine-foot scaffold for one last check on her own work. Small and agile, she had supreme confidence in her footwork on ladders and beams. This time, however, haste and nerves tripped her up. She lost her balance and dropped. To her own chagrin and everyone else's dismay, her heel dented the anvil and her clutching fingers bit into the rim of the perfected wheel.

Tilden rescued her with one hand while "he tore his hair with the other," as she told it. She wasn't hurt, but no one thought of anything but the dent and claw-marks. The mayor walked in almost immediately after, all smiles and goodwill. Sculptor and students stood paralyzed.

"I will explain to him," Nonette sighed to Tilden, "I'll tell him what happened right now." But as she started forward from the group, the mayor walked over to the fountain and looked squarely at the dented anvil.

"Perfect! I like that," he exclaimed heartily. "Old iron is being used. Only a genius would think of it."

"He likes it," Nonette signed to the bewildered Tilden. "He likes it *just as it is*."

The sculptor rapidly wrote on his pad what had happened, and the mayor read it amid deathly quiet. He wrote his reply, "Leave it as it is," Tilden read—and sighed; for he was a perfectionist who could see only the dents.

"As for you, young lady," the mayor said to Nonette, "any artist who so loves her work that she will hurl herself into space for perfection deserves a reward. If ever you want to open a studio in my city, I promise you I will furnish it completely for you."

He was to keep his word. After graduation, Nonette studied at The Art Student's League in New York City. George Gray Barnard, foremost among American sculptors of the era, spoke of her as one of his most gifted students. On her return to San Francisco she set up a studio on Jones Street, near Chinatown and the Bohemian section where young artists lived and worked. Jack London, Maynard Dixson, George Stirling—these were the promising talents among her associates and friends. Gutzon Borglum, of later Mt. Rushmore fame, was in love with Nonette. In fact, he was snowbound for three weeks in our Truckee home. But in spite of propinquity, he had too strong a rival in sculpture, to which she was delivered over at that time, body and soul.

—•—

Since Truckee's beginnings, one building had served for elementary grades and high school. Few high school students stayed in town. Most, like June and Nonette, were sent to accredited schools in towns down below. Now, with three

The first Meadow Lake High School, built in 1901.

children in high school and three younger ones coming along in that direction, Papa decided this was nonsense. It was high time Truckee had its own dignified high school building and a fully accredited staff and curriculum.

Into this project he threw all his intensity. To start it, he donated the land for the school, a site three blocks west of the Rocking Stone where he was already clearing the land for his own house.

Long active on the school board, he now found himself empowered to push forward the high school's interests to the utmost. Without waiting for the building to be done, he appealed to the State Board for accreditation.

It was granted without delay, in 1901, while the high school still consisted of one room in the grammar school building. Mrs. Mertie Thompson Kruger, recently wed to one of Truckee's leading lumbermen, was principal at the time, assisted by two able young women.

A year later, Meadow Lake High School, an impressive two-story building set high on the hill above the old site of Coburn's Station, opened its doors to thirty students and a senior class of seven. The enrollment had tripled since the edifice was begun.

Now my grandfather could turn full attention to the family home, about to rise beside the Rocking Stone.

178

Chapter Fourteen

1900 - 1910

This was the decade of fulfillment for Papa, the sunlit time spangled with graduations, five weddings, and the first wave of grandchildren. Even his long dream of a monument to the Donner party began to materialize.

He soon realized that the monument fund had to have strong organizational thrust and backing. In his heart, he wished the Native Sons of the Golden West would take it on as an appropriate project. He had friends in the N.S.G.W. all over the state, as well as in Donner Parlor, and whenever he could suggest it gracefully, he did so.

To his immense gratification, one of Truckee's leading citizens, Frank M. Rutherford, introduced the idea as a resolution before the Grand Parlor held at Nevada City in 1898. It was accepted. Before any attempt to raise funds, the members agreed, a three-year preliminary campaign of education would be feasible, and for this big job they named George L. Jones, a good friend of my grandfather's and, later, Superior Court Judge of Nevada County.

It was not until 1901, therefore, that the Native Sons were ready for a Donner Monument committee and the actual work. To head this all-important committee, they chose Dr. C. W. Chapman, a Nevada City dentist.

Chapman was a short, stocky man of sandy coloring and pale blue eyes whose rounded jowls and compressed lips spoke more of tenacity than of vision. He was undoubtedly an excellent choice for the long-range project this turned out to be. Deliberate of pace, unshakable, he would persist to the end. Ironically, this same virtue was to work for the effective blighting of any joy and satisfaction my grandfather might take in the monument that he had been the first to envision. Two years after the unveiling and dedication of the beautiful bronze and stone memorial in 1918, Chapman would initiate a sudden, mystifying course of action, described in detail in my grandfather's letter to the N.S.G.W. written in June, 1920. I will quote from this later.

At this point, it suffices to know that my grandfather and Chapman hiked around the cabin sites in 1901 while Papa explained fully his reasons for selecting the Breen lot for the monument. Chapman nodded his head in thoughtful appreciation of such facts as the Breen brothers' positive identification of the cabin site and the existence in 1879 of clear outlines that all could see. He agreed that this was, beyond doubt, the Schallenberger-Breen location, and gave every sign that he concurred in the choice.

"You can tell the boundaries of the lot from the ducks-on-rocks and that blaze on the pine over there," Papa said. "Joe Marzen, who owns the meat market and most of the local beef, deeded the land surrounding the cabin to me for the express purpose of a monument. He bought up all the pasture along Donner Creek, you see, to graze his stock. Now, I promise you I'll sign the deed over to the Native Sons the day the cornerstone is laid, if you'll use this exact site. And of course, whatever you decide, you can have the five thousand vials of Murphy wood to sell."

Chapman conveyed that he'd made his decision and gladly accepted both offers. They shook hands cordially at parting.

Nearly a decade was to pass before the cornerstone was laid on the Breen site. Meanwhile, Papa turned his mind to current enthusiasms. Although this was the year of his white-hot interest in the new high school going up on the hill, and also the year that he began blasting huge rocks from the land for his home, most thrillingly, to him, it was the year June came home from Hastings with her law degree. He had had a new sign painted above his office that read "McGlashan and McGlashan."

When June first started college she had said, "I'm going to be a mathematics teacher." At that time the whole family took for granted that Earl would be a lawyer. Certainly Papa did.

When Earl was ten, Papa told him, "Son, you will go to the best university and law school in the country," and misconstrued the frown between his son's gray-blue eyes to mean earnest attention. His mother alone read the frown for the scowl of dissent it was. He had moved nearer her, as he always did in body or spirit, for they lived in each other's hearts, as June lived in her father's.

By Earl's twelfth year, the whole family knew how he felt about law. He wanted no part of it—or anything else, apparently, his father might choose for him.

"Well, then, what do you want to be, if not a lawyer?"

The boy shrugged and frowned at the toe of a scuffed shoe.

"Look at me! Take your hands out of your pockets and stand up straight. Now. I asked you a question."

It was hopeless. Nonplussed by what he called Earl's bull-headed glum silence, Papa was torn between anger and sorrow. "Why, he's already twelve—nearly thirteen," he stormed to Mama. "He ought to have some idea of what he wants to be."

"Leave him alone, Mac. Give him time. He's still just a boy."

"A boy! When I was his age . . . well, never mind."

"He'll decide and tell us when he's ready, dear. Anyway, there's no hurry, is there?"

But she knew and Earl's sisters knew that he had set himself against his father in that ancient, strange, tragic way of so many fathers and sons. If his father asked it, he would no more be an attorney than paint himself green and purple for life. At the same time, a subterranean inexpressible love for his father coursed through the boy's turbulent heart, making the impossibility of communication between them intolerably painful. Mama saw the love, the conflict, and the pain. She tried to interpret each to the other, but failed. It was no use. Whatever the trouble, it ran too deep. The boy and the man must work it out.

June instantly suffered for her father when she learned from hints dropped in letters from home that young Earl, in a show-down with Papa, had declared utter rebellion, if not war.

"Then I'll be the lawyer," she announced to Nonette, who was still in art school and shared the small flat. "I'll be graduating in June. I'll enroll in law school in the fall."

"But . . . you know how you hate speaking in public," Nonette said, recalling the agonies of stage fright June endured before every oral report in the classroom. "You'll have to plead cases in courtrooms. Before juries, June. How can you do it? How can you do this to yourself?"

"I know, Nettie, I know." June had the liquid brown eyes of a deer and was as shy. "I won't let myself think of that side of legal work now. Maybe I won't even have to plead in court. But I'll be Papa's partner if Earl won't, no matter what it takes. Poor dear Papa." Her voice cradled the name with all the protective warmth of a mother's arms. Nonette knew that no sacrifice would be too great for her sister if it spared their father the pain of disappointment.

However, devoted as June was, she was to be no silent partner in the firm. Excruciatingly shy (before pleading a case in court she clenched her fists with dread until her nails bit blood from her palms), she was Papa's match in verbal gifts. Sparks flew about their downtown office over points of law. He loved such debates for, in his eyes, her college diploma and law degree merited his highest respect. He had longed for her to have such education and now, when she won a bout and proved her point, he was delighted with her. He would throw back his head and laugh until he had to wipe away the tears with one of his slippery white silk handkerchiefs. If he won the argument, he could scarcely hide the jubilance that shone from every pore of his face and made his mustache bristle.

When June married George Frank Kelley in 1909, the partnership ended. But she remained in Truckee with her dentist husband, who practiced law on the side, and she served the county as deputy district attorney. Since Papa was a defense attorney and she the prosecutor in every case, father and daughter enjoyed lively jousts. The ring of steel and clash of swords brought juries and witnesses to the edge of their seats. They insulted each other in sophisticated, polished displays of a high intense disdain that drew on the dramatic instincts of both to the fullest.

By the time the judge declared a recess for lunch, the staring courtroom would expect the attorneys to stomp off in opposite directions to nurse their grudges. Instead, Papa would bow to his

June (Mrs. G. F. Kelley), attorney-at-law, second woman admitted to practice in California Supreme Court.

Dr. Earl L. McGlashan, D.D.S.

Dr. George F. Kelley, dentist, with Dr. Joseph Bernard, M.D., in chair, circa 1912, at Truckee.

fiery tall daughter in the old-world courtly manner born to him and offer her his arm.

"Come, my dear. Shall we have lunch?"

"Yes, Pa. Wait a minute while I fix my hair. I'll meet you in the hallway."

In their long close association, June became her father's confidante. More than any other of the daughters, she had empathized with his thoughts, hopes, beliefs and dreams from her childhood on, since the June day of 1885 when together they discovered the *meletaea* butterfly. Of them all, she took seriously his interest in the stars and the sale of his little star maps. From him she learned the rudiments of botany. Whenever she could she went with him on butterfly hunts and on walks deep into the woods where they found treasures of stone and flower to bring home for study.

She was the only daughter who learned from his own lips the principles that underlay many of his attitudes and actions. He had discovered early that few people care about another's reasons for doing what he does. He never explained himself. He merely walked his road, and anyone who wished might follow.

There was, for instance, his attitude toward money.

"He said once," June told me in later years, "that he thought he'd given away about half of everything he'd ever earned. He tried to, anyway. It was his belief that the Lord meant money to circulate, to flow through open hands. 'Money comes to me for my needs, and then it should be passed on,' he used to say. He believed that the use of money was a matter of faith."

I remembered how often he mused over the words, "Consider the lilies of the field; they toil not, neither do they spin; yet Solomon in all his glory was not arrayed as one of these."

Another quotation he made bone-of-his-bone was: "The servant is worthy of his hire." I remember him as a lavish tipper on our train trips to the City. His tips assured us lively service but even as a child I suspected a deeper reason for the green bills that slipped into hands serving us with such care. He must have recalled days of his own youth when his services returned him board, tuition, anything but cash—and he'd needed cash.

He went beyond this, of course, and watched for struggling

young townsmen who needed a helping hand. More than one got a start in business from a secret loan he didn't have to ask for or pay back with interest. A few revealed such secrets after my grandfather's death; otherwise, his left hand never suspected what his right was up to.

—•—

I have already said that the house my grandfather built in 1903 would have stood out anywhere in the world—unique, original, a paradox of ornate simplicity. Among homes designed with a hard eye to the weather, it shone from the hill like sheerest fantasy. With its white regiment of pillars, multiplicity of glass panes, and the unexpected tower joined to its side by an umbilical bridge, it was a jaw-dropping sight. Even the encircling granite wall, peppered with glittering black mica like diamonds in the sun, fed the imagination.

And after dark, with a single light bulb for a dangling star at every window, the effect dazzled. In the dead of night, however, illumined only by moonlight on snow, it looked truly enchanted.

Aside from calling it "McGlashan's glass house" and predicting that its flat roof would collapse soon under a ton of snow, Truckee people took the house calmly. Old-timers were long used to Mac's spectacular departures from the norm. Any newcomers who had lived through his progression from lone icicle to lavish ice palace and thence to annual winter tourism were more inclined to watch and wait than to smile. Like the hourly pageantry of the S.P. depot, his activities had become one of Truckee's spectator sports, followed with kindly amazement.

The castle he gave the town in the architecture of his home went deeper than whim or gesture. Friends recognized that. He built it, for one thing, immediately on the heels of the handsome high school to which he had subscribed with agressive urgency. He intended both edifices to be signs of bold encouragement to Truckee-ites. Those who loved the town as he did, knew it.

The fact was, by century's turn, Truckee had crested the zenith of its potential for the era that begot it. This was not obvious to everyone as yet. After all, the feisty community had won every major goal. Although deadly shooting scrapes would erupt over

View of the McGlashan home and Rocking Stone Tower. Taken from an angle that does not show the height of the surrounding wall, which was approximately thirty feet at its highest point.

the next fifteen years (Jake Teeter had been killed in Hurd's Saloon in '92), they were fewer and farther between. A smooth-functioning court system had greatly controlled the rowdy-dow element. Jibboom Street still flourished but with diminished fanfare. More than one madam had discovered that her business acumen qualified her for a legitimate business (milliner or dress shop, perhaps) and had gone on to respectability in some midwestern town. Of those who retained him as attorney, Papa had persuaded several to return to a daylit life.

And the Chinese were gone—banished by boycotts, harass-ments, and finally by a shameful episode of mob action in the 1880s called "running the Chinamen out of town." Thus, Truck-ee's substantiality looked certain on the surface, even visible, like the paunch of success on middle age. The big new house on the hill and the imposing high school affirmed, "We are part of that paunch; so don't lose faith. Our town has a future we can still build on."

186

My grandfather foresaw what the advent of the automobile might do to a railroad economy, but he would not give in without resistance. He had learned from Ann the power of encouragement, the power of the dream. She had first taught him this when he lay sick in bed in Healdsburg, a runaway twelve-year-old.

"Dream big, little brother," his sister had said. After that, was there anything Peter's children hadn't been able to accomplish?

The house he built on the hill in 1903 was a rallying banner for the town. Ann's words were implicit in its fantasy of wood, glass and stone. Other pioneers and old-timers caught his message. Like himself, they missed the boom and zest of the early days when the excitement of the Comstock reverberated throughout all the mountain towns. The more settled stability of the mid-eighties and nineties, following the Comstock's demise, was what they'd wanted in the first place—a solid town of solid worth in which to harbor their families. That they had achieved. But now, even though lumber mills still operated on the banks of the river and within the forests of the basin; even though refrigeration had not yet been invented to hit the Boca ice industry; even though the S.P. depot's continuous entertainment still attested to the health of the railroad—even though all these patterns and threads still held, those who knew the town best sensed that unseen fingers, future-oriented, plucked away at the fabric's underside.

Our airy sunlit rooms filled gradually with treasures that set the scene for my own childhood and youth. Each of the chairs so personally selected in San Francisco found a sacrosanct niche. Mama grouped her low rocker, music stand and guitar permanently by the first window of the rotunda's circle, where the wall telephone would hang for nearly thirty years. Her inherited share of Persian rugs, shipped by her mother around the Horn, she scattered from rotunda to back parlor, over the wall-to-wall carpeting installed against winter cold. The parlor, a library-music room, was soon eloquent of Nonette, whose exquisite small sculptures and wall plaques, classic in style, gave the room a touch of formal elegance—a word over-used in that day.

Nonette also made two cabinets for the phonograph records that Papa brought home from his trips below. The two large boxes of thick wood were covered on all surfaces with burntwood ornamentation. Flowers and fauns and nymphs interwove in a skilled artistry of charred wood.

The cases filled over the years with red-seal and Brunswick and thick Edison records. Family listenings were as mandatory as the after-dinner reading aloud. Papa bought the earliest graphophones as they evolved from cones to discs. A large music box, too, found its place in the parlor. This was a glorious thing to hear. The perforated metal platters were a foot across and the revolving steel pellets beneath them gave out full-throated bell tones, waterfalls of rippling sound.

My mother, Maqueda, claimed the upright Baldwin piano. Mama had this tuned twice a year for decades by the same little man who became grayer and slighter until he no longer came at all.

Papa was delighted with Maqueda's musical talent. She was to have the best of teachers and music schools.

"But can you earn a living at the piano? I think not, child. So you must choose a vocation and prepare yourself for it. Music is an avocation."

She was curled in his lap and they sat in his big leather chair in the rotunda. Small for her ten years and a quiet child, her one show of aggression lay in a daily rivalry with her juniors for Papa's lap. Even when she was too old and already in college, her petite four-foot eleven inches allowed her to perch on his knee. It endeared her to him that she still did so from time to time.

"I'll be your secretary," Maqueda told him that day in the rotunda. "How do I learn to be one?"

"Well, there's Heald's Business College. But first I want you to go to the university, you know."

She looked into his face with her tawny gold eyes—"tiger eyes," her sisters called them—and without more ado her future course was plotted. A precocious child, she was then, at the age of ten, about to begin her freshman year in high school. She would have time for business college before she was old enough for the university. She would even have time to be his secretary for a year or so, and then to marry and give me birth. And then, no time at all.

—•—

Elizabeth May, foster daughter of the McGlashans, in high school graduation photo. She later became an osteopath and married Dr. V. V. Manning, also an osteopath.

Elizabeth (Mrs. W. W. Gilmore).

Lotus (Mrs. Jackson Gregory Sr.)

Ximena (Mrs. J. C. Howard) was known as the "Butterfly Princess."

The 1906 San Francisco earthquake galvanized every fraternal lodge into action. First on the scene was my grandfather's favorite, the Knights of Pythias. As a top-ranking officer of what was then the Uniform Branch, he was immediately charged with the overall supervision of relief. The purpose of the Uniform rank was to provide the nation with a trained militia for emergency defense. And in setting up camps and a good kitchen, the Pythians moved with the speed of disciplined efficiency. As Brigadier General of the California brigade, with old comrades like Tim Crowley under orders and at his side, my grandfather's joy in ideal fellowship was almost fully realized. From this time on, he was known as "the General," a title he carried well.

He had been one of the founders of Truckee's Pythian Summit Lodge, Number 54, in 1879. The fact that he was working at white heat on the Donner history when he was installed that spring as Chancellor Commander makes this incredible—and typical.

In Freemasonry, which he also loved, he attained the Thirty-third Degree and, a month before his death, a fifty-year gold button.

"Here, Maqueda, take this," he would say just before he put me on the train for a visit "below" with one of my aunts. From his watch chain he unfastened the Masonic emblem and pinned it to the lining of my jacket. "If ever you are lost or in trouble, show this emblem to a train conductor or any official. If he is a Mason, he will take care of you like his own child."

Thus he counted on the fraternal bond. I am sure that in those days he had good reason for it. Pioneer western history abounds in deeds that show how seriously the members of brotherhoods took their charitable responsibility toward each other. This was especially marked among the Masons during the great migration of caravans across the plains. The Knights of Pythias, organized in the wake of the Civil War, held the sentiment of brotherhood aloft even by its name, derived from the mythical Greek friendship of Damon and Pythias. Pythianism spread rapidly. In the aftermath of a war that set American against American, thousands of men like my grandfather saw dire necessity in its ideals.

The earthquake, of course, destroyed Nonette's studio on Jones

190

Street. "Come home, child, and work here in Truckee," Papa suggested. "You can use the basement room, for the windows give plenty of light." He had installed a room for his butterfly work in the stone-walled cellar and put windows facing the river along the south side. He had even ordered a basement lavatory for greater convenience. The room was his workshop but he gladly gave it up to his artist daughter.

Nonette's career in San Francisco had been very successful, replete with commissions from private individuals and civic organizations. She came home happily, bringing with her the unquenchable sense of fun she would always combine with the subtle aura of burning intensity, courageous fortitude, and the prophetic vision of a seeress. Gallantry moved with her diminutive figure, in the lift of her chin and the set of her slim neck, and especially in the instant flicker of response her discerning gray eyes gave to someone's need. Her hands were as ready to help as they were to sculpt. Selflessness? Rather, she carried her self in her hands and seemed always free to give herself completely, either to creative work or to human beings.

She was not to nestle her tools and clay into the new studio forever. In the spring of 1908, at twenty-nine, she married a tall, thoughtful, brilliant man of dry humor, named James S. Hennessy. He was City Superintendent of Schools and principal of the high school at Grass Valley. The famed gold town became Nonette's home for many years to come. Here she continued sculpting, although pregnancies came in quick succession. As mother of three, she exhibited a statue in the 1915 World Exposition at San Francisco. Soon after, with the birth of two babies more, she chose to put art in the corner. During her long life she would give her family the full benefit of a great creative talent. In the serenity of an alert and spiritually rich old age, my aunt, Nonette, would never be called unfulfilled.

The household in 1906, then, was comprised of Mama, Papa, June, Nonette, Elizabeth, who was home from college and teaching elementary grades, and the three "young ones," Lotus, Ximena and Bliss. Zip, the shaggy terrier, was still playing comforter and petted companion, under foot and in and out of laps. But these were not all. Lizzie May, thirteen, daughter of Al

W. May and his wife Louise, came to share and live as one of the family about that time. Her story is involved with my grandfather's interest in mineral springs discovered five miles up the Truckee River canyon on the way to Lake Tahoe. The springs were found by Al May, who detected an odd odor in the waters bubbling on his property. After a taste or two he had no doubt of their nature.

"What do you think, Mac?" How he happened to take Papa to inspect his find has been lost to us.

"Well!" Papa's eyes sparkled as he dipped the tin cup into the spring for another swig of the charged waters. "It beats Shasta water, Al." (Only Shasta water was on the market at the time.) He immediately saw the gold mine on his friend's land. "Do you know what you've got here? Why, this is alive, man! Any more tang would blow your head off."

May nodded, his blue eyes speculative but noncommital. He was a lean man of average height, who walked slightly bent from the waist like wiry men of tough sinew often do. He had come originally from the midwest and married a beautiful Indian girl, Louise, who bore him two girls about the ages of Lotus and Ximena. One day when Louise was berry-picking near Colfax with several Indian women, a hunter fired a shotgun into a clump of moving bushes without first investigating. Buckshot riddled one side of the young woman's face, blinding an eye. The hunter ran and was never identified. In due course, Louise's good eye dimmed until she was totally blind.

By this time, Al May had established himself in Truckee as salesman for a San Francisco tailoring firm. His wife and daughters, Minnie and Elizabeth (Lizzie), were well known to our family and the town.

On this day of the conversation over the mineral waters, Al spoke to the enthusiasm in Papa's brown eyes. "It would take capital to develop these springs, Mac. I just don't have that kind of money."

But Papa was already several giant leaps ahead. The upshot of the parley was a partnership, with himself manager of what they decided to call The Tahoe Mineral Springs. The location was ideal for shipping, since a narrow gauge railway ran right past it

View of the road past the house and Rocking Stone Tower leading to the first high school and on down to McIver's Dairy and the highway.

between Tahoe and Truckee. With only one competitor of stature, they both foresaw a tremendous future for a bottling works, which they were to set up without delay.

According to the first-hand witness of Ximena, who was then in high school, the history of the springs ran thus:

"Papa eventually bought the springs from Al May, who then served as manager, and the title was changed to McGlashan Mineral Spring. All flourished and McGlashan mineral water was in every saloon from Reno to Seattle. Earl came home from Stanford in 1907 and Papa wanted him to learn all about the operation. Earl went to San Francisco to learn the business and to have the water analyzed. Since he was at loose ends it seemed a happy solution for him and Papa was delighted.

"Then an iron precipitate showed in the bottles after three to six months. The rusty color spelled the end. It was unsalable. Although the high charge and the iron itself gave it a delightful taste, the entire business came to a standstill. For years, people camped near the springs just to drink the water. You can imagine the grief to Papa when he learned it could no longer be marketed after so much effort and heavy investment."

Men working at the Boca ice plant, harvesting ice from the Truckee River.

Clearly it had been to Earl that Papa's mind leaped over the first taste of the waters. He himself didn't need another involvement or even the profit. Between himself and his son, now nineteen, the chasm had been widened by Earl's apparent rebellious waste of his college years. He had quit in midstream and come home that past winter. His father didn't roar or harangue. He did worse. He signed him up at the Boca ice plant as harvest labor.

"And I want you to show my son no favors," he told the foreman. "He's to work just as hard as the rest of the men. Harder, in fact."

Soon Papa learned that because he was McGlashan's son Earl was invited in from the cold to eat lunch with ranking staff. This indulgence came to an abrupt halt thereafter. "My son is to find out what kind of work he'll do without an education," Papa said, although he probably suspected that his wrath had betrayed him into something of an exaggeration.

Mama was not long in protesting the severity of the object

194

lesson, for Earl's heart was not strong. Cutting and hauling solid ice blocks all day long was the last thing he should be doing, she let Papa know. Elizabeth, who had always been her brother's comrade on hikes and outings, sympathized with him now. June, of course, upheld Papa. The atmosphere bristled with nettling remarks and pointed silences. At the end of harvesting, Earl came home and Papa tried to warm their relationship with a hunting trip. But the hurt, mutually felt, would take long to heal. The mineral spring seemed a gift from heaven to solve their basic problem. Here was a business "whole cloth," that a young man might put himself into if he would.

Earl did—which made the failure doubly disappointing.

The two May girls had come into Papa's ken during his association with their father and he was indignant when he learned that authorities insisted on putting them in the Carson Indian School.

"Why that's no better than a trade school! Those bright girls! Why, they should have the best education possible."

Mama listened while the seed he had just planted in his own mind sprang to full growth. How well she knew him was implicit in the caution of her question: "What do you have in mind, Mac?"

"Well, now. I'll have to talk to Al and his wife, of course. But . . ." He turned to her with his most disarming charm and gently pressed her knee. "What do you say, my dear? Their mother's blind and may not want them both away. But the government might take them if we don't. What do you say? Can't we bring them here with our own girls? Send them through college, if they want to go? Oh, love, let's do it, why not? If Al and his wife agree, that is."

So the girls came and fitted into the family with ease. The older, Minnie, who was a mature fifteen and very pretty, knew she wasn't the scholar, however, that Lizzie was. The notion of what seemed interminable schooling failed to stir her to enthusiasm. Highly intelligent, she opted for honesty about her feelings, and didn't stay. Nevertheless, she always remained close to the family in spirit and heart. She is a widow now (Mrs. Peter Martini), full of wisdom and years, and one of Truckee's most respected matriarchs.

Lizzie May remained with us, taking part in the after dinner family reading or listening-to-music sessions and all phases of life in the big house. She, too, was an attractive, full-figured girl, with flashing intelligence and humor in her eyes. Her willing helpfulness endeared her to everyone and, according to her own word, she was fully a part of the family.

One of her most memorable contributions was the nature lore she passed on to us. One day when June came home from the office late for lunch, she found her lying, face-up, against the outside stone steps, staring at the sun.

"Oh, don't look at the sun, dear," June cried out, "you'll go blind!"

Lizzie glanced at her laconically; then went back to gazing straight into the sun's high noon, summer-time blaze.

"It doesn't blind you, June. People always say that, but it isn't true. I've got a headache and this takes it away."

After graduation from high school in 1909, she went to the University of California on a Bonheim scholarship.

"Now what do you mean to do for a living, Lizzie?" The inevitable question was put to her as to all of Papa's girls.

She thought it over, then chose to become an osteopath. One of her aunts was an osteopath at Leavenworth, Kansas. There, she took her own training and married another student, Dr. V. V. Manning. Together the couple practiced their profession in Leavenworth for many years. Widowed, she died there, in 1969.

"Soon after Lizzie and I went to live with the McGlashans," Minnie once told me, "a government man came looking for us. He told your grandfather we belonged in the Carson school and he meant to take us there. 'Oh? And how do you propose to do it—at gun point?' Mr. McGlashan asked. The man went away and never came back."

—•—

In 1909, the Donner Monument Committee was ready to break ground. In the presence of Dr. George F. Kelley and the Honorable Frank M. Rutherford, now a State Senator, Dr. Chapman ceremoniously handed Papa the spade to turn the first earth.

196

"Right here, General, where I've marked it. We agreed, I think, this is the exact center of the Breen cabin, and that's where I want the first ground broken."

One year later, on June 10, 1910, standing beside three of the survivors and the finished cornerstone, my grandfather gave the dedication speech. Under the huge block, twenty feet square and four feet high, Eliza Houghton and others had buried relics of the tragedy, together with a bound copy of his *History of the Donner Party*.

"My cup runneth over," he said to Mama that evening when the two of them sat alone in the rotunda.

Ever since Nonette's spring wedding two years before, joyous occasions had multiplied. Six months later, Elizabeth had married William Wiley Gilmore, the blond viking beau of her college days. Nationally known as an Olympic Club athlete and shot-put star, he had graduated from U.C. in civil engineering in 1906.

June and George (Doc) Kelley were next to marry, soon after the groundbreaking ceremony of 1909. Kelley, a dentist, guided Earl into dentistry, his true niche. To have Earl pursuing a clear-cut goal eased his father's mind infinitely.

The following May, Maqueda, twenty, a bride in powder blue, stood in the rotunda and married a young Sacramento attorney named Carl L. Shinn.

"My cup runneth over," said Papa.

He was eminently content with his new sons-in-law. Clear-eyed, straight-talking, uncomplicated Doc Kelley was the most universally liked man in town. Born in 1880 at Susanville, California where his father was a judge, he had come to Truckee in 1900. The town attracted him, especially the fishing streams and lakes so near it, and he decided to return after dental college. Returned, he joined seven lodges and gave himself to Truckee's life, both civic and social.

With a friend who worked at the Truckee Lumber Company, he launched the first gasoline-propelled boat on Donner Lake. George Gillespie, his partner in the project, was a skilled woodworker. He built the boat during the winter months while they awaited a 32-horsepower inboard motor, ordered from the east. By the time he wooed June, Doc had been president of the

197

Rod & Gun Club and had headed so many fire brigades he was made Fire Chief and then Fire Commissioner. At the time they married, he was Justice of the Peace.

Elizabeth had been Doc's first choice. After her marriage, a loss he took in stride, his fondness for the whole family prevented his looking beyond it. June was his age and single, but how would a sociable sportsman (who even played drums in the town dance band) win an introverted lady lawyer? The obvious thing was to study law himself. This he did. Thus he triumphed over two notable rivals, passed the bar exam, and was able to set up the firm of *Kelley and Kelley* after the honeymoon. He also kept his dental practice. He simply hung out a double sign and, as Assistant Deputy to his wife's Deputy District Attorney of Nevada County, continued on with his dental patients.

Maqueda's husband was the son of Albert L. Shinn, a noted attorney whose conservation bills in the state legislature served our forests well. He and Papa had long been good friends.

Snapshots of Maqueda's wedding day abound. In these Papa is shown clean-shaven for the first time. Moreover, his teeth are out, or rather, not yet in. Doc Kelley had recently persuaded him to relinquish his own teeth for full dentures. Unfortunately, these were not ready in time—a fact that he seems to think a great joke. In the photographs he laughs heartily, gums to the wind. Mama joins in, a pixie-twinkle to her smile that I was seldom to see. The quicksilver flash of her sense of fun gave way in my time to the slow smile of abiding love.

Implicit in the joy of that day was news that Nonette was pregnant for the second time. Mary Nonette, born August 8, 1909 had been the first grandchild. June's baby, due this August of 1910, would be the second. Life was bursting out everywhere. With the monument cornerstone planted like a seed, even that would be born. How good was life! *I am the Life, saith the Lord.*

"My cup runneth over," Papa said.

The following December, not a month after the family had rejoiced over Nonette's newborn son, Lotus eloped with Jackson Gregory. Since she was only in her junior year at U.C., Papa was less than happy. But he liked Gregory and took the *fait accompli* with good grace.

198

The younger daughters were elated. Jackson Gregory was the principal of their Meadow Lake High School. They knew him well and had hoped that one of their sisters would bring him into the family. Grandson of Teresa de la Guerra Hartnell, he had inherited Spanish charm and a dark, lean personableness they thought romantic. In his late twenties, as a principal and teacher he was able to combine discipline with high scholastic demands and still be popular with the students. At U.C. he had been editor of *The Blue and Gold*. He hankered to write. Often a dinner guest at our home, his gift for story-telling won him the family's heart. He and Papa enjoyed constructing plots together.

Like Doc Kelley, he had first courted Elizabeth, accepted defeat, then realized his affinity for the entire family. Lotus was one of his pupils. Sixteen and pretty, she was going to be beautiful, he saw. She had her mother's wonderful gray eyes, black-lashed, and the same perfect nose, the petal skin. In fact, her face and figure were such that one year later, when she began her freshman year at Berkeley, the dean of women summoned her into the office.

"Miss McGlashan," said the dean with a puzzled frown, "might I ask you not to wear that rose in your hair to classes? The instructors are complaining. It distracts the male students."

"Oh! Why, yes, of course . . . yes of course . . . " her hand flew to the rose tucked in the long brown curls. Blushing, Lotus drew it out and dropped it in the wastebasket beside the desk. She never knew how she made her way out. Horribly embarrassed, she thought maybe she should quit college and go home. To Papa? No, she remembered his face when Earl came home from Stanford. She must go on. But what was the matter with men, that they were so stupid over a rose!

The matter was herself. She had more than physical beauty. She had a sharp mind, a provocative wit—and yet more. She walked in a perfume of charm that, for Jackson Gregory, increased every time she came home for the holidays. He began to commute from the mountains, courting her.

Papa had built a small frame house near the Kelleys', down the hill from the Rocking Stone. This Jack and Lotus occupied after the impetuous elopement. Jack finished out his school term, then took off a year to write short westerns. Ready sales to "the pulps" led him to extend the year to a lifetime, and the stories to novels. Most of his westerns were made into moving pictures, many of which starred William S. Hart and Pauline Fredericks.

Within weeks of this latest marriage, the entire family jubilated over the birth of a son to Elizabeth and Will Gilmore. Born in Sacramento, where Will's insurance firm stationed him, David Keiser Gilmore was the fourth grandchild. Maqueda's baby would be fifth, due in mid-March.

"My cup runneth over."

Then came news of Earl's marriage to the niece of Joe Dyer, a Southern Pacific vice-president whose private railroad car was often, in friendship for Papa, put to our family's use. Henrietta Leherberger had black hair, Rapunzel-length, and a flashing dark glance. Earl married her almost immediately on the heels of graduation from dental school. President of his class, he had graduated with honors. Papa attended the ceremony and embraced him afterwards.

"I'm proud of you, son," he said. Earl heard it but made no answer. That he heard it was perhaps enough. Between the two the truce warmed, but remained, on Earl's part, a truce.

On March twelfth a wire came from Carl Shinn. Maqueda had had a baby girl. Mother and child were fine. They were in a San Francisco hospital.

My cup runneth over.

Another week and another wire told that Maqueda was no longer fine. She had high fever. (That she had had the baby in a hospital disturbed Mama from the start.)

"Oh, my God, Mac, bring her home!"

Twenty-foot snow drifts buried the roads up the hill from town. How they brought her on a stretcher from the train to the house, I do not know. I was taken to Mama's sister Laura, who still lived on the promontory of High Street.

Maqueda was two weeks in delirium. Bliss, fifteen, was the only girl at home now, for Ximena had gone below to State Normal at San Jose. My mother's moans and cries rang through the house. When Bliss came home from school she fled through the kitchen and up the back hill to sob against the granite breast of

Maqueda (Mrs. Carl L. Shinn), mother of the author.

Blunderbore. The sounds of her sister's agony were inescapable. Beyond ear-shot, memory carried them.

"Believe! Believe!" Maqueda raved in delirium. "You think you believe but you don't. If you believed, God would do anything, anything. He would even make it rain if you asked."

On April fourth, twenty-one years old, she died.

The town mourned with the family. Schools closed on the day of the funeral. Stores closed from two to four that afternoon. According to the newspaper, the Reverend Graves spoke briefly at the graveyard. The coffin was then "lowered into a grave lined with lilies, carnations and smilax."

And then, as the mourners turned silently to leave, from a clear sky in a season of snow, a little baptism of rain fell on them all.

VOL. I   APRIL, 1914   No. 8

THE BUTTERFLY FARMER

A MONTHLY MAGAZINE FOR
AMATEUR ENTOMOLOGISTS

XIMENA McGLASHAN
Publisher and Proprietor
TRUCKEE, CALIFORNIA

C. F. McGLASHAN $\left\{ \begin{array}{l} \textit{Associate Editor} \\ \textit{Business Manager} \end{array} \right.$

A Comprehensive Correspondence Course in Entomology,
Conducted Under the Auspices of The Agassiz Association,
Will Be a Leading Feature During the Present Year.

Subscription, in advance, $5 per Year.   Single copies Fifty Cents

Copyrighted 1913 by Ximena McGlashan.   All rights reserved.
Entered as Second-class matter October 25, 1913, at the Post-Office at Truckee, California.

Chapter Fifteen

1911 - 1921

My grandfather was sixty-four, Mama fifty-seven when I came into their lives, and in that time of sorrow a new baby in the house was most likely, as they termed it, "a blessed distraction." Papa hired a nurse to help with those infant requirements more distracting than blessed. But Bliss, who rushed home from high school every afternoon to spend time with me, did more than any nurse. Next to my grandparents' warm laps and comforting arms, her bouncy brown curls and mobile young face were home and security.

Around my unawareness, family history continued to unfold—events that I would later glean from table-talk as much as from the testimony of those concerned. One such event, with unexpectedly far-reaching results, occurred when Ximena came home with a teacher's diploma but small inclination to teach. Not, at least, in "some little country school" to which she was sure she'd find herself assigned.

"Well, dear, what *do* you want to do?" Her father kept his eyes on the worktable where a number of inert moths and butterflies lay waiting his inspection. With a large, round, magnifying glass in one hand he had been peering at wings, feet, and antennae for damage before pinning each insect with infinite care and exactitude to the cork lining of a box. Of all his children, Ximena had been the scientific one, the only one to ply him with questions about his butterfly hobby. Even at this moment he felt her dark eyes assessing every facet of the operation.

"Father, I just don't know. I'll have to think. I only know that teaching all grades in some little school far away from everybody . . ."

"You know, darling, you could earn a living doing this."

Her eyes widened in surprised skepticism. "I could? How?"

"If you would catch, prepare and ship butterflies and moths to Dr. William Barnes, a dealer in Illinois, you could make more money than you ever could teaching." He put down his forceps and glass and looked directly at her. "Would you like me to prove it?"

"Would I! I'd like nothing better!"

Thus began a fruitful father-daughter collaboration that resulted in what entomologists today affirm was one of the first and certainly the best butterfly farm of its time in this country.

Public interest in the farm was phenomenal. Syndicated press stories featured Ximena as "the butterfly princess" (for her name means princess). These were translated by foreign newspapers and periodicals around the world. In a day when women seldom ventured into professional fields other than teaching or nursing, a nineteen-year-old girl who made a living off "bugs" was news. When she confided to reporters that she planned to return to college on her savings for a degree in entomology, her encouragement to other young women brought a snowy storm of grateful letters. Many fans became her students, whom she taught by circular letters soon replaced by a well-organized course.

In September, 1913, the partners published "The Butterfly Farmer," an attractive, lively little magazine that carried a twelve-month entomology course for the layman. Published under the cordial auspices of the Agassiz Society, this correspondence course excited the interest of every entomologist, many of whom contributed information to its pages. The warm personal style invited a stream of mail that poured in from nature lovers, dealers, or casual readers, in addition to regular mail from hundreds of enrollees. "How to" information abounded for the would-be farmer. How to breed and preserve specimens and, most important, *where* to market them were pressing questions in beginners' minds. Along with answers to such needs, the course gave its students a thorough foundation in the science, presented in clear language and with a contagious enthusiasm.

Many people, some famous in their own fields, climbed the hill from the depot to pass time between trains. For nearly twenty

C. F. McGlashan and daughter, Ximena, the Butterfly Princess, circa 1912.

years the Rocking Stone Tower had been the main attraction. Now there was the butterfly farm with its glass jars and covered cages, busy with tiny, moist, winged or crawly creatures. Gene Stratton Porter, whose novels were doing much to quicken public interst in nature's wonders, spent time in Truckee, much of it with Ximena. She came to the mountain town in the interests of the projected movie version of her novel, *Girl of the Limberlost*. She frequently said that Ximena was the inspiration for the film's heroine.

Meanwhile, Papa was enjoying the unprecedented chance to share his knowledge and joy in the subject so dear to his heart. Universal interest had mushroomed where little or none had existed before. Although this was due in part to the novelty of Ximena's role in the enterprise, serious and active interest in the science can only be explained by timing. Hundreds of people were ready for either just such a hobby, or for the remunerative aspect of butterfly farming—a decidedly uncrowded field.

The last of the twelve issues of *The Butterfly Farmer* appeared in August, 1914. This heralded Ximena's enrollment at the Univer-

Below: An unidentified visitor studies C. F. McGlashan's butterfly collection on display in Nevada County Courthouse. The cases were invented and patented by McGlashan in 1886. Right: Detail of the display. Although a few of the 20,000 specimens have deteriorated, they are remarkably well preserved after more than 90 years.

sity of California. A year later she transferred to Stanford, where David Starr Jordan, then president, personally guided her studies. Soon after graduation in 1916, she married John Cary Howard, son of a prominent Oakland attorney. Although she now had her degree in entomology, fame and a career for the taking, she chose the career of an army wife. Jack Howard had planned to join his father's law firm on graduation, but World War I changed his life. Selected by the University of California with one other honor graduate to take officer's training, he entered the regular army, which he made his career. For many years he was Commandant of the U.C. Military Department, until his death in 1952 at Berkeley.

The butterfly farm closed down after Ximena left for college, but even if the partnership had remained in full strength, public attention was turning to life and death matters. By 1916 the war in Europe was purpling the skies of our own future. Americans were uneasy, if not deeply disturbed.

Despite political assurances that we would stay out, Papa did not believe we could stay out of war. As early as 1884 he had said in a Fourth of July speech:

"America has more to do than to develop her own magnificent resources if she fulfills her legitimate destiny. She has a world-work to perform. She has to achieve the practical unity of the human race. The slender conduits of a flower or leaf, the finest nerves in an insect's eye, all are regulated by unerring laws. Surely, then, the career of a great nation like America is not without its appointed orbit."

Even while he bandied dinner-table politics with his sons-in-law, predicting that "the next war will be fought in the air" and other progressions, privately his interest was captivated by cosmic implications of a world embroilment. Scriptural prophecy drew him with compelling attraction to his daily Bible study. This had become a very private delight, like a secret cave or hidden treasure. He rarely mentioned it and never imposed his beliefs on others, although he would come out loud and clear and publicly with his "Gawd be with you" or "Thanks to the good Lord for" everything from health to all varieties of weather. I particularly noted this habit as I grew into the self-conscious

207

teens, for by then the "dusty answers" of the 1920s were fashionable. Faith, hope, and God were not.

With Mama he had full and open communication in the realm of their Christian faith and they were to need all its resources before the decade closed. Papa had already sustained the deaths of all his sisters but Martinette Kinsell. Mama alone therefore took the personal losses yet to come, first in the death of her sister Laura, followed by Ella's death in 1919.

Together, however, they bore a loss nothing could have prepared them for when Earl died.

Pneumonia, following the 1918 influenza, was more than his heart could stand. He died December 4, 1919 at his home in San Francisco where he had established his dental practice. He left Henrietta with two small children, Robert Charles, four, and Elizabeth, not yet two.

For Mama his death was one of the fathomless sorrows that turned her to stone, tearless and deathly calm. Papa's grieving may well have been tortured with regrets. He had reached San Francisco too late to see Earl alive. There was no moment together to convey "I'm sorry, son" by word or look. Every year since his marriage, Earl had hunted bear and deer with his father. Reconciliation had taken place, surface-wise, long ago. But there is reason to doubt that they could, either one, wholly forget the past. Both had tried. Earl had named the first baby for his father—Charles Fayette McGlashan.

"No, please, Earl, don't give him that name!" Papa had said when he heard of it. "Not that name, Earl, I beg of you."

"Sorry, Pa, it's time we buried that old superstition. I want him named for you and that's the way it's going to be."

Henrietta too had begged him. "I can't help it, Earl, I don't care if he *is* the healthiest baby in the world. I'm afraid. Your brother Fayette was healthy too—but he died!"

"Poppycock!" Earl laughed away everyone's superstitious fears. Beautiful, bright, physically perfect and well, the baby died of pneumonia, three months old. Earl had grieved for his son. Henrietta would waken in the night and find him standing in the corner where the crib had been, crying. Although this personal tragedy drew them closer, father and son still found it hard to communicate fully. Earl was thirty-two when he died, and throughout his life he continued to kiss his father when they met after an absence.

My grandfather was seventy-two in 1919. Straight-backed and vigorous in his stride, he never considered retiring from his law practice, but left for the office each morning at the same time I left for school. However, this was the year his health began to suffer the invasion of infection to kidneys and bladder. Earl's death took its own toll, and for the first time he discovered with cruel suddenness that to a stranger he might look not aging but actually old. I was with him when this happened.

Six months after my uncle's death, Mama and I accompanied Papa on a business trip to the city. We stayed, as usual, at the Golden West, an unpretentious but good downtown hotel near our favorite restaurant. Flu masks were no longer required, I remember, for Mama observed aloud that the waitresses looked different unmasked. True. Our favorite with the beautiful eyes now revealed a mustache.

One evening Mama said:

"I think I'll rest and read tonight, Mac. You two go out for dinner. Bring me back some fresh fruit if you want."

Assured that she felt tired, not ill, Papa agreed and we left. We must have chosen a new restaurant, because we took a streetcar. On the ride home, darkness had fallen. The car was crowded with people. Papa steered me through the jammed aisle to the only vacant seat, put me in it, and hooked his fingers cheerfully through the strap above my head. I sat on the aisle side and held his free hand.

Suddenly a young woman rose from beside me.

"Sir, take my seat."

Aware that she spoke to him, he smiled attentively, but obviously didn't grasp the intention of her words.

"I beg your pardon?"

"Take my place, sir, here."

"Oh, no no no no . . . " he spluttered, but the girl had stepped smoothly into the crowd; there was nothing for it but to sit down. I couldn't look at him. I felt rather than saw the white head, always held so high, now lowered almost to the level of my own. I understood the hunched shoulders. I slipped my eight-year old hand into his dry warm one and we sat hurting together to the end of the ride.

"Mac! What's happened?" Mama said the instant we walked in the hotel room. He tossed his black felt hat on the lamp table and kissed her.

"A girl offered me her seat on the streetcar. Gave *me* her seat, Nona—a young woman! Do I look so...Can it be I look so...Darling, am I...are we...?"

She watched his face intently and within her own a strange glow, like a heart-smile, began to dawn. Before he could say the hated word, she sang in a voice still fairly true: "Darling, we are growing old, silver threads among the gold..."

She didn't sing much more than that, for he looked into the look she had for him and they smiled at each other. I think this began the most wonderful part of their marriage. His last partnership was to be with her, beginning that moment when she introduced him to old age, and gave it the coquetry of an invitation to the waltz.

—•—

Thus, as the second decade with its terrible war drew to a close, sorrows walked side by side with joys in our family. Not only were births celebrated frequently—Papa once walked down the hill flanked on either side by three very pregnant daughters—but on June 6, 1918 the Donner monument was finally unveiled.

Instead of reconstructing the jubilation of that longed-for day from the standpoint of my grandfather, I give the words of Eliza Donner Houghton in a letter to her niece, written within two weeks of the event:

We reached Truckee at eight-thirty P.M., June fourth. We were met by Dr. Chapman and a delegation from Donner Parlor 162, who escorted us to the Sierra Tavern, which was headquarters for all officials of the NSGW and NDGW...Clara [her daughter] and I were delightfully settled in a pretty, cozy, sweet looking room, newly furnished and conveniently located—and Ida [Ida Babcock represented Eliza's sister Georgia] at a private home near by. We had dined on the train and after a little brushing up I descended to the parlor where I was surprised to find many officials and their wives waiting to meet and welcome "Captain George Donner's youngest daughter." I should have mentioned that as I reached the lowest step a smiling man asked, "Are you Mrs. Donner? I am John App. Rebecca is here." She knew me at once. She was neatly dressed in black and very happy to have a place in line of reception which continued until eleven o'clock . . .

At ten o'clock on the morrow, Clara, Ida, and I were taken out to get our first view of the monument. Near the monument I met DeRome, who supervised the casting of the bronze figures. He had been associated in business with his father years before the latter signed the contract for the bronze work of the Donner monument. The father died soon after, and the son, embued with his father's love and interest in the work, assumed the responsibility, put his heart and soul in the great undertaking and produced the memorial . . . .

I was up at 5:30 on dedication morning to see the sunrise, to feel the wonderful throb of stirring events that already were marking the . . . day. There, under the same roof with me were the Governor of California, the Governor of Nevada, officers and wives of the Native Sons of the Golden West, the President of the University of California.

Of the dedication, Eliza says:

I wish that you could see that sacred spot as it appeared when our little party reached the old campground. There loomed the veiled monument, the Bear flag and the Stars and Stripes . . . the school children stood in line amid a large concourse of people from surrounding counties. A gentle breeze murmured through the pine trees and fanned the heat waves from the waiting crowds with the clicking cameras.

I took the place assigned me at the right of the speaker's table and the end of the row of survivors and descendants. My thoughts wandered. I was a child again on the spot where mother had entrusted us to the care of God and given her three helpless little ones to be saved by the Relief. There she had kissed them goodbye and hastened away to their father's side. I saw her small figure move unfaltering over the spot through those pine trees among which we now sat and I could know, as a woman and mother, how her heart ached . . . Then the sound of the gavel and the ringing voice of the Grand President of the NSGW brought me back to reality. " . . . Donner monument, I dedicate you to the memory of the party whose name you bear and the memory of all overland pioneers to California." Two little girls in white had drawn the cords and the veil dropped, and all eyes were fixed upon the magnificent memorial. Tears were in many eyes as the throng bared their heads in spellbound reverence...A thrill of thanksgiving ran through my being, for I had really lived to see and participate in the dedication of the Donner Monument."

Eliza was in her mid-seventies at this time.

Two years later, on the last Friday in May, when the snow still lingered on Sierra hillsides, Chapman dropped into my grand-father's office casually and without an appointment. Wholly off-guard and sincerely pleased to see the man who had brought the monument through to achievement, Papa gave him a cigar and sat back to enjoy a friendly chat.

But Dr. Chapman had something on his mind. He quickly came out with it. The inscription in bronze letters on the base of the monument, he said, must be changed.

Still not too concerned, Papa said, "Ah? How so? What must be changed?"

"The first word ON—where it says ON THIS SPOT..." he took from the side pocket of his long coat a sheet of folded paper with a typed copy of the inscription. "See, Mac, it says here 'On this spot stood the Breen cabin'... Well, that has to be changed to *Near* this Spot..."

Now he had drawn blood. Papa put down his cigar very carefully and his voice was soft, a danger signal if Chapman had known it.

"What do you mean it has to be changed to Near this Spot?"

"Well, naturally it has to be changed because it isn't true."

"Who told you, sir, that it isn't true?"

"Why, you did, Mac. You said it was...uh, well, some thirty or so feet from there."

"*I*? *I* said *that*?" his voice was still quiet but his inflection was picking up a razor thin edge. "When in God's name did I ever say anything BUT THAT to my certain knowledge, corroborated by the Breen family and other survivors, the monument stands ON THE VERY SPOT of the Breen cabin? When, sir? I ask you to tell me, for I seriously think you have gone mad."

Chapman had hold of a bone and was not letting it go.

"Meet me at the foot of the lake, Mac, and I'll show you what you told me eleven years ago, when we laid the cornerstone. You pointed out a place several feet beyond—I'll show you where.

And I say we should bring shovels and see if we don't turn up bricks from the Breen fireplace."

It was no use to say that all that had been done years ago, that yes, the fireplace had been found ON the spot where the monument now stood. No use to say that he, Chapman, had heard McGlashan state publicly at the cornerstone dedication and again at the monument ceremony that THIS was the Breen cabin site, preserved down the decades for the monument site. Papa promised to meet him and they set the day and the time.

On that day he rose in a dawn of stinging cold and set out on foot. He strode briskly, his white silk kerchief drawn masklike over his nose to blunt the icy knives his lungs drew in. He needed the solitary hours before Chapman came. He wanted time to ponder the strange belatedness of the man's challenge. Surely he would admit his mistake after this morning's last-ditch conference. Or would he?

Arrived at the lake he gazed upward at the burnished figures of the pioneer family atop the cobbled stone pedestal. He reached out one hand and lightly caressed the base. Chapman and John McQuarrie, the sculptor, had conferred with him and with Nonette on every phase of the model, as well as on the story told in bronze relief around the high base.

"ON THIS SPOT . . ." Why, he thought, that one word ON makes all the difference between champagne and water. That decisive, confident, bold, two-letter word gathers up the memorial's whole meaning and shoots it like an arrow straight into the heart of the Donner tragedy.

But wait—what about the concession he'd made on the change in the name? It was dedicated as the Pioneer Monument, not the Donner Monument.

"Look, Mac, if we're to get a funding bill through we may have to present it with a broader purpose. Why not a memorial to all pioneers who came west the overland trail? What do you say?"

He'd said he didn't like it. The idea had always been to erect a monument to the Donner party.

"I know. But look, Mac, we'll get faster results if we broaden out."

Faster? He'd waited nearly forty years already. But he had given in finally. Fool that I am, he thought, and here I've gone on thinking of it as the Donner monument. He saw now how the name change shifted the emphasis. It robbed the Breen site of significance. Only a Donner memorial needed that special spot for dramatic poignance. Suddenly he knew with unwelcome and blinding certainty that Chapman would never back down.

Chapman arrived for the rendezvous at eleven, accompanied by two Truckee men, T. C. Wohlbruck and John Cabona, for witnesses. On a little tablet, Papa had written in pencil and in duplicate the following:

Memorandum: (Donner Monument, May 29, 1920)

Dr. C. W. Chapman and C. F. McGlashan are, and have been for many years, staunch friends.

Yesterday, May 28, 1920, Dr. Chapman first told McGlashan that the site of the Breen Cabin is thirty (30) feet from the foundation of the Monument.

McGlashan is positive the base of the monument is directly over the site of the Breen cabin.

By amicable agreement they will today excavate the site pointed out by Dr. Chapman to ascertain if evidence can be found to support Dr. Chapman's contention.

C. F. McGlashan

Signed in duplicate in the presence of _____

Chapman read the memorandum.

"Yes, I'll sign this, but it should be changed to read 'the spot is the one pointed out by you to me.'" Without waiting for further discussion, he and Wohlbruck walked to a spot some yards distant and began digging.

According to my grandfather's report to the NSGW, the two men quickly turned up four burned and blackened "carefully matched stones, fairly flat and level" and a score of smaller stones, a handful of charcoal and several bits of rotten wood. All these Papa placed in or around his silk kerchief. Chapman was sure this was the Breen-Schallenberger fireplace.

While I knew this was not true, I realized that Dr. Chapman and Wohlbruck were thoroughly convinced and no argument would undeceive them ... The stones indicated to me a campfire but nothing

214

Right: Dedication of Pioneer Monument at Donner Lake, June 6, 1918. From left are: Governor E. D. Boyle of Nevada, Martha J. Reed Lewis, Eliza P. Donner Houghton, Frances E. Donner Wilder, and Governor W. D. Stephens of California. Below: Loading a portion of the monument on a boxcar for transport to Truckee. This figure was approximately sixteen feet tall when completely assembled.

resembling a hearth to a fireplace ... There was a brick kiln and brickyard just west of Truckee, about a mile and half east from the Monument in the years from 1868 to 1873. Sisson, Wallace & Company erected a brick building in Truckee during the days when the Central Pacific Railroad was being constructed; and many chimneys and other buildings were built with these bricks. Old discarded brick from this yard ... were often used by fishermen and others in their campfires. It must be remembered too that just across the road from the Monument, during those days of railroad building, there were several dwellings and a store, and on Donner Creek about a hundred yards west of the Murphy cabin was a saw mill owned by Towle Brothers. Bricks were found in abundance in the ruins of these old buildings in those early pioneer days following the completion of the road when I first came to Truckee.

While they were examining Chapman's findings, Surveyor E. C. Uren and Chapman's two sons arrived. One of the Chapman boys looked at a brick and immediately said he had seen other bricks like it "around here." Going to an old campfire site fifty yards away he brought back five more bricks of identical appearance.

Once more, before they parted, my grandfather reviewed for Chapman the long story of his guardianship, but in spite of his efforts, Chapman conceded not an inch.

Heartsick and alarmed, my grandfather clung to the hope that the Native Sons of the Golden West would not agree to the change. Arrived home, he found a letter from J. R. Knowland, chairman of the NSGW Historic Landmarks Committee.

Papa wrote an answer in full detail, even to the meeting with Chapman at the lake that same week. He described the site as he first saw it in 1879:

In 1879 the site was marked by the stump, the excavated floor, and by the fireplace ... The ashes were sifted, but the burned earth and foundation of the fireplace stood undisturbed and formed a blackened landmark liberally covered and surrounded by bits of broken, charred remnants of charcoal by which I mean the small black coals left from a wood fire. The excavated space showed the size of the cabin, and with the stump and fireplace as markers anyone could find the site of the Breen Cabin from 1879 until 1910.

216

To the letter he applied every plus of his legal and journalistic experience to convince with facts and to convey persuasively his heartfelt concern that the Donner monument rise on the square of ground so central to the Donner party's tale. It was a long letter, including even a recapitulation of all the public occasions on which he had unequivocally stated "this is the spot where the Breen cabin stood." He pointed out that on several occasions Dr. Chapman stood nearby and heard every word. Not until May 28, 1920 had he ever challenged it.

The letter was strong, its facts were strong. The Native Sons printed it, as was customary, in a pamphlet to be circulated among the members of all parlors before the issue came up for vote. There can be little doubt that everyone believed my grandfather's statement. The majority had always accepted without a flicker of questioning the location he gave for the Breen site.

But the change was made. So it reads today: NEAR this spot . . . Did the change of one word seem inconsequential? That could be. Because Dr. Chapman had no argument other than his own statement that my grandfather had told him, eleven years before, something different.

Papa never visited the monument after that. He never spoke of the matter in my hearing. But he no longer took our guests to the monument. To him, that word NEAR made all the difference.

"Mac" and Nona at Donner Lake campground, near road he cleared of rocks for exercise.

218

Chapter Sixteen

"The last of life for which the first was made."—Robert Browning

Although he was not a Christian Scientist, Papa quietly refused medical help during his prolonged illness. He had been exposed to Christian Science by his sister Laura who, in middle age, had begun to be a sick-a-bed lady, perennially ailing. One day, in desperation, she reached under her bed and brought up Mary Baker Eddy's book which she had flung down without reading two weeks earlier. On opening it, she found the pages radiantly meaningful. When her brother next saw her, Laura met him at the door, once more a vital active woman. Impressed, he read the literature she gave him and liked its stress on positive thinking. This he put into practice by suppressing all thoughts and spoken words of complaint. He did not deny, however, the reality of his illness.

He turned increasingly to faith, prayer, and meditation on the Scriptures, but he did not appear to seek a miraculous healing. He often mused aloud, quoting: "Verily, I say unto you, that whosoever shall say to this mountain, Be thou removed and be thou cast into the sea; and shall not doubt in his heart but shall believe that those things which he saith shall come to pass, he shall have whatsoever he saith." The problem of perfect trust was to become a passion with him. Yet, as far as possible, he tried to help himself by natural means. Foremost of these means was physical work in the outdoor air and sunshine.

We were a family that loved the earth and needed it—not as farmers, for ours had not been a vocational approach to the soil. We loved it in the manner of American Indians.

"I can't wait for summer," June or Elizabeth or Mama would say. "I crave the feel of earth on my bare feet. I need to sit by a rock or tree and absorb the sun and earth for hours."

Each family had its chosen lot on the eighty-acre tract at Donner Lake. Mama and I had ours. Every summer until 1926, when she was 72 and I, fifteen, we camped there. Two sparkling creeks babbled down the mountain at some distance on either side of us. The other campsites lay along these streams; therefore Mama was centrally located and accessible to her girls. Papa set up a platformed tent for her, a cot under the stars for me, an outdoor kitchen among the firs, and a woodburning stove. Alone and unaided, he cleared the boulders from the hill above us and laid a pipe that brought water to our kitchen.

He then returned to Truckee and his law business, but whenever he could steal time from work during the week he hired a driver and car to bring him to the lake. The car stopped at our barbed wire gate while he swung down from the high seat above the running board and gave out his Indian war whoop. This was a staccato Ah-Ah-Ah-Ah-Ah that he made by patting his lips on a sustained falsetto "Aaaah." Hearing it, my cousins and I raced from the water in our swim suits to spatter him with wet hugs and kisses. On such weekday visits he wore a flat-topped straw hat but his oldest shoes and trousers, for he carried a pick and shovel. Around the neck of his collarless shirt he wore one of his 30-inch square kerchiefs.

"I'm building a road to the right of your mother's camp, up the hill," he would say when asked about the pick and shovel. We all knew that if he really wanted a road he would hire a man and equipment to build it in short order. Instead, single-handed, he tackled the large boulders that obstructed his path until sweat trickled down his face. Summer after summer, until he was seventy-nine, he used his road-building for sun, air and exercise.

On Sundays, he spent all his time with Mama. Before the day ended, the daughters and their families gathered informally at our camp. Dressed in camp attire or sweaters over bathing suits, everyone sprawled or sat on the ground in a convivial circle, the center of which was "the General" and his lady. They, too, sat on the warm earth with a rock for backrest.

220

We children gradually stopped our play to slip into the group and listen to the grownups talk. For this we engaged our peculiar radar system, lifting our antennae to the silent unseen, the *felt* only, the *guessed-at*, which somehow became surer knowledge than all that reached us through the noise of words. We appeared to occupy ourselves with the gritty, beige-gray earth that churned between our toes with the industry of ants. But without exception we were Grandpa watchers. And Grandma watchers as well. For us they moved and spoke and had their being in a magnetic nimbus, an intensification of ordinary light, that riveted our attention in unforgettable fascination. Not one of us could then, or since, have explained why this was so. At the fore of our knowledge was the position of our grandfather in this circle. As years moved on and we grew taller with the strength of youth, we would see the toll of age and sickness in his face. We would see the shortened stature. But still the piercing eyes would command; still his presence would be the key-piece that joined the families in unity, just as Mama's was the grout-like cushion that smoothed the human mosaic, holding the pieces firm in this union.

No day of summer passed without a visit from one or several of Mama's daughters. She was the confidante, the wise woman who spoke little but emanated sympathetic understanding. She never repeated confidences. Sons-in-law loved and appreciated her more and more as the years revealed her refusal to take sides in a quarrel. Wives who stalked wrathfully down the slippery pine-needled hill "to mother" with lamentations, returned silent and thoughtful.

"The General is all very fine," the men would say, "But your mother—there's a real woman."

It wasn't just her prudent wisdom they loved. The young sons-in-law inspired her to amuse. When "the girls" were together, they knew each other's thoughts so well that the conversational ball bounced from one to another without a single sentence finished. But the husbands watched Mama for the moment when she would clear her throat and mildly offer, "I'll tell you an anecdote." Then Jack or Doc or George or Will would grab the ball and hand it to her with a loud "Let your mother talk!" There

221

could be no doubt where their interest lay. Her anecdotes were always on target to the topic under fire and, if never risqué, had juice and spice enough to delight the young men. "Just a dash of purple," was the way she termed it.

Her motto was "Least said, soonest mended." To the end of her life she never ceased to be watchful of her tongue. When she spoke therefore, we all knew that it behooved us to listen.

—•—

Until I went below in my turn to high school and then to college, I shared my grandparent's life all the more intimately for being the only child left in the house. The Kelleys moved to San Francisco in 1919. Bliss, a war-time bride, had married and moved away in 1918. During the long white winters, our small unit of three (and Brownie) was especially close-knit.

Heavy snowstorms often jailed us in the house for days at a stretch. Schools closed, stores kept short hours, the doctor and dentist cancelled appointments, and Papa stayed home from the office. Housebound children stared through snow-plashed panes at a gray, hypnotic swirl of endlessly falling particles that inexorably buried the town. Such days could be unbearably restrictive for a child. But I was lucky. Papa knew exactly what to do with

> . . . . . interminable afternoons
> When the slow, thick, feather-float
> Muffles to silence the vari-keyed tunes
> Of a railroad town and the train whistle swoons,
> Stifled in Truckee's throat.

First, he hefted a freshly cut wedge of red-barked pine into the stove's deep craw, jolting the indolent flames to a fierce roar. Then he went to the parlor, unlocked the hinged glass door of a tall bookcase, and selected a novel for us to read aloud. Mama and I drew our chairs close to his beside the stove, now red-hot. Then, with Brownie dozing at Papa's feet, we dove like Alice down the rabbit hole, into the carnival world of imagination.

He introduced me to this world at the age of six with *Lallah Rookh*, Moore's narrative poem of the queen for whom the Taj

222

McGlashan house in the snow.

Above: Rear entrance of Rexall Drug Store in Truckee. Below: Front Street, waist deep in snow.

A Truckee winter means shoveling snow—off the roof!

The 1917 McGlashan family reunion, held at Gilmore's home in Berkeley. Back row: Jackson Gregory Sr., Lotus Gregory, Elizabeth Gilmore, Wm. W. Gilmore, June Kelley, Dr. George F. Kelley, Bliss Isabel McGlashan, Undine Raymond, Dr. Earl L. McGlashan, Robert C. McGlashan, Ximena Howard, John C. Howard. Second row: Nonette Hennessy, James S. Hennessy Sr., Henrietta (Mrs. E. L.) McGlashan, Baby Elizabeth McGlashan, Ella Keiser Greenleaf, Leonora G. Keiser McGlashan, Charles Fayette McGlashan, Martinette (Nettie) Kinsell, Nonette (Mrs. J. S.) Hennessy, June Hennessy. Front row: Jackson Gregory Jr., Douglas M. Kelley, George M. Kelley, Naida Gilmore, Natalie Raymond, David Gilmore, Nona McGlashan, James S. Hennessy Jr., Albert Raymond, John V. Hennessy.

224

Mahal was built. *The Arabian Nights* followed logically, and I was ready at seven for Dumas' *Count of Monte Cristo* and Stevenson's *Treasure Island*. Lest I become addicted to exotic romance, a year later he started me on our shelf of Charles Dickens, which we had read straight through by the time I was ten. His favorite of these was *David Copperfield*, I later learned; for he compared David's two marriages to his own. Mama, of course, was the Agnes of his personal story. For mystery and adventure we interspersed novels by James Fenimore Cooper, Joseph Conrad, Jack London, Sir Rider Haggard or Conan Doyle, all among his favorites.

Patiently, he made sure I understood every word. He explained words whose meaning lay beyond my wildest surmise until I learned to use the well-thumbed Webster's. He and I took turns reading, and though he was patient with my vocabulary, with my reading voice he was not.

"Read that again, Maqueda, the whole sentence. And give it some expression. Don't swallow your words. E-nun-ci-ate!"

How many times I had heard the story of his own training in reading aloud. His blind father, Peter, would have no one but Fayette read to him and, with a musician's ear made doubly acute by the loss of sight, Peter could not tolerate an artificial "reading" tone.

"Hard as it was on me—and I, just a boy in those days—my father's constant correction helped me in my later life. It put me ahead of my rhetoric class at Williston, and served me well in all the years of public speaking."

So Papa always ended the story, but it gave me small comfort. I didn't intend to do any public speaking.

Mama didn't read, but listened with her hands quiet in her lap. I knew she would gladly have busied those talented hands during the long reading sessions, for we read all day, with breaks only for meals or to stretch our legs. But Papa had long ago legislated against "fancy work." "I will not read or talk to the top of a head," he said. The womanly arts of knitting and crocheting had no encouragement in our house.

Papa gave each novel total response. Death scenes and partings between loved ones brought out the kerchief for nose-blowing and unabashed tears. I could not follow him to his heights and depths of involvement from my low plateau of experience. But thus he pointed the way and encouraged my imagination to follow.

These days held but one dark hour for me, the hour he helped me with arithmetic. In this area he was the stern teacher, inclined to be abrupt and irritable with my dim grasp of the subject, which only increased my "block" against numbers. For, although he had gentled over the years since my mother's death, Papa was ever a strict disciplinarian. His sternness over our arithmetic lesson never failed to conjure up the memory of my fourth birthday, when I had found a drum among my gifts. I began to beat the drum at a time when Papa and Mama were chatting quietly in the rotunda after lunch.

"Maqueda, stop beating that drum," Papa said.

I gave it a tentative tap.

"Come, come now, Maqueda, I told you to stop that noise. If you beat that drum once more I'll . . . I'll put it in the stove."

I gave it one more tentative tap.

Without another word, he gently took the drum strap off my shoulder and the drumsticks from my fingers, lifted the lid from the stove, and dropped all in the fire.

In 1923, the enchanted circle he drew around our winter solitude ended. Heart pains had troubled Mama for several months and Dr. Joseph Bernard, successor to the town's line of beloved family doctors, advised a lower altitude. "At least during the cold months," he said. Thus, she and I spent a winter at Auburn where Lotus and Jackson Gregory had a spacious, brown-shingled home overlooking the American River Canyon. The following year I entered high school and we went to Elk Grove, California where Bliss was teaching in the high school. But the third year, 1925, Mama put her foot down.

"I will not leave you for another day, Mac, let alone another winter. Let Nonie stay with Bliss at Elk Grove. The child's fourteen and needs an active young woman like Bliss."

Papa did not argue. The two long winters, alone with Brownie, had been enough of restaurant meals and solitude.

Bliss, only fifteen years my senior, was like a young mother as well as an older sister in my life, although she had two small girls

Bliss (Mrs. G. H. Hinkle), principal of Tahoe High School.

of her own. Of all my gifted aunts, I have always believed that Bliss, with her lightning-swift perceptions, was the most brilliant. Her greatest gift, however, was an ability to comprehend the adolescent heart and mind. Sympathetic but never soft, she could pinion me or my peers on a shaft of induced self-knowledge. Wounding, if need be, to heal, she still won our undying affection. She was that much-needed friend in an adolescent's confusion, a friend whose influence followed many of her pupils into their adult years.

227

Two days after the dedication of the Donner monument, she eloped with George Henry Hinkle, PhD., like herself a native of Truckee. These two talented educators were to spend their short lives teaching, he on a college level, she as principal of the Tahoe City High School. Just before her death at fifty-three of cancer, they co-authored *Sierra Nevada Lakes*, a scholarly but entertaining book on the history and lore of their native region. (It is one of the American Lakes Series, published by Bobbs Merrill.) George's death, of heart disease, followed hers a year later, in 1950. Ten years before, in 1940, George and Bliss had edited a Stanford University Press printing of the McGlashan *History of the Donner Party.*

Throughout high school and on into college, I went home once a month for a weekend, and always for holidays and summer vacations. During these visits, I soon noticed that my grand-parents were simplifying the externals of their daily life and turning ever more deeply to faith and prayer. They never exhorted or preached. But I sensed the inaudible thunder of their faith—a subterranean river that coursed beneath all they said and did.

For one thing, they were developing a life-style which I could either join or not, as I wished. For the most part I did not. This did not bother them. They had, in wisdom, toppled me early from a nest they might not live to guard until I grew up. I began to realize gradually what they had known all along and this was that our roads were to diverge radically.

On our long-ago evening walks to the McIver barns, Papa had loved to raise his baritone in song: "O ye'll tak the high road and I'll tak the low road, And I'll be in Scotland af-o-o-o-ore ye..."

I now knew they would be in Scotland "afore" me. They, who had been part of my heartbeat, were moving away from me, and Brownie with them. Brownie was Papa's shadow down the hill to the office, in deep snow or summer dust; at home, he sought Papa's feet, not mine. They were all departing on a mysterious journey where I could not follow. Not yet. I had my own adventure to confront. Verbal communication between us all but ceased as adolescent taciturnity took over my speech. This they accepted without comment. Steadfastly, they gave loving example. And all unconsciously, as I had in early childhood, I made them the object of my profound attention. I watched, I listened, but I did not analyze.

I saw that they lived by rules that governed their conversation as well as their routine. Gossip was off limits between them. So were complaints. Aches or pains and sleepless nights—I never heard these mentioned. There was a third prohibition—the past. One might refer lightly to a shared memory, especially a humorous one, but they didn't dwell on it long. When the dinner table was enlarged to seat our summer flurry of visiting relatives, they would let themselves be pressured into telling an anecdote or two, not more. Always my grandfather took the lead in circumventing conversation that would point backward. He was adept at drawing out each son-in-law by unfeigned and earnest interest in whatever concerned the young man. And of the present and future, he would talk at any length.

"I guarantee that you or your children will see a man put on the moon," he said the summer of my 18th year. He was then 82. No one at table believed him, of course. Why would anyone want to put a man on the moon?

Mama had her own preposterous prophecy. "I believe women will one day wear trousers—like Chinese women."

"Oh, mother! Trousers? You mean pajamas?" Lounging pajamas had just come in. Girls wore knickers, of course, for sports and hiking.

"I mean pants, like men, only in pretty materials and colors. Feminine fabrics and bright colors would make all the difference. And I think it would be a very sensible mode of dress." The term "slacks" had not been heard extensively, if indeed it had yet been coined.

Health foods, as we know them today with their stress on vitamins, were just beginning to be taken seriously in the late 1920s. Papa immediately investigated the stores down below that carried raw sugar, whole wheat breads, and vitamins, pronounced with a short "i." I came home on holidays to find all manner of such foods on the table, with Fleischmann's yeast cakes and semi-cooked vegetables "to preserve the vitamins." In the

229

back yard he started a vegetable garden that put radishes and fresh lettuce and green beans on our table. Sometimes I found we were having a spell of one food only—corn meal mush is the one I recall vividly—for breakfast, lunch and dinner.

I knew why Papa seized upon this new science of nutrition. His red-rimmed eyes and the puffy flesh beneath them told me of pain-ridden nights, and day-hours, too, of excruciating discomfort. Were pain and illness the testing ground of his faith, I wondered? For he still refused to see a doctor. For Mama he called in Dr. Bernard at once. But for himself, no.

Along with exercise and health foods there was another kind of help he accepted. This was proffered by his son-in-law, Jackson Gregory, with consummate tact and delicacy. When sub-zero temperatures were prolonged in Truckee, we often spent a week or more with the Gregorys at Auburn, in the foothills. Jack put aside the novel he was working on and brought out the chessboard. From dawn until late evening the two men huddled over their games. They played the slow game, with hour-long contemplation between moves. Then, "Checkmate!" one or the other announced, and "the General's" delighted shout told of surcease from pain.

To stretch their legs, they strolled together under the loquat trees by the swimming pool and discussed their favorite shared interest—plots. Jack's westerns were selling very well, particularly in the British market. Reviewers called him "the Zane Grey of England." By the 1920s nearly all of his books had been filmed in this country. Of all my grandfather's sons-in-law, Jack Gregory was the closest to his heart.

When I went away to school, my grandparents continued to read together. Over breakfast, they talked quietly, then Papa read a Psalm or chapter from the New Testament. Sometimes he read a page from *Daily Word*, a Unity publication that Mama favored. Then he lit up a cigar, leaned back, and glowed while the two of them shared their reflections on the reading. Whatever the night-hours had brought him of their dark bounty, he readied himself to meet the new day as a friend.

"See this orange," he once said, holding up the sliced half as if it were an unbelievably precious jewel. "How marvelous it is. Such perfection! And to think the dear Creator provides something so lovely for our mere food." The miracle of a peach and its brilliant sunset around the stone, the artistry of Jack Frost on the window pane, or the simple wonder of being alive brought words of responsive gratitude. He always left for the office "trailing clouds of glory" never lost with "lost childhood."

After lunching at noon on his favorite combination of "soup, pie and tea," he and Mama retired to the rotunda for the half hour that gave him "poise," as he said, for the afternoon. Often he put a red-seal record on the Brunswick phonograph that had long since replaced the old brass-horned machine. He loved opera and all vocal music. Galli Curci and Nellie Melba were among his favorites and, of course, Enrico Caruso. For convenience, our chests of records were moved to the rotunda. There, too, was the large console radio Papa had purchased as soon as the market offered powerful radios. At night they enjoyed Amos and Andy after the news.

On the floor at their feet lay the newspaper, discarded section by section, as Papa finished with it. Mama and I picked it all up after he left for the office. Two papers came to our house—the San Francisco Examiner (Democrat) for Mama, and The Chronicle (Republican) for Papa.

"Well, now, Nona," he had said when women got the vote. "What are you going to be, a Democrat or a Republican?" The question was purely rhetorical, for he was sure of the answer. What else would a woman be whose father and husband "ran" the Republican newspaper in a Republican town for years?

"Well, Mac, since you're a Republican, I'm going to be a Democrat. Just for the sake of argument." Ever since, she had diligently studied her side of all campaign issues and Papa never lacked for stimulating political discussion.

During these days, Papa came home around four in the afternoon to hoe his garden. After an early supper, Mama rested on the couch in the living room and he read aloud from the Old Testament, which they had begun to read straight through. After this spiritual reading they took up a secular novel or a novelette from one of the many periodicals they subscribed to and Papa continued aloud from the marked page where he had left off. If

C. F. McGlashan gave his last public address at the age of 79, at the dedication of the Donner Summit Bridge, in 1926.

the mood was on them, I found that they might sing together instead of reading at this time. They had a small paperbound book of the old songs, *Annie Laurie, Swing Low Sweet Chariot, Billy Boy*— songs that Papa often sang spontaneously on his way to the vegetable garden or while simply walking through the house.

For Mama, religion was just as Scripturally oriented as for him, but Papa read the Bible more than she. Beside her bed she pasted these words in large print on the wall where she would see them on waking: BE STILL AND KNOW THAT I AM GOD. One felt that in her control of speech and the wisdom that impregnated her words, religion was something she experienced deeply. It was far more a life that she lived than something she intellectualized either in reading or in discursive thought. She had healing hands, she believed, but rarely did I hear her mention this. She never encouraged charismatic gifts in herself. But during a time that I suffered sties on my eyes and painful boils elsewhere, she laid her warm dry palms on the affected part and prayed silently. I felt the warmth become heat. A current, it seemed to me, passed from her touch to my suffering flesh. Soon after, the sty or boil was gone.

—•—

Papa had taken on his last murder trial in 1915, and that only reluctantly. Remembered in Truckee as the case of Doyle vs. Smith, it involved two prominent citizens, both of whom were his good friends. He had won the case for the accused, but retired thereafter to the quieter aspects of a local legal practice. In 1926 on the occasion of the dedication of the Donner-Summit bridge, he gave his last public address. The following summer, just before his eightieth birthday, he rode horseback with me through the backwoods along unbroken trails. Even I, a thoughtless sixteen, could see that, ill as he was, he rode only by sheer iron grit. Still erect in his walk—"Stand straight, Mac, you're stooping," Mama reminded him—his frame was settling, shrinking.

In heavy snows, if the trail down the hill was open, he never excused himself from the office. On one such afternoon, followed by Brownie, then fourteen, he had gone to work as usual and we looked for him to return at four o'clock. The weather clouded and chilled two hours before and Mama and I stood watching for sight of him as four o'clock approached. Storm clouds darkened the summit. We couldn't see the trail because of the stone wall. We could only hope that soon his black hat and overcoated figure would appear at the lower stone steps. At four-fifteen I dressed in snow-gear and sluffed across the yard to peer over the top of the wall. I saw him lying prone, face forward in the snow, with Brownie standing a few feet ahead.

"Papa!" I called out in panic. I meant to scream, "Wait! I'm coming!" But something stopped me. I saw that he had struggled to his knees. Only one thought commanded me then: Don't let him know you have seen this. I hurried to the house to assure Mama he was on the way, but had fallen and was delayed. We agreed not to mention the fall if he did not.

He slipped on the snow-packed hill and fell heavily forward, his feet straight back on the slope. He gloveless hands burned with cold and found nothing to grip. But he must get to his knees! Stupidly, it seemed to him, his feet kept skidding backward.

Brownie stood patiently waiting, just out of reach. "Good dog, come! Come, Brownie!" If he could just catch hold of the furry shoulder or rump. But the old dog was as deaf as a snow drift. He didn't understand anything beyond that he must wait for his master, if need be, forever. That he would gladly do.

Tired from his efforts, he lay still a moment, thinking. This was ridiculous. Were his overshoes so worn, then, that the soles no longer gave traction? No, the cold had intensified since noon and iced the path, he decided. Again he tried to rise, and again slipped back. For the first time since he had fallen, panic touched him. Why, I'm perfectly helpless here, like a baby, or a doddering old . . . Lord, Lord, he cried out in his mind, Thou knowest that I have to get up! Oh, help Thou me!

Just then Brownie sniffed the Artic air currents that riffled his long silky ears and came to his master's outstretched hand. With something to grasp at last, Papa pulled himself to one knee and with the other foot gained a foothold. Leaning on Brownie, he pushed himself up. "Blessed dog, dear old dog!" he said.

"Lean thou on Me," said the Lord. Together they walked up the hill.

More than once after that, in the two years left to him, I heard my grandfather say, "If the Lord had not walked up the hill with me today, I would never have made it."

In August, 1930 he celebrated his 83rd birthday. This was the summer I discovered how mightily he strove to overcome the irascibility attendant on his illness. One day when I had brought down on my head a short but sharp scolding, he let the situation fade into the passing hours and then told me about Nick, the barber.

"You know, Maqueda, I've wondered lately what was the matter with that man. He's been snapping at customers until once I felt, in friendship, I should tell him, 'Nick, you won't have any customers if you jaw at people like you do.' Then, just last week I found out that the man suffers from excruciating migraines. He can't find any relief for them and I'm told he becomes almost suicidal sometimes from pain."

I understood. I had been scolded not by himself but by the dark companion of his days and nights. Almost every day thereafter he would announce toward evening, "You know, I went through this entire day without losing my temper once." Sometimes this came as a mild surprise to us who had possibly trod eggshells in his vicinity.

The Big Depression found him worried about money, as everyone was. But he did not let me know this. In 1928 he launched a Christmas tree project and hired men to cut firs on his land and ship them to city markets below. He was among the first to market Christmas trees. He didn't have strength to oversee the operation or the personnel to carry it out and he did not resume the enterprise in 1930, the final year of his life.

On March 12, 1929 he patented his last invention, a collapsible bird feeder that he called a Bird Lure. He and Mama fed the snowbirds outside the rotunda windows during winter and they had devised a feeder made of pie tins strung one below the other. This fed more birds at a time than any I have ever seen since. In those days, commercial bird feeders were not common.

In September, Mama suffered a heart attack that put her to bed under strict orders to rest. Papa moved a bed downstairs to the parlor where he had long since installed his own brass

UNITED STATES PATENT OFFICE

CHARLES F. McGLASHAN, OF TRUCKEE, CALIFORNIA

BIRD LURE

Application filed Mar

This invention relates to a bird lure,
especially to a lure which is adapted to
suspended outside a window or from post
trees and from which wild birds may be
5 without being in danger of cats or other a
mals of prey.

Individuals, associations, municipal g
ernments and States spend vast sums
money in feeding famishing birds dur
10 periods of heavy snows, during migrat
seasons, and whenever occasion dema
Untold numbers of housewives feed ev
scrap, crumb and morsel of food to birds
teach their children to do so year after y
15 Individuals who shudder at keeping bird
captivity purchase grain and feed to
wild birds and to attract them to their
dow sills and doors—in fact, inhabitant
cities can scarcely realize the almost
20 versal custom of feeding birds which
vails in the rural districts.

The placing of feed for wild birds on
ground, on a shelf or table attracts the bi
but they are in danger and in constant
25 of enemies such as cats and other animal
prey that cannot be seen without spe
effort, and hence the birds cannot be f
studied and appreciated.

Everybody is interested in watching

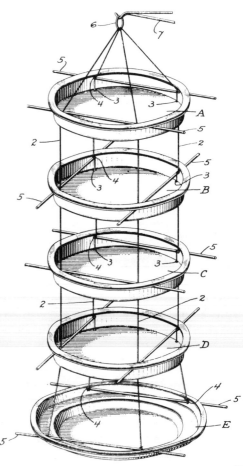

March 4, 1930.

C. F. McGLASHAN

1,749,49

BIRD LURE

Filed March 12, 1929

INVENTOR.
Charles F. McGlashan
BY
Townsend, Loftus & Abbett
ATTORNEYS.

C. F. McGlashan was 82 when he patented this bird lure, his last invention. Photo (left) was taken from inside the rotunda. Above, U.S. Patent Office descriptive pages, shown three-quarters actual size.

bed. Thus he could care for her constantly. The top floor was closed off except for my use when I came home from college.

His own health had deteriorated since I left for the fall term of my junior year. He welcomed the excuse to stay home with Mama and read to her books and magazines. *Popular Mechanics* was her favorite periodical, for her artist's fingers also understood tools. We never called in a repair man or electrician. Mama fixed it. If anything was beyond her ken, our neighbor, Ed Baldwin came. Baldwin was an old-timer of Truckee and a friend of long standing. It was he who cared for Brownie and looked after the house when we were away. A comfortable man to be around, I thought him, from a child's point of view. I remember him for a tobacco-stained mustache, but mainly for the feeling he gave of durable devotion to our family.

"Ed took the Keeley Cure with your father," Mama once told me.

"Keeley Cure? What's that?"

"A cure for drinking. Tabasco sauce essentially. The idea is to . . . "

I remembered then. This belonged to the story of How Papa Got Thirty Men to Take the Cure. In my early teens I noticed that he never partook of wine or beer with the uncles at our table. When I asked about this, the story unfolded.

In the 1890s, when Papa was promoting the Truckee ice carnivals, Mama asked him to forego the matter-of-course drink at the bar over a business deal and the almost daily after-work drink with friends that had become, over the years, an integral part of his life.

"But you sound as if I drink too much!" he remonstrated.

As far as she was concerned, any amount was too much. She was the daughter of one Quaker parent, and the other, her mother, viewed alcohol dimly. Nona's first romance had been blasted by drink. She had never before objected to Mac's social and business drinking, at least she had not made a point of it. But now she did. Bliss was the baby, they had many mouths to feed, money was short, and treating a round at the bar cost money they could ill afford, if nothing else. There was something else, of course—her fear that alcohol would take hold of him.

He didn't take her seriously until, when day after day she had sniffed whiskey on his home-coming kiss, she said one day, "Mac, if you don't stop this I'm going to leave you." Even then, her wish struck him as preposterous and he ignored it. Only once more. The next afternoon he looked up from his legal ledger to see whose shadow had suddenly darkened the page. There stood Nona, surrounded by all the children. All were dressed for traveling and the oldest, June and Nonette, carried handbags.

"Well, goodbye, Mac," she said. "We're catching the afternoon train."

Thus she extracted a promise that he would take the Keeley Cure at Los Angeles. She had all the literature on it. "But I don't need to take a cure," he sputtered. "Damnation, I'm not a drunkard!" Nevertheless, those were her terms and he decided that if he, who didn't need the cure, had to take it, then by thunder! he'd take some others with him who did need it. Legend has it that thirty men went with him. Mama's threat of leaving was probably sufficient cure for him. He never touched liquor again.

In November, 1930 Papa tried to sell Mama's Santa Clara lot. He also offered for sale a property near Horseshoe Bend, east of the summit, that he had always hoped the town would use for winter sports. No one at this time had money to buy land.

A bright moment cheered him when a Masonic delegation came to the house to give him his fifty-year membership gold button. They took a snapshot of him on that cold day. He drew himself up tall and proud and smiling. Only the one clenched hand at his side revealed the constant suffering. His clothing hung large and loose on his wasted frame.

Three weeks later, he hemorrhaged from the bowel. This time he listened to Mama's plea and called Dr. Bernard. In his lower abdomen the doctor felt a growth the size of a lemon. Nonette, who lived in San Francisco, came at once when Papa wired her. Dr. Bernard told her that although the growth might be malignant, surgery would not help now.

I was not told that anything was amiss; therefore I was shocked when, in the midst of December midterms, I received a wire from Nonette that read, "Papa dying. Come home at once."

I arrived home to find him sitting beside the living room stove,

238

McGlashan's last photograph, taken at age 83, less than two months before his death. A Masonic delegation had just presented him with a gold fifty-year membership button, which he is wearing in his lapel. His faithful spaniel, Brownie, looks on from the top of the steps.

fully dressed from the waist up even to a celluloid collar and necktie. From the waist down, however, he wore longjohns covered by a laprobe. Mama waved to me from her bed in the parlor. They had opened the wide dividing doors and turned the bed to let her participate in all that went on in the living room. From his chair by the stove Papa frequently turned his head to exchange a smile with her or to throw her a kiss. Neither knew which would go first, but both were aware that for one or the other death would come soon. Brownie, now sixteen, pressed close to Papa's feet as if he too were aware.

During the weeks since Nonette had come home to care for them Papa had set her the task of searching the Scriptures for references to the Holy Ghost. As an eight-year old boy, he told her, he had walked two miles to Sunday school, "from Cook's Bar to Michigan Bar in Sacramento County." On the way home one Sunday, he had realized in unforgettable clarity "that the Holy Spirit is the most important thing in life." Now, before he died, he longed for the experience of that Spirit, Whose nature he understood to be divine Love. Nonette therefore underlined every mention of the Holy Ghost while she read aloud to him from the big red Bible.

Just before her wire to me, he had hemorrhaged once more. I could see through the laprobe's smooth covering that the growth was now the size of a cantaloupe. With the third outrush of his life blood, which occurred a week after my homecoming and in my presence, the end began in earnest.

On the afternoon before, he had done a strange thing. First, he had asked our help to face his chair toward the window. "Closer, girls," he said; so we moved it to the window, where he could view the southwestern hills. He thanked us and then said, "Go on about your business now. I must think."

Dismissed, we sat in the rotunda. Here we could see him and yet give him privacy. We talked in low voices, Nonette over a piece of clay that she modeled and remodeled. "My knitting," she called it. I simply sat. But soon Papa's expression caught our attention. Intense, absorbed, his unseeing gaze bored through the mountainside. Sometimes he shook his head, as if he negated something vigorously. He clenched and unclenched his fists, and sometimes, with his elbows on his knees, he grasped his head between his hands. Then he returned to the mountainside and continued his tremendous, silent self-communion. I recalled his lifetime habit of seeking privacy to examine his life on the eve of every birthday.

At long last he spoke. We listened with held breath and knew he was not addressing us. "I will be remembered," he said, "for the history of the Donner Party."

That was all. He tried to rise and we hastened to help him. All the while, my nineteen-year old being mutely protested, Oh no, not for just a book, Papa! I will remember you for so much more than just a book! For what you *are*!

That evening, Nonette and I couldn't speak of casual matters. I found myself possessed by a need to know how Papa's faith held up in the face of death. How often I had heard him state with firm conviction, "There is no such thing as death. Life goes on, but on another plane." If he really believed that, if it were not a form of whistling in the dark, then he should have no fear now. I watched for a sign that would tell me what I wanted to know. It came at dusk.

"Take me out to the back porch, girls," he said after he had eaten a light meal. We were unaware that it was time for the moon to be new, but he had been waiting for this moon of the New Year. We went with him, one on either side, through the kitchen and out the door. From the middle of the long plank porch we looked up and saw it—a silver scimitar, in a clear, clean sky. The thought raced through me, maybe he'll think it means he isn't going to die. But his only comment answered all my questions.

"What a sweet moon to go on," he said.

That night he hemorrhaged again, then lapsed mercifully into a coma that took away all pain. For two weeks Nonette and I took turns beside him day and night, dropping water into his parched mouth. He moved his head restlessly as though he dreamed, and seldom slept quietly.

By the hour I held his hot dry hand. "June?" he would sometimes say. "Yes, Papa." June was bedridden at this time with an illness from which she never fully recovered. Now he believed that she was with him, as undoubtedly she was in her thoughts.

C. F. McGlashan left his beloved Truckee for the last time in January, 1931. His home, at upper left, was "lyrical, imaginative, large-souled and free . . . an architectural portrait of the man who built it." In March, 1935, it burned to the ground, leaving the Rocking Stone Tower intact.

On January sixth, 1931, the strong heart finally stopped. January sixth is the feast of Epiphany, celebrated in some countries as Little Christmas, and in all Christian countries as the day that the three wise men arrived at the Bethlehem manger. We would have more comfort in the thought of this in later years than we did at the time.

The Knights of Pythias in full uniform regalia conducted the funeral. Doc Kelley made the arrangements for cremation and accompanied the body to Oakland. According to Papa's wish, his ashes would be buried "in the same grave with Nona."

Before he lapsed into a coma he had said: "I realize my whole life has been a life of love. How much love I have received in my lifetime—from my sisters, my family, friends . . . " Perhaps this realization was the prelude to the "anointing" he longed for by the Spirit of Love.

—•—

Mama never walked again. The doctor thought that the shock, always present where a loved one's death is concerned, may have caused this. She felt her hips were "locked," she said. She went to Nonette's in San Francisco, where she lived until her 80th birthday, February 18, 1934, the day of her death.

Little Brownie remained in Truckee. Within six weeks of his master's death, the faithful spaniel, wasted with grieving, was himself laid to rest.

Nonette needed surgery soon after Mama came to live with her and I was recruited from college to help.

Mama's hearing loss was acute. Bedridden as she was, she practiced the guitar without an instrument. We propped her music before her on the bed and, fingering imaginary strings, she "played" the complicated chords. Her eyesight was equal to an hour of this, but not to prolonged reading. Therefore it was difficult for her to pass the long hours. Once I asked her, "What are you doing, Mama?" She had been lying still, gazing through the window, without anything really to see beyond it.

"Well, dear, I'm walking through a garden and I'm smelling the flowers," she said, her voice vibrant with interest in the pastime. "But I'm having a hard time remembering how violets smell. Can you imagine the perfume of violets?"

I soon discovered that a deck of cards and "Chinaman's solitaire" could pass the time for both of us. I would play and she would watch and by the time I wore out the backs of one deck we had become very close. My adolescence was over and the age gap had closed. My engagement at this time pleased her very much for she wanted.to see me settled before she died. She had warm wisdom to impart to me, as well.

"Young love is all very beautiful," she said once, "but it can't compare to the love of two hearts bound together by cobwebs of time."

Another time she said, "When a girl marries, her heart is only big enough to hold her husband; but when a baby comes along, she finds her heart has grown to include both of them. And it grows with each baby thereafter, until finally her heart holds the whole world."

A year before her death she had a remarkable dream.

"I dreamed that I was a young woman and I was expected to play the guitar on stage before a large audience. I said 'Oh no, I haven't played for years before a crowd. I just can't do it without time beforehand to practice.' Then a beautiful young man came up to me and said, 'Never mind, just go through the motions on stage and I will play the music.' So I took up the guitar and sat before that vast audience and went through the motions of playing. And out came the most wonderful music! I have never heard such beautiful music. Afterward I ran behind the scenes to find the young man and thank him. 'Who are you? Tell me your name?' I begged him. He turned and looked at me full in eyes. And he said, 'My name is Jesus Christ.'"

When she died, Doc Kelley, whose devotion to her had been that of a true son, escorted her body by train to Truckee, where she was buried next to John Keiser in the family plot. Papa's ashes were placed in her grave.

Epilogue

When he died January 6, 1931, all major newspapers of California mourned Charles Fayette McGlashan as "a pioneer historian, newspaperman, scientist, educator, and barrister." San Francisco's Hearst papers honored him with feature columns, amply illustrated with photographs of himself, his home, and the Donner monument. The *Sacramento Bee* News Bureau immediately provided *The Superior California News* with a well-prepared and complete biography that not only pointed up the many-faceted character of the man but furnished anecdotal color and depth.

On January 15, the State Legislature adjourned in his honor. The purple-bound testimonial that was sent to his widow praised him as one who served California "with distinction and unswerving fidelity, not only in our legislative halls as a former member of this Assembly, but also in private life as a faithful instructor, an able Counselor at our State Bar, and a distinguished Historian; one whose admirable personal traits and character have won for him a warm place in the hearts of all who knew him."

In scientific circles, the Pacific Coast Entomological Society devoted its leading article in the January 1931 edition of "The Pan Pacific Entomologist" to his memory. This quarterly, published in cooperation with the California Academy of Sciences, solicited the chairman of its Publication Committee, E. O. Essig, to render a full and warm account of McGlashan's life as well as his contribution to the study of moths and butterflies.

All of the obituaries referred to his colorful legal career. Of this the *Sacramento Bee* said:

245

McGlashan was noted in California bar history as a criminal lawyer. He was counsel at various times for Crown Williamette Paper Co., Hobart Estate, Southern Pacific, Boca & Loyalton Railway and, of late years, acted as deputy prosecutor of Nevada County. From 1903 to 1910 he was a partner in private practice with his daughter June . . . who was one of the first women admitted to the California bar. McGlashan had all the mannerisms of a Kentucky colonel and could plead a case with a fervor and zeal that gave him a wide reputation in case pleading. Mrs. Kelley is said to have inherited her father's oratorical ability.

Dr. George F. Kelley, himself an attorney and dentist, told me that when my grandfather died "he was the best known defense attorney on the Coast" and, according to his colleagues, "the best paid." He was often called the Clarence Darrow of the west coast for his passionate interest in the rights of labor and for his ability to get his clients off "scot-free." An investigation of his court trials alone would inspire an engaging book, touching as it must the history of California courtrooms and crime.

On December 6, 1968 the California Press Association formally announced his election to the Newspaper Hall of Fame. The closing paragraph of the award-plaque says:

He [McGlashan] proved small towns and small papers can have big men. Editor, politician, inventor, author—and above all chronicler of the drama, tragedy and courage of those who pioneered their way to California across plains, deserts and mountains. McGlashan had great self confidence, was daring and courageous but at the same time polite, tender hearted and sentimental. He was the true outdoors type who greatly admired nature's wonders and honored those who pioneered their hard way to his beloved California. . . . This is the eve of the one hundredth anniversary of *The Truckee Republican* and also of the completion of the transcontinental railroad on which Truckee is an important stop. May men of vision and great influence continue to let their light shine from the desks of the small town newspapers!

Present at the award luncheon, held in San Francisco at the Clift Hotel, were three generations of McGlashans. Michael Enfield, a great-grandson and the grandson of Bliss Hinkle, accepted the plaque for our family. His infant daughter, Susan, representative of the "great-greats," slept throughout her father's graceful speech in a portable bassinette under the table.

246

The photo of C. F. McGlashan was then placed in the State Capitol among those of his good friends James McClatchy of the *Sacramento Bee* papers, Fremont Older of the *Oakland Tribune*, and Friend Richardson of the *Berkeley Gazette*.

Thus the world saw him and thus it spoke of him *in memoriam*. Thus a biographer might have written of him, filling this book with his public words and achievements. But we who knew him intimately were aware of another dimension to his personality— the spiritual dimension. I do not refer to his religious orientation alone. In every human being lies a capacity for aspiration toward an ideal value. In some it is weak and can be suffocated by satisfaction with material goods. But my grandfather was like Daniel of the Old Testament—a "man of desires." He hungered, one might say, not only for God but for the spiritual freedom to preserve his own uniqueness.

Following his election to the Hall of Fame, I visited Truckee for the first time in many years. It was hard for me to look at the hill where our house had been. On a bitter March night in 1935 it had burned to its granite foundation. Only the Rocking Stone Tower was spared. Papa's butterfly collection was then placed on display at the Court House in Nevada City, while the Donner relics were transferred to the museum at Sutter's Fort. In place of our white castle strung with columns like a harp, I saw a monstrous quonset hut constructed during World War II. The little tower had been replaced by a baldachin, a roof-like canopy to protect the rocking stone—which no longer rocked. It had been shored up with stones to forestall activity on the part of vandals, I presumed.

When Papa was nearing his last days in 1930, Truckee too seemed near its own demise. But now I found a resurgence of youth and vitality. New industries had sprung up. Westward toward Donner Lake, a new and modern section of Truckee had sprouted like a tunneling root that seeks nourishment beyond the parent tree. Donner Memorial State Park, all new to me, now surrounded the commanding monument. And in the Donner Museum I discovered my grandfather's photograph smiling at me from a display wholly devoted to him as author of "The History of the Donner Party."

I recalled his prophecy that he would be remembered for the Donner history. And I recalled my own prophecy and protest: "Oh, no . . . not for just a book." The museum guide and supervisor, Bert Troelsen, proved to be an ardent McGlashan enthusiast. He had devised the display and read all he could find about my grandfather. He gave me access to the files that contained valuable research materials and, thanks to Mr. Troelsen, my first research for this book began.

In the town, later, I found that the memory of my grandfather still thrived after nearly forty years. Those who knew him were passing down stories of him to their children, like heirloom brooches, bits and pieces of a legacy. Most of the memories concerned his charities. He was of the stuff of legend.

I went home then and began my nine-year journey into another century, another time. Others may write of the influential people Papa knew or of his manifold achievements. I have preferred to write of what he valued:

"You can have the metropolises of the world—*give me a mountain meadow.*"